Christmas's

Mo

Also in the Most Wanted™ series

The 1950s' Most Wanted™: The Top 10 Book of Rock & Roll Rebels, Cold War Crises, and All-American Oddities, by Robert Rodriguez

The 1960s' Most Wanted™: The Top 10 Book of Hip Happenings, Swinging Sounds, and Out-of-Sight Oddities, by Stuart Shea

Basketball's Most Wanted™ II: The Top 10 Book of More Hotshot Hoopsters, Double Dribbles, and Roundball Oddities, by David L. Hudson, Jr.

Cats' Most Wanted™: The Top 10 Book of Mysterious Mousers, Talented Tabbies, and Feline Oddities, by Alexandra Allred

Dogs' Most Wanted™: The Top 10 Book of Historic Hounds, Professional Pooches, and Canine Oddities, by Alexandra Allred

Chicago's Most Wanted™: The Top 10 Book of Murderous Mobsters, Midway Monsters, and Windy City Oddities, by Laura L. Enright

Ireland's Most Wanted™: The Top 10 Book of Celtic Pride, Fantastic Folklore, and Oddities of the Emerald Isle, by Brian M. Thomsen

The Super Bowl's Most Wanted™: The Top 10 Book of Big-Game Heroes, Pigskin Zeroes, and Championship Oddities, by Walter Harvey

Christmas's Most Wanted™

The Top 10 Book of Kris Kringles, Merry Jingles, and Holiday Cheer

Kevin Cuddihy
and
Phillip Metcalfe

Potomac Books, Inc.
WASHINGTON, D.C.

Library of Congress Cataloging-in-Publication Data
Cuddihy, Kevin.
  Christmas's most wanted : the top 10 book of Kris
Kringles, merry jingles, and holiday cheer / Kevin Cuddihy
and Phillip Metcalfe.— 1st ed.
      p. cm.
  Includes bibliographical references and index.
  ISBN 1-57488-968-0 (pbk. : alk. paper)
  1. Christmas. 2. Christmas music. 3. Christmas films.
I. Metcalfe, Phillip. II. Title.

GT4985.C75 2005
394.2663—dc22
                                                2005002644

Printed in Canada on acid-free
paper that meets the American National Standards
Institute Z39-48 Standard.

Potomac Books, Inc.
22841 Quicksilver Drive
Dulles, Virginia 20166

First Edition

10 9 8 7 6 5 4 3 2 1

Contents

List of Illustrations   ix

Acknowledgments   xi

Introduction   xiii

Christmas Firsts   1
Holiday firsts and starts

Christmas by the Numbers   5
Facts and figures on Christmas

Where in the World Is Santa Claus?   11
Geographic holiday fun

Why Do We . . . ?   19
The story behind traditions that stand today

It Was Tradition Somewhere   25
Odd worldwide holiday traditions

I Am Santa Claus   31
Gift-givers around the world

Home, Home on the Range   37
All about the North Pole

O Christmas Tree, O Christmas Tree   41
All about Christmas trees

To See if Reindeer Really Know How to Fly   **47**
All about reindeer

Eight Isn't Enough   **53**
Ten of the most famous reindeer

**Bing, Nat, and Frank—No Christmas Is
Complete Without the Classics**   **59**
Classic Christmas songs

Sing It and Swing It   **67**
Jazz vocals to play by the fire

Merry Christmas and All That Jazz   **73**
Jazz instrumentals for the season

That Old-Time Christmas Rock and Roll   **81**
Rock oldies for Christmas

**Both Types of Christmas Music—
Country AND Western**   **89**
Great Christmas carols in country music

I'll Have a Blues Christmas Without You   **97**
The best in Christmas blues

Get Down at Christmas   **105**
The best Christmas soul, R&B, and funk

Nollaig Shona   **113**
Celtic holiday music

Holiday Movie Classics   **121**
Top Christmas movies

Not-so-Classic Holiday Movies   **129**
Bad and offbeat holiday movies

Ho Ho Ho and Ha Ha Ha   **135**
Christmas comedies

Not Just *A* Christmas Carol   **143**
Ten versions of the Dickens classic

No Small Parts, Only Small Actors   **149**
Holiday movie bit players

**It's Only Christmas Rock and Roll,
and I Like It** **155**
Classic rock's best Christmas songs

Send in the Clowns **163**
Christmas novelty songs

The B-Side **171**
Non-title holiday cartoon songs

Twelve Ways of Christmas **177**
*'The Twelve Days of Christmas' performed
ten different ways*

As Seen on TV and Heard on Your Hi-Fi **183**
Christmas albums from TV stars

'Tis the Season to Be Jolly **189**
Christmas's most fun songs

Mass Appeal? **195**
Popular, but bad, Christmas music

Christmas Present **203**
Great modern Christmas music

As Seen on TV **211**
TV holiday specials

Classic Christmas Cartoons **217**
Top holiday cartoons

Not-so-Classic Cartoons **225**
Bad and offbeat holiday cartoons

No Small Parts, Only Small Cartoons **233**
Holiday cartoon bit players

Merry Birthday **239**
People who were born on Christmas

Merry . . . Arrrgh! **245**
People who died on Christmas

The World Doesn't Stop on Christmas **253**
Historical events from Christmas day

The Toy's the Thing   **259**
   Top holiday toy fads

Tasty Treats   **265**
   Holiday food and drink

All You Need is a Reason   **271**
   Other things to celebrate around Christmas

Say That Again?   **279**
   Ten translations of "Merry Christmas"

Bibliography   **281**

Index   **283**

About the Authors   **289**

Illustrations

Statue in Santa Claus, Indiana 14

Christmas Tree Farm 43

Arthur Fiedler 63

Burl Ives 87

Roomful of Blues 101

Rudolph and Hermey the Misfit Elf 172

Perry Como 213

"Cast" of *Rudolph the Red-Nosed Reindeer* 220

Snow Miser and Heat Miser 237

Texas-shaped Fruitcake 266

Acknowledgments

Phillip Metcalfe wishes to thank Kevin Cuddihy for inviting him to help write this book and for driving the whole project. Thanks so much. It was fun. Additional thanks to the Potomac Books editors for their help with the manuscript. Thanks to my parents for their encouragement, to the Nebbias for the annual Christmas cookies, and to Teresa and Aaron who make every day like Christmas for me. Teresa—you support and challenge all my ideas and I am forever grateful for your love. Aaron—you bring joy and creativity to my life every day. Special thanks to the tiny babe in the straw who has brought warmth and light to the cold winter of my heart.

Kevin Cuddihy wishes to thank his co-author Phillip Metcalfe for the brainstorming sessions, the ideas, and his extreme musical knowledge. You're certainly Professor Phil, Doctor of Music. Thanks as well to my family for always making Christmas something to look forward to. Special thanks to friends, co-workers, and online message boards for letting me bounce ideas and thoughts off of you and listening as I prattled on and on about the latest bit of holiday fun that was stuck in my brain. I'm sure many of you will see some of your ideas and feedback folded into the book, and for that I'm extremely grateful. I'd name names, but there are so many that I'm sure I'd forget a few, so I'll just thank you en masse. Thanks especially to Don McKeon at Potomac Books for allowing this project to go forward, and to Christina Kahrl for providing the most appropriate subtitle.

Both authors would like to thank the production and marketing teams at Potomac Books. Without them, this book would not be in your hands right now. So thanks to Julie Kimmel, Michie Shaw, Judy Coughlin, Claire Noble, and Sam Dorance. Candy canes for all of you!

Introduction

It's the rare bird that doesn't like Christmas; sure there are Scrooges and here-and-there cries of "Bah humbug," but Christmas is a time for celebration, for giving, and trying to be just a little nicer to your fellow man. As the song goes, "if every day could be just like Christmas what a wonderful world it would be."

While obviously we (the authors) recognize that Christmas is a religious holiday, this book is a celebration more of the secular side of Christmas—the songs, the movies, the television shows, the commercialism, the people, the laughs . . . all that and more. So in these pages you'll see such things as ten different versions of both "The Twelve Days of Christmas" and *A Christmas Carol.* You'll find out about how different song genres celebrate Christmas in music. You'll relive the great—and not-so-great—Cartoons of Christmas Past. You'll find out which television celebrities "graced" the world with their very own albums of holiday tunes. And you'll find out about births, deaths, and historical events that occurred on Christmas. You'll laugh, you'll smile, and hopefully you'll learn a lot of cool and interesting stuff about Christmas that you didn't know before.

So curl up before the yule log, pour yourself some egg nog, bite into a gingerbread cookie, and enjoy Christmas's Most Wanted™. Merry Christmas, from our families to yours.

Christmas Firsts

We start our book, logically enough, with Christmas firsts. No, not the first Christmas. There's no discussion of wise men, mangers, or myrrh—whatever that is—here. All of the following items or symbols are relatively commonplace today, but they all had to start somewhere. Where did they start? Who came up with them? Why did they persist? And why do we continue them today? Well, read on.

1. TURKEY DINNER

Golden, delicious, and full of tryptophan, ensuring a nice nap after dinner—you gotta love turkey! But before Ben Franklin's favorite bird became the standard main course for Christmas meals, rich households would feast on goose, beef, or a boar's head instead, the boar's head often prepared with a tasty mustard. Yum! The Christmas turkey first appeared on English tables in the sixteenth century, and while it didn't immediately replace the above, thankfully today turkey is preferred to boar's head by almost everybody. Except the turkeys, I suppose. Gobble gobble!

2. CHRISTMAS CAROLS

Christmas carols came into popularity at about the same time as the Christmas turkey (although we doubt any of the songs were celebrating getting rid of that nasty boar's head . . . but we can't say for sure). It's still called "wassailing" in some circles—generally older circles, mind you, like the kind Grandma Edna hangs out in—which comes from the old Norse "ves heill" or "good health." The earliest English collection of these songs wishing good health for the holidays was published in 1521. Sadly, "Feliz Navidad" was not included.

3. CHRISTMAS HOLIDAY

Christmas has been celebrated for centuries, but in the United States it wasn't always an official holiday with days off, closed post offices, and shorter hours at stores. It wasn't until 1836 that Alabama became the first state to recognize Christmas as an official holiday. The other states followed suit, but not quite in rapid succession. The last state to declare Christmas a holiday was Oklahoma, an amazing seventy-one years later in 1907. Surprisingly, that was thirty-seven years after the United States declared it a *national* holiday, on June 26, 1870.

4. CHRISTMAS CARD

England seems to have a monopoly on some of these Christmas Firsts, but this next first was a few centuries after the others. Perhaps weary of writing notes to friends and relatives and having to dip and redip that quill pen, the English in 1842 found a happy solution. On December 9, 1842, the first Christmas card was created. There's no word on whether that first card included a mass-produced "Here's what our entire family did in the past year" newsletter update inside with detailed reviews of Aunt Sally's scurvy and Cousin Jim's graduation from blacksmith school, but today Hallmark is ever-grateful for this tradition.

5. WHITE HOUSE CHRISTMAS TREE

Today it's a media event, televised and taped as it is lit for the first time each year. Each president tries to outdo his predecessor, and each president tries to put his own personal touch and a taste of his home state on the nation's most famous holiday tree. The only one who didn't feel the need to one-up the previous occupant was Franklin Pierce, as he became the first president to decorate an official White House Christmas tree during his presidency of 1853–57.

6. SLEIGH AND REINDEER

Santa Claus didn't always come around on a sleigh with reindeer; that depiction is less than 150 years old. In an issue of *Harper's Weekly* on January 3, 1863, a cartoon by Thomas Nast first depicted old Kris Kringle with the help of the now-standard reindeer-powered sleigh. Titled "Santa Claus in Camp," it shows Santa Claus delivering presents to soldiers during the Civil War.

7. CHRISTMAS LIGHTS

For years, people placed candles in Christmas trees to help decorate them, illogically ignoring the flammable nature of the trees and keeping a close watch while the candles burned. No more, thanks to one American, Ralph E. Morris. Following Thomas Edison's invention of the light bulb, Morris in 1895 came up with the idea of placing these newfangled things on Christmas trees in place of those dangerous candles. While Christmas tree fires still exist, they surely don't occur in such high numbers as when candles were involved.

8. POSTAGE STAMPS

Today the U.S. Post Office distributes a number of different postage stamps designed to celebrate Christmas—including religious, artistic, kitschy, and Santa-related—but that wasn't always the case. The first postage stamp to commemorate Christmas, in fact, came not in the United States but in Austria, in 1937.

9. MERRY CHRISTMAS SUBJECTS!

While King George V was the first English monarch to broadcast a Christmas message to his people, Queen Elizabeth was the first to do so for the bright lights of the cameras. On December 25, 1957, her Christmas message was broadcast on television for the first time. The BBC would continue to televise the yearly statement and proclamation into the next century.

10. EASTERN EUROPE

Those pesky Communists messed everything up, even outlawing Jolly Saint Nick among their people! Shades of the Burgermeister Meisterburger and his outlawing of toys in the classic cartoon special, *Santa Claus is Comin' to Town*. Never fear, though, as the celebration of presents, food, wassailing, and—oh yeah, a birthday—returned to Eastern Europe with the fall of the Berlin Wall. For the first time in decades, the former Communist countries were allowed to freely celebrate Christmas Day in 1989. For those more sedentary folk, church masses were broadcast on television throughout the area for the first time in history.

Christmas by the Numbers

How much, how often, how little, and how big—this list takes a look at some of the figures associated with various Christmas traditions and Christmas itself, exploring the numbers behind the holiday.

1. SHOPPING

Black Friday (the day after Thanksgiving) is traditionally the official kickoff of the Christmas shopping season with sales in every store and early start-times to create a festive atmosphere. While the Saturday before Christmas is usually the busiest shopping day of the year, Black Friday comes in a strong second and occasionally takes first place. In 2003 Wal-Mart counted sales of $1.52 billion in the one day, and in 2004 Visa reported that its customers purchased more than four billion dollars worth of goods. As to the season as a whole, according to the U.S. Census Bureau, solely in December 2002 the toy industry reported $30.6 billion in sales. In December 2003 department stores reported $31.1 billion in sales and online and mail-order businesses reported $14.4 billion of sales.

Overall, 14 percent of a department store's sales take place in December; for jewelry stores that number climbs to 24 percent.

2.   WHERE TO SHOP

Heading to the mall for your Christmas shopping? There were 47,104 shopping centers in the United States at the end of 2003, reports the Census Bureau. That's a whopping 10,000 more than were around in 1990. Not sure what to buy? According to the Bureau's latest figures in 2001 there were "151,668 clothing and clothing accessories stores; 10,374 department stores; 10,783 hobby, toy and game shops; 33,678 gift, novelty and souvenir shops; 22,468 sporting goods stores; 29,780 jewelry stores; and 11,559 book stores." And should you not want to leave the privacy of your home, there were 11,086 electronic shopping or mail-order businesses from which to choose.

3.   PHYSICS OF SANTA CLAUS

What if a fat man really *did* fly around the world delivering presents to each household on one festive night in the year? Is that possible? What would happen? Thanks to a piece in *Spy Magazine* by Richard Waller titled "Is There a Santa Claus?" we now know. According to figures Waller used at the time, he estimated that for Santa to deliver a present to each child who celebrated Christmas, he'd be visiting 91.8 million homes in thirty-one hours of Christmas (thanks to the rotation of the earth). That, wrote Waller, works out to 822.6 visits per second. To keep this brisk schedule, Santa would have to travel at 650 miles per second— about 3,000 times the speed of sound.

Limiting each child to two pounds worth of toys, that would add up to 321,300 tons of packages. Even if you give Santa's magical reindeer ten times the pulling power of earthbound reindeer, claimed Waller, that would necessitate 214,200 pullers. Finishing up, Waller calculated that the weight of sleigh-plus-reindeer traveling at 650 miles per second would put 14.3 quintillion—that's seventeen zeroes—joules of energy per second on the lead reindeer, which would lead to the entire team being vaporized in 4.26 thousandths of a second. And finally, before he was vaporized as well, Santa would be pressed back against the sleigh by more than 4.3 million pounds of force.

4. CHRISTMAS AT DISNEY

Disney World is where adults can become kids again, so it's no surprise that Christmas at the theme park is a special time of year. Disney decks the halls with more than 140 tractor-trailers full of decorations, including 14.2 miles of garland and 1,600 holiday trees. Epcot Center gets into the act as well with eleven of the countries dressed up for "Holidays Around the World" and 30,000 lights covering the bridge between Future World and World Showcase. Finally, according to the Disney website, there's a "100 percent chance of 'Florida snow' flurries during Mickey's Very Merry Christmas Party, taking place on select holiday nights at Magic Kingdom."

5. FLOWERS

Surprisingly, according to a consumer-trend study Christmas is the biggest flower-selling time of the year, beating out Mother's Day, Easter, and even Valentine's Day in the top four of sales for specific calendar occasions. A whopping 31 percent of flowers sold for a holiday are sold for Christmas, with 48 percent of those being gifts and 52 percent bought for the purchaser's use. What's one of the biggest draws? Poinsettias, which make up 88 percent of the total sales for flowering plants at Christmas.

6. WHITE CHRISTMAS

Bing Crosby may have been dreaming of a white Christmas, but it's doubtful he meant this much snow. According to the U.S. Census Bureau, eight locations in the United States average an amazing two feet or more of snow in the month of December: Valdez, Alaska; Mount Washington, New Hampshire; Blue Canyon, California; Yakutat, Alaska; Sault Sainte Marie, Michigan; Marquette, Michigan; Syracuse, New York; and Muskegon, Michigan.

7. IT'S ALL CHINESE TO ME

"Made in China" just might be second only to "Merry Christmas" in holiday slogans. Almost a billion dollars worth of Christmas ornaments were imported from China in the first three quarters of 2003 according to the Census Bureau. In that same time period, the United States imported $93 million of artificial Christmas trees from the Asian nation. And $820 million of stuffed toys were imported from China for sale in the United States as well.

8. CHRISTMAS CARDS

The Greeting Card Association has reported that U.S. consumers purchase roughly seven billion greeting cards each year, with about 30 percent of those—or 2.1 billion—being Christmas cards. Christmas is by far the most popular seasonal card purchase, and even ties "birthday" as the biggest occasion to purchase a greeting card overall. And should Hallmark not fit your style, there are roughly 3,000 greeting card publishers from which to choose instead.

9. TRAVEL

Christmas sees a lot of traveling—not only over the river and through the woods, but over interstates and through the air as well. According to a study conducted in 2001–02 by the Department of Transportation's Bureau of Transportation Statistics, during the Christmas-to-New-Year's time period, long-distance travel (defined as more than fifty miles) increases 24 percent over the rest of the year's average. That's 16.5 million one-way trips *each day*, compared to 13.3 million daily over the rest of the year. Of those numbers, roughly nine in ten will travel by personal vehicle rather than a plane or train.

The average travel distance is 275 miles, fourteen further than the yearly average. Just because we travel, though, doesn't mean we stay. Half of all holiday visits are same-day trips. However, of the other half the average stay is almost four days.

10. SHIPPING

Even when you can't travel you still may want to send gifts, and shipping around the holidays picks up tremendously. According to the United Parcel Service (UPS), the company's busiest day in 2004 was December 21 when approximately 20 million packages were delivered—roughly 50 percent more than an average day for "The Brown." That corresponds to an amazing 230 packages *every second*. Over the entire 2004 holiday period, UPS expected to deliver 340 million packages globally.

Federal Express sees a rise in its business as well. Its busiest day in 2004 was December 20, when an estimated 4.6 million packages were shipped by way of FedEx Express. December 20 was also the biggest day for the United States Postal Service, as an estimated 280 million cards and letters were delivered; that's triple the average card-and-letter delivery for the USPS.

Where in the World Is Santa Claus?

Carmen Sandiego, the computer game detective, isn't the only geographic whiz. Santa and various Christmas names make the rounds of the world with holiday names appearing on maps in the United States and worldwide. Below are ten of them.

1. CHRISTMAS ISLAND

As Jimmy Buffett sings, "How'd you like to spend Christmas on Christmas Island?" Christmas Island is an Australian territory, and like in Australia, Christmas comes in the summertime. As such, expect shorts and T-shirts on your Santa Claus should you travel there for the holiday: The average December high is 82 degrees Fahrenheit. Located roughly 1,500 miles west of Perth, Australia, the tiny island (52 square miles) has 1,500 inhabitants, not counting tourists.

The island was named by Captain William Mynors of the East India Ship Company, as he discovered it on Christmas Day 1643. Today tourism is its chief draw, with amazing flora and fauna to discover. And, according to the U.S. Census Bureau, from 1999–2003

Christmas Island exported an average of $327,800 worth of goods to the United States each year. Surely some of those were for Christmas presents from Christmas Island.

2. NORTH POLE, ALASKA

Where else but a town called North Pole would you find the slogan "Where the Spirit of Christmas Lives Year Round"? According to the town's website the name was selected to attract toy companies to the burgeoning area under the lure of being able to advertise their toys as "made in the North Pole." Apparently toy manufacturers enjoy warmth too much, because they failed to flock there. The name, however, stuck, and the town rallied around it. There are streets such as Snowman Lane, North Star Drive, and Holiday Road, and the street lights have a candy cane motif.

3. SANTA CLAUS, INDIANA

There are two competing stories as to how the town of Santa Claus, Indiana—originally named Santa Fe but forced to rename in 1852 when it was decided another Santa Fe in the state had the name first—took its holly, jolly name. The first declares that during a meeting on Christmas Eve the townspeople couldn't decide on a name everyone liked. Suddenly, however, the door opened and a child cried out, "It's Santa Claus." With that, so this story goes, the town took its name. The second story claims the town sent request after request to the postmaster with new town names, but all were rejected. During the holiday season they sent "Santa Claus" as a joke—but instead it was accepted, becoming the new name.

The town postmarks roughly a half million letters and cards every holiday season, and receives—then replies to—tens of thousands of children's letters to Santa Claus each year. If they ask, you can tell your kids that Santa's zip code is 47579. Of year-round interest is Holiday World—formerly Santa Claus Land, which, when it was built in 1946, was the world's first theme park. Ironically, however, it is *not* open on Christmas. (Admittedly, Santa has other obligations that day; also, not many people want to visit an outdoor amusement/water park in Indiana in December.) The main attraction aside from the park is a twenty-two-foot-high Santa Claus statue, complete with Star-of-Bethlehem base, that weighs in at more than forty tons.

4. CHRISTMAS, FLORIDA

Christmas, Florida, twenty miles east of Orlando, takes its name from the nearby Fort Christmas. Two thousand soldiers arrived to build the fort on December 25, 1837, and just like Christmas Island, they named the location after the date of its "discovery." The fort, built for use in the Second Seminole War, remains open for tours and souvenirs. As with Santa Claus, Indiana, the town's post office (zip code 32709) does a brisk business around the holidays.

5. SANTA CLAUS, GEORGIA

Much smaller than the Indiana town of the same name—fewer than 250 residents as compared to more than two thousand—Santa Claus, Georgia, is two-tenths of a mile squared in area and sits six miles southeast of Vidalia. While there's no post office, the town invites people to stop by the Santa Claus Town Hall and get the official Santa Claus postmark put on cards and letters.

Statue in Santa Claus, Indiana.
Spencer County Visitors Bureau

6. NOEL, MISSOURI

Calling itself both "The Christmas City" as well as "Canoe Capital of the Ozarks," Noel, Missouri, lies in the southwest corner of the state, on the Elk River and surrounded by the Ozarks. Noel started stamping their "Christmas City" postmark in the 1930s, and with the help of publicity from singer Kate Smith, more than a half million pieces of mail went through tiny Noel each holiday season in the forties and fifties. Today the mail numbers "only" in the tens of thousands—this in a town with a population of roughly 1,500—and the holiday postmark can be accessed by mailing letters (with postage on each one, of course) to Postmaster, Noel, MO, 64854.

7. JOLLY, TEXAS

All residents of this small town in Clay County, Texas, have a "Jolly" Christmas each year. With a population numbering in the hundreds—up, however, from the dozens that called Jolly home for most of the twentieth century—there is no longer even a post office. While it has a festive name, Christmas spirit played no role in the naming of the town. Instead, the town was named in 1891 after a farmer/rancher in the area, William H. Jolly.

8. RUDOLPH, WISCONSIN

But do you recall . . . the most famous reindeer town of all? Okay, Rudolph, Wisconsin, wasn't named after the red-nosed one but rather after Rudolph Hecox, the first Caucasian child born in the area. The tiny section of Wood County, Wisconsin (the village has a population of slightly more than four hundred, while the surrounding town of the same name holds almost two thousand) does celebrate its famous name, however. The "Welcome to Rudolph" sign on Highway 34 features a photo of the lead reindeer, complete with glowing nose, and "Rudolph Wisconsin, Home of Rudolph the Red Nosed Reindeer" can be imprinted on outgoing mail.

9. BETHLEHEM, GEORGIA; PENNSYLVANIA; AND WEST VIRGINIA

O Little Town of Bethlehem, indeed! Georgia's version of the still-lying town, in the Atlanta metropolitan area, has a population of roughly seven hundred. The area took its name in 1884 from the local Bethlehem Methodist Church, and street names such as Manger Street and King Avenue add to the holiday spirit as does a lighted star that has shone above the town during each holiday season since 1951. As with the other holiday towns, the post office maintains a brisk business every December with more than 100,000 cards and letters postmarked.

West Virginia's version holds around 2,600 residents; still small overall but bustling when compared to Georgia. Horror fans may recognize the town from scenes in the film *Freddy versus Jason*.

And finally is Bethlehem, Pennsylvania, founded by a German Count on Christmas Eve 1741 and named in honor of the special date. Today more than 70,000 people call it home, and the city celebrates with the nickname "Christmas City USA" and an eighty-one-foot-high electric Star of Bethlehem on South Mountain.

10. MCADENVILLE, NORTH CAROLINA

If you're scratching your head trying to figure out how "McAdenville" is a holiday name, take it easy. None of the three kings were named McAden, it's nothing like that. But every December the tiny Gaston County town transforms itself into "Christmas Town USA," where four hundred trees ranging from four to eighty feet tall are strung with almost half a million lights. In addition, a life-size nativity scene highlights the town. Every December 1 since 1949 the town has been set aglow with lights burning nightly through December 26, and millions have taken the full tour over the years to view the amazing spectacle. However, don't expect to arrive past 9:30 at night and see the lights. According to the town's website the lights shut off by automatic timer at half past nine. Why? McAdenville is a textile town, with plants running twenty-four hours a day. The night shift starts at 10 p.m. so traffic needs to be clear by then to allow the workers to make it to work on time.

Why Do We . . . ?

Traditions are a big part of Christmas, and many families have their own traditions that have been passed down from generation to generation to make the holiday unique and special for them. Christmas in general has some traditions that weren't always the "in" thing to do as well. Have you ever stopped to ponder the genesis of some of these traditions, asking "Why do we . . . ?" about some of the things we do by memory? Following are some standard traditions and common activities or actions, and the explanation behind them.

1. WHY DO WE CELEBRATE CHRISTMAS ON DECEMBER 25?

Many scholars believe Jesus Christ was born not in the winter but rather in the spring. For centuries Christmas was a movable feast, celebrated at different times of the year. So why is it now on December 25, other than to allow for dreaming of a white Christmas (because let's face it, that wouldn't happen in the spring in most areas)? It was in the fourth century A.D. that Pope Julius I tabbed December 25 for Christmas celebrations. Why? It was picked to coincide with the pagan celebration of Winter Solstice, or Return of the Sun, in an effort to replace the pagan celebration with one of a more religious character.

2. WHY DO SOME CELEBRATE CHRISTMAS ON JANUARY 7, THEN?

What do you do when days just disappear from the calendar? Well, for some people the answer is "celebrate Christmas on January 7." In October 1582 ten days were dropped to realign the calendar because of the previous improper understanding of leap years. While the Catholic world switched from the Julian calendar to the Gregorian calendar immediately, the switch spread slowly elsewhere, and England and its colonies didn't adjust until 1752. In 1923 the Eastern Orthodox Church made the switch as well; by that time the number of days to drop had risen to thirteen, and thus the December 25 of the old calendar was now January 7. Some sects, called "old calendarists," therefore celebrate Christmas on January 7.

3. WHY DO WE START CHRISTMAS SEASON SO EARLY?

For years, Christmas was a much shorter season, not the monstrosity we have now where one can actually purchase candy canes to give out to little trick-or-treaters on Halloween. (By "one" we mean one of the authors of this book. And the kids love it!) For the current length of the season, merchants have World War II to thank. With thousands upon thousands of sons, brothers, friends, and other soldiers overseas, it was necessary for stateside Americans to mail gifts early to make sure the troops received them in time to open them Christmas morning. The merchants, of course, know a good thing when they see it and reminded the public to shop and mail early . . . and the beginning of the protracted holiday season was upon us.

4. WHY DO WE SEE THE SALVATION ARMY EVERYWHERE?

This tradition was born in San Francisco in 1891. Short of manpower but needing to collect money to pay for a charity Christmas dinner, volunteers simply set a large crabpot down on a San Francisco street. Obviously this first Salvation Army collection kettle was a success, as today stores nationwide host these kettles and their bell-ringing accompanists every Christmas season.

5. WHY DO WE HANG MISTLETOE?

The simple answer to this question is "to get a little smooch from that hot guy/girl at the holiday party!" But how did that tradition, and that meaning, start? Once revered by the early Britons, mistletoe was considered to have magic powers by the Celtic and Teutonic people. It had, they believed, powers of both healing and—ah, here we see it—fertility. At one point, people believed that a kiss under the mistletoe would lead inevitably to marriage.

6. WHY DO WE HANG EVERGREENS ON THE FRONT DOOR?

Seems pretty farfetched, doesn't it? "Hmm, I think I'm going to wrap some of these branches in a circle, and then nail them to my door!" This practice is borrowed from the New Year's wish of good health by the ancient Romans who would offer branches of evergreens to their friends and neighbors. Called "strenae" after the goddess of health Strenia, it became customary to bend the branches into a circle and hang them in doorways. Additionally, ancient Celts saw evergreens as symbols of everlasting life in the midst of bleak winters, whereas Vikings in Scandinavia wanted to show their allegiance—with greenery—to their god, Balder.

7. WHY DO WE PUT LIGHTS ON CHRISTMAS TREES AND IN WINDOWS?

Before Christianity, people in many countries believed that branches of evergreens brought inside could keep ghosts, witches, evil spirits, and diseases out of their homes. Then, others of our nature-worshipping ancestors in Northern Europe started the custom of placing candles on Christmas trees under the belief that they helped shelter the *good* woodland spirits when all the other trees had lost their leaves in the winter. In Germany, thanks to the inspiration of a sixteenth-century church reformer, Martin Luther added candles to his Christmas tree to remind him of the starry winter night.

As for lights in windows, that dates back to the time when Christians were persecuted just for being Christian—and celebrating Christmas was a pretty big tip-off to that. So they developed a code: A candle in the window meant that mass would be celebrated there that night.

8. WHY DO CHRISTMAS CARDS SHOW A ROBIN DELIVERING MAIL?

Well, they *all* don't, but if you look closely at some of the more artistic cards, you'll see a simple robin with a letter in its beak. How did these two things come together? As we learned in Christmas Firsts, the first Christmas card was created in England, and the practice became extremely popular in that country. The British Post Office evolved from the delivery of royal dispatches, and as red was a color associated with royalty the uniforms and letterboxes of the new Post Office were red as well. With these red uniforms, the postmen quickly became tabbed "robins," and it was thus the robins that delivered the Christmas cards.

9. WHY DO WE HAVE A SILENT NIGHT?

As those with kids can attest, Christmas is hardly a "silent" night. So where did this song come from? While the story is debated, according to popular legend, on Christmas Eve 1818, Austrian priest Josepf Mohr was told that the church organ was broken and it was not possible to repair it in time for Christmas services. Depressed at the thought of a Christmas without music, he sat down and composed a carol that could be sung to guitar music rather than the organ. Later that night the Austrians in attendance performed "Stille Nacht" for the first time.

10. WHY DO WE SOMETIMES REFER TO CHRISTMAS AS XMAS?

Many maintain it's an effort to "take the Christ out of Christmas," that the abbreviation is a way to remove the most obvious religious reminder of the holiday. Not so. The abbreviation of Christ to X comes from the Greek letter "chi," the first letter of the word "Christ" in that language. Xmas was in fact originally used in ecclesiastic tables and charts to save space and provide room for more information.

It Was Tradition Somewhere

To people from other cultures, some of the American Christmas traditions must look quite weird. Santa coming down the street on a float in the Thanksgiving Day parade? Yeah, sure . . . whatever you say. But just the same, there are traditions around the world—some current, some that thankfully have passed—that likely drew a raised eyebrow from all but those who celebrated them. That doesn't make them any less traditions . . . simply more unique ones.

1. LA QUEMA DEL DIABLO

December 7 in Guatemala sees the celebration of La Quema del Diablo, or The Burning of the Devil—harsh punishment! It's all part of Advent in the Central American country, as during the first week of Advent the devil runs wild, even to the point of men dressing up as the horned one and chasing townfolk (usually children) around on the street. This builds up to La Quema del Diablo, which helps reinforce the Advent message of preparation for the baby Jesus. People clean their homes, piling useless items in front of their houses where they'll be set on fire. The fires both chase away the devil and assist with the season of housecleaning, both literally and figuratively.

2. THE KING OF THE BEAN

Although not seen as much today, a mock ruler was long a standard of holiday celebrations. A man, usually chosen by luck, lorded over the celebration of Twelfth Night, or Epiphany Eve, mostly in Western European countries. "The King of the Bean" was so named because he was chosen by baking a bean into a cake, and whoever found the bean in his piece of cake was King. (If a woman found the bean, she would appoint a king of her choice.) Said king would make silly proclamations, utter infantile demands, and in general attempt to assist in the merry-making of the evening. Today the tradition is alive with the "King Cake" of Mardi Gras, as whoever finds the token baked into the cake (different families use different tokens) shall have good luck for the coming year.

3. KILLANTZAROI

According to Greek legend, the Killantzaroi are goblins that live in the middle of the earth and are said to appear only during the twelve days of Christmas, between Christmas and the Epiphany, gaining entrance through the chimney. They're a mischievous lot, playing pranks such as souring milk, riding on people's backs, and braiding a horse's tail. Some further believed that babies born during this time had to be kept a careful watch over and protected, otherwise the Killantzaroi would possess them. To keep the scoundrels out of their houses, Greeks will bless their house with holy water each of the twelve days and traditionally keep a fire burning until Epiphany to bar the main means of entrance.

4. FORTUNE TELLING

Polish folklore has it that the Christmas period, and Christmas Eve in particular, were especially powerful times for fortune telling. Much of the fortune telling was done by the young women in the family as they attempted to predict suitors and even marriage by events and luck of the draw. For instance, from whichever direction a dog barked on Christmas Eve, that's where a woman's husband-to-be would appear. Other young ladies drew colored straws from underneath the tablecloth; different colors determined if they would be wed soon, or if they would see only spinsterhood.

5. SECOND CHRISTMAS DAY

Sometimes one is not enough. The Scandinavians really like Christmas; not only is December 25 a holiday in Denmark and some of its neighboring countries, but December 26—Second Christmas Day—is a holiday as well. Second Christmas Day is usually spent like Christmas Day, visiting relatives that one didn't have time to visit the day before. Often with married couples the time breaks down into spending one day with the wife's family and one day with the husband's. For Scandinavians who don't have that much family (or don't want to visit them), theatergoing is a popular alternate activity, and many plays start on December 26 to take advantage of this.

6. MARI LWYD

One of the most unique holiday traditions, the Mari Lwyd is seen only in Wales and involves a combination of hand puppets, caroling, and the television show *Whose Line Is It Anyway?* The Mari Lwyd itself is a horse's skull, decorated with sheets and ribbons and other assorted coverings, so much so that someone can hide underneath the sheet and work the jaw up and down. Bands of men, with the Mari Lwyd in tow, go from house to house like carolers, but rather than singing carols they engage in improv banter and insults with the families they visit. These "discussions" can continue until one side can't think of any more retorts, at which point the group is invited in for drinks.

7. SHOOTING IN CHRISTMAS

Here is another tradition related to spirits or gremlins. According to Norwegian folklore, much like Ebenezer Scrooge of *A Christmas Carol* fame, families receive visitors on Christmas Eve as their dead relatives come back for a visit. Some go so far as to leave out a plate of food at the Christmas feast so those spirits will not go hungry. If the good guys are coming back, though, that means so too can the evil spirits. The custom of shooting in Christmas counters unwanted otherwordly visitors, however, as bands of men go from house to house, saluting each with a volley of gunfire in the belief that the loud sudden noise will scare away any evil spirits that happen to be approaching.

8. WREN HUNT

Although thankfully out of favor today, in past centuries rural areas of the United Kingdom would celebrate the day after Christmas with an organized wren hunt. Large groups of men and boys would hunt this tiny creature, beating it with sticks and stones after a sometimes-long chase. Others would make the unfair fight even more so by using pistols or archery bows to make the kill. Upon return to the homestead, the group would display the "impressive" catch to the town, often leading a parade or singing songs about the hunt. Even though this practice is virtually extinct, for some odd reason the wren remains a somewhat minor symbol of the Christmas season, appearing alongside or sometimes instead of the more popular robin on cards, decorations, and ornaments.

9. BONDI BEACH

With Christmas a summer holiday in Australia, it makes some sense that many celebrate the holiday at the beach. At Bondi Beach near Sydney, up to 40,000 people have spent Christmas roasting themselves rather than a turkey. Until 2004 many toasted as well as roasted, and trees decorated with beer cans were a common sight. However, in 2003 lifeguards had to rescue more than one hundred revelers from the waters, many of them drunk, so in 2004 local authorities instituted a ban on alcohol at the beach. Roasting, however, continues.

10. URN OF FATE

And you thought your office holiday gift exchange was harsh. In Italy (and parts of other European countries) the Urn of Fate is stocked with gifts—including some empty wrapped boxes. Each person takes a gift in turn, with much laughter for those who choose an empty one. Never fear, however, for the Urn of Fate always contains one "real" gift for everyone; just wait until the next turn and try again!

I Am Santa Claus

While the fat man in red slides down chimneys to bring toys to all the good girls and boys here in the United States, he doesn't have a monopoly on gift-giving. A wide variety of folks are the traditional givers in different countries around the world. Following are some of them.

1. **ITALY**

Italian children write to La Befana with their gift requests. La Befana comes from the Italian word for "epiphany," and she is also sometimes called La Strega, "the witch," or La Vecchia, "the old woman."

According to legend, La Befana lived alone and was busy with household chores when three men stopped by and asked directions to Bethlehem. These were the three wise men, who invited her to go along with them to rejoice in the birth of the Christ child. La Befana refused, citing her mounting chores, and sent the three on their way. Later she regretted her decision and tried to catch up with them but failed. To this day, the story goes, she wanders from house to house each year trying to find the Christ child and leaving presents for children who have been good over the past year.

2. RUSSIA

Prior to the Revolution of 1917, holiday gifts in Russia came from Baboushka, a grandmotherly figure with a story very similar—almost exact, as a matter of fact—to Italy's La Befana. After the Revolution, however, the government frowned upon tales involving religion, and as Baboushka was searching for the Christ child she was disenfranchised, replaced by Grandfather Frost, or Dyed Moroz. Further, the government promoted him as bringing gifts on New Year's Eve, a secular holiday, rather than the religious Christmas Eve.

3. ENGLAND

Today, Father Christmas is Santa Claus in all but name, but that wasn't always so. Originally Father Christmas didn't distribute gifts but rather was a symbol that represented the mirth and happiness of the holiday season. Although debate still exists on how long he's been around, Father Christmas has been in England at least since Renaissance times, if not longer. His usual appearance is in a green or red robe with a green crown of holly. Some picture him as an old and thin man, a la Father Time, but the more popular depiction is of a hale and hearty soul. Charles Dickens's "Ghost of Christmas Present" is a popular representative of that period's standard picture of Father Christmas.

4. GERMANY

The Christkindel, or Christ child, brings gifts in Germany as well as parts of Austria and Switzerland. There are varying iterations of the Christkindel, with some saying it is the child Jesus whereas others view it as an angel, a young girl with flowing hair, golden wings, and a long robe. In some areas Hans Trapp used to accompany the Christ child; he was the punisher, the "bad cop" of the two.

The Christ child started his giving ways in the seventeenth century as a way of teaching children of the blessings that come directly from God. St. Nicholas was fine and dandy, but he still wasn't the direct link to God that the Christkindel was. Over time, of course, the name changed into Kris Kringle, which today is simply another synonym for Santa Claus.

5. SPAIN AND SOUTH AMERICA

Many Spanish-speaking countries exchange gifts on Dia de los Tres Reyes, or "Three Kings Day," rather than (or sometimes in addition to) Christmas, and as such their gift-givers are the Three Kings, or Magi. The Magi, of course, would be traveling through each town on their way to Bethlehem to see the baby Jesus on January 6, the Epiphany. Children (only children received gifts from the Magi) leave out their shoes, as well as straw for the camels, and wake in the morning to find them overflowing with gifts.

Another tradition is similar to Mardi Gras's "King Cake," as bakers insert a tiny doll into a special "Three Kings Cake," and whoever finds the doll in his or her slice of cake will be blessed with good luck in the forthcoming year.

6. SWEDEN

The Jultomten, or Christmas elf, is possibly the most playful of the gift-givers. Often depicted as a stout gnome with the standard red hat (think of the garden gnome from Travelocity commercials), the Jultomten lives in a dark corner of the house, under the stairs, or perhaps up in the attic. Only on Christmas Eve does he emerge to leave small gifts in hiding for the children to find. Showing a wise eye, the Swedish custom suggests leaving out items such as liquor or tobacco to appease the gnome and keep him from making merry havoc in the house. Other Scandinavian countries have similar figures—Denmark's Julnissen, Norway's Julenissen, and Finland's Joulutonttuja—taking on similar appearances and actions.

7. POLAND

Christmas celebrations in Poland focus on the Star of Bethlehem, and as such their gift-giver is Star Man, usually the village priest or a family elder decorated with stars on his clothing. The Christmas meal, or wigilia, does not start until the appearance of gwiazdka, or little star. After the meal the Star Man sometimes quizzes the children with religious questions, rewarding them with presents when they answer correctly (even if they need a little help to do so).

8. JAPAN

Although there is no official celebration of Christmas in Japan—such a small percentage of the country is Christian—there is a secular celebration that has evolved over the last century. The Japanese god of Hoteiosho brings gifts to good children, allegedly helped in his spying by eyes in the back of his head. This merry soul looks to be a cross between Santa and a sumo wrestler.

9. BRAZIL

Brazilian children are visited in the summer heat by Papai Noel, who is similar to Santa Claus but differs for very logical reasons. Because of the extreme heat, he's often dressed in silk rather than the standard fur of the more northern climates. And because most houses in the country don't have chimneys—no need, really—Papai Noel comes in through the front door rather than down the chimney. Finally, Papai Noel officially arrives each year from his home country of Greenland (rather than the North Pole), and his mid-December arrival by helicopter to a soccer stadium always draws a huge crowd.

10. **TURKEY**

Many countries look to St. Nicholas to deliver toys, yet the Turks feel a special attachment, because the real St. Nicholas lived in what is now Turkey during the fourth century. Toward the end of his life he served as bishop of Myra, on the southwestern coast of Turkey, and the Church of Saint Nicholas (built after his death) is there today. A bit away from the church is a modern statue of the saint surrounded by children and, as proof of his gift-giving attitude, a bag of toys. As with Father Christmas, St. Nicholas is depicted as a tall, rather thin man rather than the rotund figure we recognize as Santa Claus.

Apparently not all Turks feel the same attachment to St. Nick, however. In March 2005 the town of Demre replaced a bronze statue of the native son with a statue depicting the modern-day Santa Claus, claiming that this image of St. Nicholas is the more recognized one and would bring more tourists to the area.

Home, Home on the Range

As even the smallest of children know, Santa Claus makes his home at the North Pole, freezing his tuchus off and making good use of the cheap elf labor available to him. But what are the facts on the North Pole? What else is up there? What's Santa seen through the years, and who might have joined Santa in the past for a neighborly meal? Read on and find out.

1. GEOGRAPHY

Santa doesn't actually own a piece of land at the North Pole—but only because there's no land to own. The North Pole is rather part of the ice cap on the northern tip of the earth, some six to ten feet thick as it floats on the Arctic Ocean. At its biggest, the ice cap is roughly the size of the United States; it shrinks to half that size in the "heat" of the summer.

2. CLIMATE

The "heat" of the summer, however, really isn't all that hot. July is the North Pole's hottest month, with an average high of 32 degrees Fahrenheit. That's right, the average high is right at the freezing point. February sees the coldest temperatures when the average drops to 31 below. That's not counting the wind-chill, either,

which makes it an even less welcoming environment.
No wonder Santa doesn't have many neighbors.

3. EXPLORERS

Santa may not have a lot of neighbors, but he's had a
fair number of visitors over the years. Robert Peary
and his team (including Matthew Henson and four
Eskimos) are believed to be the first explorers to reach
the North Pole, on April 6, 1909. However, recent data,
based on some of Peary's writings, shows that he may
have unknowingly been as much as twenty miles short
of the pole. The first airplane reached the pole in 1926,
flown by Richard E. Byrd, and in 1968 the United
States' nuclear-powered submarine *Nautilus* was the
first vehicle to view the North Pole from underneath.

4. TRAVEL

Santa's atmosphere has become a bit noisier in the
semi-recent past, and he may see more traffic sometime soon. With the end of the Cold War, Russia now
allows flights over Siberia and onward to the North Pole,
allowing for much shorter flights from Europe and the
United States to Asia and the Pacific Islands. And many
scientists say that with global warming and the shrink-
ing ice cap, sometime in the next century or so the elusive "Northwest Passage" could become viable in the
summer months. The would allow shipping through the
Arctic Ocean and cut thousands of miles off the current
journey from Europe to Asia, which now goes down to
Panama, through the Canal, and back up again.

5. NIGHT BEFORE CHRISTMAS

For Santa Claus, the night before Christmas is always a
long one . . . and not because he's spending it finishing
up on toy-making and cookie-eating and all those deliveries. No, there's only one "night" at the North Pole, and

it takes place from September until March. The sun rises at the North Pole on the spring equinox, usually March 21, and rises then falls through the sky for six months of daylight until it finally sets again on the autumnal equinox, on or about September 21. From then until March again, it's a long winter night for Santa.

6. POLAR BEAR

Santa would do well to avoid the polar bear on his sojourns around the North Pole. The polar bear is the world's largest carnivore, but as yet there have been no reports of them chasing a fat man in a red suit. Rather, they subsist mostly on a diet of seals with the occasional walrus thrown in, as well as whale carcasses. Contrary to what many believe, polar bears do not eat penguins. That, of course, is because there *are* no penguins at the North Pole; they reside in Antarctica.

A male polar bear can grow upward of eleven feet long, and can weigh as much as fifteen hundred pounds. And while polar bears may appear white, their hair is actually clear. Their entire body is covered with hollow fur, allowing for sunlight to be transported to their skin quickly.

7. NARWHAL

The polar bear isn't the only animal that might pay Santa a visit. The narwhal—also called "the unicorn of the sea"—lives in the icy waters of the Arctic Ocean. Average as whales go, the narwhal draws its nickname from one of its teeth, which grows out from its mouth up to nine or ten feet long. This tusk, as one can imagine, can be very useful as a weapon in disputes. According to legend it's good luck to find one of these tusks, but it's bad luck to kill a narwhal for its tusk. Whether that's bad luck for you or for the narwhal isn't fully detailed.

8. MAGNETIC NORTH POLE

What most people commonly refer to as the North Pole (i.e., the tip-top of the earth) is technically referred to as "geographic North Pole." The "magnetic North Pole" is in a different location, and it's where your compass points. The magnetic North Pole can shift up to twenty-five miles in a single year, affected by the molten core of the earth as well as particles from the sun. Amazingly, magnetic North and magnetic South can actually switch places, and have in the earth's history; many scientists think it's not out of the question that they'll swap again. Currently, the difference between the two North Poles is roughly 600 miles.

9. NORTH POLE MARATHON

Santa must think there's some crazy people out there with this one. Yep, you read right—there's a North Pole Marathon. It's the brainchild of Richard Donovan, who won the first South Pole Marathon in 2002, and then ran a solo marathon at the North Pole in April 2002. In each year since he has organized the North Pole Marathon, and the event includes a helicopter ride to and photo at the exact North Pole. In April 2004, fifteen participants ran laps on the circular course, with the winning time of 3:43:17 being turned in by Sean Burch of the United States.

10. FORTRESS OF SOLITUDE

Who could forget about Superman's Fortress of Solitude at the North Pole? Surely Santa has the Man of Steel over for dinner and drinks when he's in the area, right? The Fortress is Superman's home away from home, a place to get away from it all and do a bit of research at the same time. Entrance to the building is simple: a giant key lies out in the open, but only someone of Superman's super strength can lift the key to use it.

O Christmas Tree,
O Christmas Tree

Alive or artificial, green or white or even pink, tall or short—they all qualify as Christmas trees. Some families bring them home and decorate them the day after Thanksgiving; others wait until Christmas Eve or Christmas itself. Fathers have threatened to find one in the recycle bin on December 26 if the kids don't behave and keep quiet while he's watching the football game (or was that just one dad?). However they look, whenever they come into the house, however they are decorated (many say there are two types of people in the world: clumpers and single tinsel stranders—which are you?), and whenever presents are placed underneath them, everyone agrees: O Christmas Tree, O Christmas Tree! How lovely are your branches.

1. THE FIRST TREE

No one knows who first had the idea of taking a tree from outside and decorating it—or when that thought popped into someone's head—but the Christmas tree was popular in Germany as far back as the sixteenth century. The first printed reference to a Christmas tree appeared in that country in 1531. Germany certainly wasn't selfish, however. Queen Victoria's husband, Albert, visited Germany, and impressed with the idea, he made the Christmas tree part of the Windsor Castle celebrations back in England. As for the United States, the earliest mention of a Christmas tree there is in the diary of a Pennsylvania man who came from Germany.

2. THE OFFICIAL CHRISTMAS TREE

The Christmas tree in the presidential White House and the one on the Ellipse are both often called the national Christmas tree, yet the actual "official" Christmas tree is neither of them. As a matter of fact, it's not even in Washington, D.C., or anywhere close. The official Christmas tree is located in King's Canyon National Park, all the way on the West Coast in California. Named the official tree in 1926 by President Calvin Coolidge and proclaimed a National Shrine by President Dwight D. Eisenhower in 1956, this monstrous sequoia—named "General Grant Tree"—is roughly 270 feet tall, 40 feet across at its base, and 107 feet around. Estimates of its age range from 1,500 to 2,000 years old.

3. HOW MANY TREES?

According to the National Christmas Tree Association (NCTA), Americans buy close to forty million live Christmas trees each year. As many as 25 percent of them come from the more than five thousand choose-your-own-tree farms around the country, cut down by the people taking them home. Although sales of live trees have been declining lately, the NCTA recently introduced a campaign to encourage the purchase of "real" trees, including a contest for children to "help Santa find the perfect real Christmas tree."

Christmas trees grow on a Christmas tree farm.
National Christmas Tree Association

4. CONSERVATION

With all those trees, there sure must be a shortage of
Christmas trees, right? Well, finding a Christmas tree
may not be as easy as in the mid-1800s when the item
first became popular in the United States—with a few
hundred million fewer residents, forests were certainly
in higher abundance—but tree farmers take careful
steps to make sure they don't run themselves out of
business. For instance, for every live tree harvested,
two or three seedlings are planted in its place. In 2003,
Christmas tree farmers planted an estimated seventy
million trees just in North America. Those trees will
take seven to ten years to reach the desired six or
seven feet high, but that's still a lot of trees.

5. TEDDY ROOSEVELT

President Theodore Roosevelt was a strict conservationist, so much so that he would not permit an evergreen tree to be cut and brought into his house—even when he lived in the White House! This was the president who established the National Park system during his administration. No cut Christmas trees didn't put a damper on the spirits of his family, however, because Roosevelt's children would evade their father's edict by sneaking the forbidden trees into their bedrooms for the holiday season.

6. KINDS OF TREES

All kinds of evergreens are used for Christmas trees—no one tree has a monopoly on the American heart. The most popular trees are Douglas fir, white pine, Virginia pine, Noble fir, Fraser fir, Scotch pine, and Balsam fir. Most trees in the United States come from Oregon, Pennsylvania, North Carolina, California, Michigan, Wisconsin, or Washington, with Oregon ahead of the pack. Worldwide, however, lovely Nova Scotia, Canada, is the biggest exporter of Christmas trees—along with wild blueberries and lobster.

7. CARE OF A TREE

The care of Christmas trees starts long before they reach the sales lot. To encourage the number of branches desired, Christmas trees are hand-clipped each spring and trimmed to reduce the upward growth while making them fuller. Trees grown in the wild are naturally sparser trees with fewer branches. In the industry these are sometimes referred to as "Charlie Brown trees," after the pathetic, droopy specimen that Charlie Brown selected for the Christmas pageant in his eponymous cartoon classic. According to the

National Christmas Tree Association, however, these less dense trees are becoming more and more popular. One guess as to the reason: room for more presents underneath them.

8. CARE OF A TREE: HOME EDITION

Okay, so what about you? What can YOU do to keep your tree looking good from start to finish? A fallacy of the season is that a live Christmas tree can be jammed into a stand that is filled up with water and be considered cared for. Not so. The most important thing to remember is to buy fresh. In that way, at least, a Christmas tree is like fruits, veggies, and Mentos: Fresh matters! Grab a branch and gently pull it toward you. Do lots of needles come off between your fingers? If so, move on. If it passes that test, pick up the tree and bounce it on its stump. While some interior brown needles are expected to fall from this force, you shouldn't see an excess of green needles being dropped.

Once you've picked your tree and have it at home, make a fresh cut in the trunk of the tree, about a half inch from the bottom, to allow for easier absorption of water. Keep the tree stand full of water, checking daily. You want at least a quart for every inch in diameter of your tree. And although a tree by the fireside is a nice picture, it's best to keep your tree away from any sources of heat. Heat will affect the moisture in the tree and let it dry out earlier than desired.

9. HUNGRY?

You all know the drill, kids. You go to bed at 8 p.m. on Christmas Eve, knowing that the sooner you fall asleep the sooner Christmas comes. Either that or you're so wired that you wake up every hour, steal a peek at the clock, and then wonder if Mom and Dad will think three o'clock in the morning is too early. When the excitement is still too much and you jump out of bed, it still takes the parents awhile to get moving, doesn't it? All those presents to be had . . . to say nothing of breakfast!

Well, we have the breakfast part taken care of now. You didn't hear this from us, but Christmas trees are actually edible (note: this doesn't apply to those fake trees. If you have one of those, go grab a Pop-Tart). If you've got a pine, a fir, or a spruce, though, dig in! The needles are a good source of Vitamin C, and if you can find yourself a pine cone or some pine nuts, those are also a good source of nutrition. Mmm, tasty!

10. SOME TREE

While it may seem more like a Halloween decoration than a Christmas one, an artificial spider and web are often seen on Christmas trees in the Ukraine, because seeing a spider web in the tree on Christmas morning is supposed to bring you good luck. There's no mention of how much luck you'll have if the spider starts spelling out holiday messages and convinces you not to cook the pig for dinner, however.

To See if Reindeer Really Know How to Fly

Hard as it may be to believe, reindeer can't really fly. And surprisingly there is not a single instance in reindeer history of one having a glowing red nose. Really, it's true! Below are some more facts about Santa's favorite mode of transportation, the means behind his nine-reindeer-powered sleigh.

1. CLASSIFICATION

Known as *rangifer tarandus*, the reindeer is of the animalia (animal) kingdom. It's in the "chordata" phylum, meaning it has a backbone with a spinal cord. Next down the line, it's of the class "mammalia," or milk-producing animals. As it's a hoofed animal, its subclass is "ungulata," and the order is "artiodactyla"—even-toed. They are of the suborder "ruminantia," as they're cud-chewers and have a multiple-compartment stomach, and are of the "cervidae" family—the deer. Finally, as mentioned, they're of the genus "rangifer" and the species "tarandus."

2. REINDEER VERSUS CARIBOU

Reindeer and caribou; caribou and reindeer. Like Patty Duke and her "cousin" of the 1960s' television program, *The Patty Duke Show*, they look alike, they walk alike, they . . . well, you get the idea. What's the difference, anyway? Turns out it's relatively simple: Reindeer are domesticated caribou. They're stouter than their wild cousins with shorter legs, too, tend to be lighter in color, and have a flatter face than the caribou. They also tend to stay in herds and run in a tight group when chased, whereas caribou will scatter more.

3. DOMESTICATION

As mentioned in the previous item, reindeer are domesticated caribou. There's evidence that this domestication occurred as many as 5,000 years ago, when natives learned to use the caribou for travel, as well as food and clothing. A Chukchi breed appears to have been domesticated the longest. Modern-day man has made efforts to domesticate wild caribou, but all of those efforts have failed. Today, the largest domestication is in Russia, where an estimated 2.25 million domesticated reindeer reside.

4. LOCATION, LOCATION, LOCATION

At their prime, reindeer could be found anywhere in the Northern latitudes. Today, for the most part because of over-hunting, reindeer are found only in the Arctic regions, with the largest herds in northern Canada, Alaska, Scandinavia, and Russia. Herds can range from roughly twenty to thousands. Because of the frozen land and scarce food supplies, reindeer herds are nomadic, wandering often in search of new food, and crossing both land and water in their travels.

5. LOOK AT ME!

Depending on the subspecies, reindeer can range from a low of 180 pounds all the way up to a whopping 600 pounds. Their height varies from roughly thirty-six inches up to fifty inches—just over four feet tall. As with most species of animals, the male is usually much larger than the female. Their fur is relatively short—not much more than an inch long for the most part—but is thick and dense, with roughly 5,000 hairs per square inch for the outer coat and up to 13,000 for the denser inner coat. During the summer the color is a rich brown, but in the winter it turns to gray or white. As with similar-climate animals, their fur is hollow, allowing the reindeer to retain warm air and shed cold water much better, a necessity in their cold, wet environs. Also perhaps because of their location, the reindeer is the only deer that has a furred nosepad.

6. ANTLERS

Unlike other breeds of deer, both the bulls (male reindeer) and cows (female reindeer) grow antlers, which are extremely useful in scratching through snow to find food. The bulls do have slightly larger antlers, which can grow up to an impressive four feet wide. Reindeer antlers typically have two sets of points, two groupings in the horns: one lower and set closer to the head, and another one taller and wider as you see with deer. New antlers are fully grown by July of each year but don't completely harden until the fall. They are covered by vascular tissue through the summer. Each sex loses its antlers every year with the male reindeer shedding theirs in the early winter while the females usually keep theirs until after giving birth in the spring.

7. HOOVES

Reindeer hooves are broader and flatter than most of their deer brethren, splaying out more with webbing between the "toes" to allow for a firmer, wider base to walk on. As most of the land that reindeer tread upon is snow or soft marsh, this keeps them from sinking down when walking—think of it as a natural snowshoe. The hooves are tough as well, as reindeer use them to dig into snow while looking for food. When walking, reindeer often make a clicking sound, the result of a tendon snapping across a bone. While it sounds neat to kids watching them prance and click, hunters are able to use the sound when tracking the reindeer.

8. MMM, MMM GOOD

As with all deer, the reindeer is an herbivore, subsisting on a wide variety of vegetation. Its main food is lichen, a fungus and algae mix. In fact, one kind of lichen is such a large part of the reindeer diet that it's become known as "reindeer lichen." It's the relative inability to replicate this lichen in captivity that makes reindeer survival in zoos quite difficult. They also eat any grass they can find along with the lichen, as well as sprouts and shrubs in the spring, green leaves in the summer, and twigs, sprouts, and even moss in the harsh winter—often having to dig a few feet into the snow just to find that.

9. MMM, MMM GOOD PART TWO

It's the circle of life, they said in *The Lion King*. Like the buffalo with the Native American, the reindeer is extremely important to the inhabitants of the Arctic regions as a member of the food chain. In addition to providing transportation, the reindeer provides meat as well as butter and cheese. Its coat can be used for clothing, the antlers and bones for utensils and tools, and the tendons in its legs can be made into thread. Reindeer meat is very lean, only about two percent fat, and is extremely high in protein. It has a distinctive taste, gamey yet relatively mild, and remains in demand in many areas despite its high price.

10.   WELL, YA KNOW, NORMY . . .

There are so many little facts about reindeer that are interesting and amazing . . . the type of information with which Cliff Clavin of *Cheers* fame might regale his barmates. For example, a baby reindeer can outrun an average human when it's only one day old—it needs to be able to keep up with the meandering herd! In another example, by eating moss, reindeer ingest a chemical that helps keep their bodily fluids warm, acting almost as antifreeze. Also, while reindeer meat is extremely healthy, reindeer milk has more fat in it than cow's milk. And interestingly enough, reindeers are extremely fond of bananas. Who knew?

Eight Isn't Enough

Now that we have learned about real reindeer, let's move on to the ones that are all about Christmas. As we learned earlier, Santa was first shown on a sleigh led by flying reindeer in a cartoon during the Civil War. Later on, a cartoon special would trace back the reindeers' ability to fly to magic corn provided to Kris Kringle. The number of reindeer with Santa usually varied until 1823 when Clement C. Moore wrote the famous poem *'Twas the Night Before Christmas,* and in the course of the action presented for eternity the names of eight reindeer. In naming them, Moore seemed to look at the three qualities necessary to pull a sleigh across the world and land on snowy rooftops: strength, speed, and nimbleness. One more reindeer was introduced more than a hundred years later, and the tenth . . . wait a second, who *is* the tenth? Will this list come up short? You'll find out soon enough. Now, sing along with us . . .

1. YOU KNOW DASHER

The first of the reindeer listed in the poem and song, you know Dasher had to be a bit ticked at giving up his lead spot when Rudolph came along. Dasher was, as demonstrated by his name, recruited for his speed more than anything, dashing through the sky for Santa (as opposed to dashing through the snow; there was just one with that sleigh, and a horse at that).

2. **AND DANCER**

Dancer is second in line, directly behind Dasher on one side of Santa's sleigh. Dancer's name might suggest that his abilities lie in his nimbleness, being able to dance along the slick and icy rooftops and not lose his footing, which would send the sleigh and all its packages hurtling roadside. That would not be a good thing.

3. **PRANCER**

Although not paired with Dancer in the song's couplets, one could probably assume that the two are related, much like twins Phil and Lil of *Rugrats* cartoon fame. The rhyming names must be a giveaway that these reinder are siblings, no doubt about it. Any sibling rivalry that might occur because of their relative positions on the line—does Prancer begrudge Dancer being ahead?—is a moot point on Christmas Eve. Prancer relies on surefootedness just like Dancer to maintain contact with the rooftops.

4. **AND VIXEN**

For awhile, Vixen was thought to be the only definite female of Santa's group. Cupid was considered to be definitely male, and the rest . . . well, for some it was hard to tell based solely on the name. Dasher, Comet, and Donder were certainly male. At least in the cartoon version, Dasher was Rudolph's proud papa, Donder was Rudolph's little sweetheart's father, and

Comet was the very male-sounding coach of the young reindeer. However, as mentioned in the previous list, a male reindeer loses his horns at the beginning of winter, while a female reindeer keeps her horns until the spring. Since almost all images of Santa and the reindeer—on Christmas Eve—depict reindeer with antlers, they simply must be females, some argue. Only Santa knows for sure.

5.   COMET

Comet, the fifth reindeer, was the coach in the television cartoon classic. He, sadly, was the one who first ordered all the reindeer not to include Rudolph in their reindeer games. Luckily, his intolerance was combated later in the show and he's since recovered from his initial shock. Comet, as you can guess from the name, has the speed and endurance to streak through the sky all night long.

6.   AND CUPID

Hooked up behind Comet on Santa's sleigh, Cupid's name comes from the mythological Cupid and his love-inducing arrows, indicating that the reindeer Cupid was tabbed for inclusion based on his speed. Like Cupid's arrow—and the love that arrow brings—the reindeer himself can sometimes get a bit out of control, relegating Cupid to the second row instead of a lead position.

7.   DONDER

Elsewhere in the book we maintain there are two types of people in the world: The tinsel clumpers and the single-stranders. Well, here's another divisive point to use: Donder or Donner? Quien es mas macho? Er, which is correct? Believe it or not, technically neither is right! In the very first printing of Clement C. Moore's poem, *'Twas the Night Before Christmas*, the seventh reindeer listed was Dunder. Later printings by Moore changed the spelling to Donder. The etymology of the word is from the Dutch for thunder, and Donder is a bit closer to the correct pronunciation than Dunder. The name Donner was popularized by the song "Rudolph the Red-Nosed Reindeer," but was seen in print occasionally even before that song. Dunder, Donder, or Donner, he's still one of the top eight.

8.   AND BLITZEN

Blitzen is another reindeer who's gone through some name changes, but no one goes around arguing about this one for some reason. In the original poem, Blitzen was called Blixem, coming from the Dutch for lightning to pair with Dunder's thunder. Within a decade, however, that had been switched to Blixen—better to rhyme with Vixen—and soon thereafter common pronunciations led to another switch, this time to the Blitzen we all know today. Fast as lightning, Blitzen helps provide the speed for Santa's sleigh.

9.   BUT DO YOU RECALL

The most famous reindeer of all? Yes, Rudolph! Rudolph wasn't a part of Moore's nineteenth-century poem but was created for a holiday giveaway at Montgomery Ward department store in 1939. After rejecting Reginald and Rollo as potential names, store employee Robert L. May settled on Rudolph and wrote a tale based in part on the story of the ugly duckling from children's literature. The rest, as they say, will go down in history (like Columbus!).

10. OLIVE, THE OTHER REINDEER

Ah yes, of course! Who could forget Olive? Olive is the fruit of a mondegreen—a misinterpretation of musical lyrics usually both common and hilarious. Some of the more famous examples include "Excuse me while I kiss this guy" instead of "Excuse me while I kiss the sky" from Jimi Hendrix's "Purple Haze" and "There's a bathroom on the right" instead of the correct "There's a bad moon on the rise" from Credence Clearwater Revival's "Bad Moon on the Rise." And while not a musical misinterpretation, there's also the old joke about Harold being Jesus's middle name, from "Our Father, who art in heaven, Harold be thy name."

Olive got her start from the many people who misheard the lyrics in Rudolph's ode as "Olive, the other reindeer" instead of "all of the other reindeer." Who was this mean Olive creature who laughed and called poor Rudolph names? Where does *she* get off? Taking advantage of the common confusion, Vivian Walsh and J. Otto Seibold wrote a book called *Olive, the Other Reindeer* that was turned into a television cartoon special as well, starring actress Drew Barrymore as the voice of Olive. However, it turns out Olive isn't a reindeer, but a dog—a dog who thinks Christmas is about to be canceled and travels to the North Pole to volunteer as a substitute reindeer. Now that's the Christmas spirit!

Bing, Nat, and Frank—No Christmas Is Complete Without the Classics

These are the songs that no matter how often they are overplayed are just so great they bring a special Christmas warmth to our hearts, a smile to our faces, and that desire to rush to the mall for one more K-Tel Record.

1. "WHITE CHRISTMAS"—BING CROSBY

This song has put the notion in millions of heads that no Christmas is perfect unless there is a good foot of pristine snow on the ground. Recorded by nearly everybody, the definitive version is performed by Bing Crosby. Bing first performed "White Christmas" live on the radio Christmas Day 1941 and hit the top of the charts with it in 1942. "White Christmas" has been one of the best-loved Christmas songs ever since. The song's sentiment and yearning for a Christmas "just like the ones I used to know" struck a very emotional chord when Bing would perform for servicemen during World War II.

Interestingly, "White Christmas" was written by Irving Berlin, a Jewish man, for the 1942 film *Holiday Inn*, which starred Bing and Fred Astaire. For the movie, Berlin wrote songs for each major holiday of the year. Unsure of whether he had captured the feeling of Christmas, Irving ran the song past Bing who proclaimed it an undeniable winner. "White Christmas" was the hit song of the movie, enough so that it spun off into its own movie in 1954, starring Bing, Danny Kaye, and Rosemary Clooney. The Bing Crosby version of "White Christmas" that we hear every year is not the original 1942 version. That master was played so often that it became damaged. Bing re-recorded it in 1947, carefully trying to reconstruct the 1942 master.

2. "THE CHRISTMAS SONG"—NAT "KING" COLE

"Chestnuts roasting on an open fire" . . . now, try to find a family in America where this is actually an essential part of its Christmas tradition. Nevertheless, this 1946 recording by Nat "King" Cole has warmed the hearts of "kids from one to ninety-two" who have had "Jack Frost nipping at their nose." Apparently no provision has been made for kids ninety-three and older.

Cole had a very successful career, both as a jazz pianist and as a crooner, recording such hits as "Mona Lisa" and "Straighten Up and Fly Right." Yet it is "The Christmas Song" that most people are familiar with today. It was written in less than an hour by singer/songwriter "The Velvet Fog" Mel Torme and his songwriting partner, Bob Wells, reportedly while sitting around a swimming pool in the summer. The title of "The Christmas Song" is not quickly recognized by most casual listeners, as this tune is often referred to instead as "Chestnuts Roasting on an Open Fire."

3. "RUDOLPH THE RED-NOSED REINDEER"—GENE AUTRY

The addition of a ninth reindeer, this one to lead Santa's sleigh with his night-light red nose, was created as a publicity stunt by a Montgomery Ward employee, Robert L. May, in 1939. While a successful inclusion to the American Christmas institution, it wasn't until May's brother-in-law, Johnny Marks, put a melody to the poem that Rudolph became the most famous reindeer of all. The 1949 recording by Gene Autry, America's Most Famous Cowboy, sold several million copies and helped Rudolph go down in history. Autry was one of the biggest movie stars of the 1940s, as well as a successful singer, and later, the owner of the California Angels baseball team. Another famous version of this song is performed by Burl Ives from the 1964 television special on Rudolph that is still popular to this day.

4. "LET IT SNOW"—DEAN MARTIN

The official title being "Let It Snow! Let It Snow! Let It Snow!" written by the famous songwriting team of Sammy Cahn and Jule Styne, this becomes a favorite of school-aged kids each year, hoping for school closures as the area weather broadcasters start mentioning the S-word. Cahn wrote for singer Frank Sinatra throughout much of the 1950s, and, although Sinatra's version is top-notch too, it is Martin's rendition of "Let It Snow" that is the most played each holiday season. This is one of those popular Christmas songs that actually has nothing to do with Christmas. It is entirely a song about frightful winter weather, but since Bing Crosby has us dreaming of a white Christmas, this song is usually only heard with collections of holiday music. Dean recorded "Let It Snow" on a 1959 album that, like the song, had more to do with winter weather than Christmas.

5.   "HAVE YOURSELF A MERRY LITTLE CHRISTMAS"— FRANK SINATRA

Yet another wartime classic, "Have Yourself A Merry Little Christmas" was written by Hugh Martin and Ralph Blane in 1944 as part of the score for the film *Meet Me in St. Louis*. This is one of those melancholic Christmas wishes with the hope that "from now on our troubles will be miles away." The song evokes a hopeful and emotional wartime sentiment, reminiscing of "olden days" when "faithful friends who are dear to us gather near to us once more" and out of harm's way. Judy Garland performed this in *Meet Me in St. Louis*, but The Chairman of the Board set the standard for this oft-recorded classic in 1957.

6.   "SLEIGH RIDE"—ARTHUR FIEDLER AND THE BOSTON POPS

Giddy up, let's go! The Boston Pops performed this orchestral classic to perfection with the clip-clop horse hooves, whip snap, and requisite trumpet horse whinny at the end. Leroy Anderson was a twentieth-century composer of what could be called light classical music and contributed many original compositions to the Boston Pops beginning in 1938. His 1948 composition "Sleigh Ride" is his most enduring work. Another song that has more to do with snow than Christmas, it has nonetheless become a Christmas standard. The Boston Pops were formed in 1885 but took off in popularity when Arthur Fiedler was named conductor in 1930, a position he held for fifty years, and it is Arthur conducting the Pops for this famous recording. "Sleigh Ride" was such an enormous success that lyrics were added in 1950 by Mitchell Parish: "Just hear those sleigh bells jingle-ing, ring ting tingle-ing too. Come on, it's lovely weather for a sleigh ride together with you. Outside the snow is falling and friends are calling 'yoo hoo' . . . ."

7. "SILVER BELLS"—JOHNNY MATHIS

The downtown shopping districts with elaborately decorated department store windows and silver bells on every street corner are almost a thing of the past now, but we can remember them when we hear this song. These days we schlep down to the mall, and are hard-pressed to find "children laughing" as we meet "smile after smile."

Arthur Fiedler conducts the Boston Pops. *Photographer unknown. Courtesy of the Boston Symphony Orchestra*

"Silver Bells" was composed by the great songwriting team of Jay Livingston and Ray Evans, the same team that composed "Que Sera Sera" and the theme to *Mr. Ed.* The standard for this song comes from the great Johnny Mathis, who included it on his first Christmas album in 1958. Mathis also released his first greatest hits album in 1958. This was the first full-length album given a "greatest hits" title, and was such a huge success that almost every artist since, no matter how many or few "hits," has had a "greatest hits" collection.

8. **"IT'S THE MOST WONDERFUL TIME OF THE YEAR"—ANDY WILLIAMS**

"The hap-happiest of all" Christmas songs, this sweeping, uplifting song from the pens of Eddie Pola and George Wyle was composed in 1963. Recorded the same year by Andy Williams, it was so well performed most other singers do not attempt to tackle it. One can only hope that the reference to "scary ghost stories" at Christmastime refers to Dickens's *Christmas Carol.* Otherwise, it can only be a reference to a Christmas tradition held by very few Americans. This song also made its way into popular culture in the late 1990s as part of a back-to-school-shopping ad. While Andy crooned about the most wonderful time of the year, the parents danced through the school supply section of the store while the children glumly followed.

9. **"BLUE CHRISTMAS"—ELVIS PRESLEY**

Nothing says Christmas like the King of Rock and Roll—Elvis Presley. He recorded "Blue Christmas" in 1957 and set the standard for great songs for people spending Christmas at the Heartbreak Hotel. Up to this point, most Christmas songs focused on the chilly weather or idealistic emotional wishes for the better times ahead of us, but The King was not afraid to say he was feeling blue. Contrary to the sentiment of "Blue Christmas," Elvis loved Christmas and his Memphis, Tennessee, home, Graceland, is still decked out for Christmas each year. In an effort to ward off feeling blue at Christmas, Elvis proposed to Priscilla on Christmas Eve in 1966. Also, Elvis's famous meeting with President Nixon took place just before Christmas in 1970. "Blue Christmas" was actually written by Billy Haynes and Jay Johnson in 1948. Country music legend Ernest Tubb was one of the first to record it, and many others have recorded it throughout the years, including a stuttering Porky Pig imitator. However, it seems as if it was written for Elvis.

10. "WINTER WONDERLAND"—TONY BENNETT

The oldest of the songs on this list, "Walking in a Winter Wonderland" was written in 1934 by Felix Bernard and Dick Smith and has been recorded by thousands of singers. A romantic song about snow and dreaming of getting married by Parson Brown may be the inspiration behind hundreds of Christmas Eve engagement stories. It may be possible that Tony Bennett left his heart in foggy San Francisco, another of his hits, to find a winter wonderland to sing of when he recorded his version on an album called *Snowfall* in 1968.

Sing It and Swing It

Jazz was invented in America, and it seems to hold a special place in American hearts at Christmastime. Even though many Americans no longer listen to Ella Fitzgerald and Louie Armstrong as much any more, they return to their warm vocals every year at Christmas. Over the years, many jazz masters have created some unique and special moments with their own versions of Christmas songs.

1. "ZAT YOU, SANTA CLAUS?"—LOUIS ARMSTRONG

A true American icon, and one of the most influential figures in jazz, Louis "Satchmo" Armstrong would be on the Mount Rushmore of twentieth-century American musicians, along with Frank Sinatra, Hank Williams, and Elvis Presley. Armstrong recorded many Christmas songs throughout his career and also added a wonderful reading of Clement C. Moore's "The Night Before Christmas" in a way that only Satchmo could. Gifted as a singer, trumpet player, bandleader, and entertainer, one of Armstrong's best Christmas recordings was "Zat You, Santa Claus?," a swinging hip number where Armstrong is preparing for Christmas and hopes the strange sounds in the house belong to the man in red. Written by Jack Fox, the song wonders who is knocking on the door, hoping Old Saint Nick is there to deliver the presents. Despite his strong belief that it really is Santa Claus, Louie still has some fear as he asks that the presents be "slipped under the door." Those must be awful thin presents.

2. "SILENT NIGHT"—DINAH WASHINGTON

Probably the most sacred and popular of all Christmas songs, "Stille Nacht" was written in Germany by Josepf Mohr in the 1800s and has remained the centerpiece of all Christmas music ever since. Most artists who have included a religious song on their Christmas recordings have recorded "Silent Night," but Dinah Washington's version is one of the most sincere and beautiful. Dinah was one of the most popular jazz singers of the 1940s and 1950s and expanded her repertoire to include blues, pop, and R&B styles. She worked in Lionel Hampton's band in the 1940s and with many different band leaders, such as Clark Terry and Maynard Ferguson, throughout her short career. An accidental overdose of diet pills claimed her life in 1963, but Dinah remains one of the most influential voices for today's female R&B stars.

3. "FIVE POUND BOX OF MONEY"—PEARL BAILEY

"Now there's a little gift that's loaded with lots of sentiment," sings Pearl Bailey. Undaunted by Eartha Kitt's request for diamonds and cars in "Santa Baby," Pearl wants the green stuff and lots of it. She admits that money isn't everything, but "it's much better with than without it." This song is delivered with perfect phrasing by Pearl who, by the end of the song, has upped her request to ten pounds worth of tens—not a bad chunk of change. Pearl Bailey was the daughter of a preacher and began performing when she was three years old. She began dancing professionally by the time she was a teenager. She performed in nightclubs, on Broadway, and in movies, won a Tony for her stage work in "Hello, Dolly!" and even hosted a variety show on television in the 1970s.

4.   "WINTER WONDERLAND"—ELLA FITZGERALD

Ella Fitzgerald is known as "The First Lady of Song," and, along with Billie Holiday and Sarah Vaughan, is among the most famous of all jazz singers. She first came to the nation's attention in the 1930s, singing her trademark song "A Tisket A Tasket" for the Chick Webb orchestra. After Webb's death, Ella went solo and toured the world for years with jazz giants such as Dizzy Gillespie, Count Basie, and Oscar Peterson. Ella was such a happy singer and delighted her audiences with her singing. Even the sad songs sounded cheerful when Ella sang them. And there was no one in the world who could scat like Ella. In 1960, Ella released the album *Ella Wishes You A Swinging Christmas*, which included, among more than a dozen swinging versions of well-known Christmas tunes, the old favorite "Winter Wonderland." Her warm vocals almost melt the snowman and do away with the need to "conspire . . . by the fire."

5.   "O LITTLE TOWN OF BETHLEHEM"— SISTER ROSETTA THARPE

Sister Rosetta Tharpe was one of the greatest "sanctified" singers of her time and one of the most controversial. She had no problem adding swing and blues stylings to her gospel songs, played an electric guitar, and often performed at night clubs and theaters (causing some scandal by bringing gospel music to the night club circuit). Sister Rosetta's innovations have paved the way for almost all contemporary pop-gospel recordings. She was born into a family of traveling evangelists and performed as a child with her mother at Holiness conventions. Once signed to a recording contract as an adult, she still sang gospel music but successfully used popular showmanship and glamor techniques to help her songs, such as "This Train" and "Didn't It Rain." Tharpe's "O Little Town of Bethlehem" takes on a swinging gospel tone, with an organ guiding the music, and Sister's voice telling the story of that night in Bethlehem.

6. "DIG THAT CRAZY SANTA CLAUS"—RALPH MARTERIA AND HIS ORCHESTRA

Though he claimed not to be a jazz trumpeter, Ralph Marteria and His Orchestra did swing, and they prove it on their version of "Dig That Crazy Santa Claus." Ralph's big band was one of the last of its kind. By the end of the 1950s, big band music was not as successful, rock and roll having replaced big band music as the musical choice for the youngsters. Ralph played trumpet with bands led by Percy Faith and Andre Kostelanetz before heading his own by the mid-1940s. "Dig That Crazy Santa Claus" uses such dated phrases as "hep cats," "really gone," and "groovy," and is a joyous number when a crazy, cool Santa (read: not your father's stuffy Santa) shows up on Christmas Eve with a bag full of crazy toys. It's crazy, I tell you. Crazy.

7. "JINGLE ALL THE WAY"—LENA HORNE

Lena Horne added such a new twist to "Jingle Bells" on her 1966 recording with Jack Parnell's orchestra that it was renamed "Jingle All the Way." For those who didn't really want to get in that one-horse open sleigh before, they did after Ms. Horne invited them. The words are slightly rearranged, and the sleigh ride becomes much more romantic and fun. Lena began performing in the 1930s and has continued to perform into the new century. She recently lent her acting and vocals to a popular jeans company's Christmas advertising campaign, looking as dazzling and beautiful as ever. Horne also had an extensive film career, including the lead in *Stormy Weather* in 1943 and Glinda the Good Witch in 1978's *The Wiz* featuring singers Michael Jackson and Diana Ross. She has had frequent television appearances throughout the years, including Rowan and Martin's *Laugh In* and showing up for Cliff Huxtable's birthday on *The Cosby Show*.

8. "CHRISTMAS EVE"—BILLY ECKSTINE

Not all great jazz vocals belong to the ladies. Billy Eckstine's rich baritone made him one of jazz's finest singers in the 1940s. He led his own big band and was influential in the career development of singer Sarah Vaughn and be-bop pioneers Dizzy Gillespie and Charlie Parker. There is no be-bop in Eckstine's "Christmas Eve," a lush and romantic number that peacefully finds Billy crooning about stockings and mistletoe in the candlelight. All the wrapping must be finished and the relatives sent home, as this song paints a picture of an "all is calm, all is bright" Christmas Eve while waiting for Santa's arrival. Additionally, Mr. B. does not leave out the manger scene, complete with star and wise men.

9. "WHAT WILL SANTA CLAUS SAY (WHEN HE FINDS EVERYONE SWINGIN')?"—LOUIS PRIMA

Evidently not everyone was sure Santa was such a swingin' cat, as Louis Prima poses the question "What Will Santa Claus Say (When He Finds Everyone

Swingin')?" in a Christmas song that flat-out swings. Even the kiddies are swinging. Prima knows the answer though, that Old Saint Nick is a swingin' cat himself, and Prima would be an authority. Prima's career was largely influenced by another Louis from his same home town of New Orleans, jazz icon Louis Armstrong. In the 1930s, Prima was the composer of one of the most famous jazz songs ever, Benny Goodman's show-stopping "Sing Sing Sing." By the 1950s, he was performing with his wife, Keely Smith, in an act that strongly foreshadowed Sonny and Cher's famous singing/comedy duo with the exuberant husband and calm wife (Smith, like Cher, also had a Native American heritage). By the 1960s, Prima performed in the animated movie *The Jungle Book* where he performed as "King Louie" (the king of the jungle, the jungle VIP). So, what will Santa say? Chances are that he'll join right in the fun and sing, sing, sing.

10. "A CHRISTMAS MEDLEY"—THE SWINGLE SINGERS

A French a cappella group formed in the 1960s by Ward Swingle, The Swingle Singers also recorded with the Modern Jazz Quartet. They include "Carol of the Bells" in their wordless scat and bop "Christmas Medley," a Christmas song most well known as the jingle for a champagne company's 1970s television ads that included the chiming of champagne glasses at each strong beat. Anyone who grew up in the 1970s cannot hear this song without the clinking of glasses lodged in their memories. The Swingle Singers give a frantic treatment to "Carol of the Bells" and transition into much smoother melodies and harmonies for the rest of the medley. The original Swingle Singers' performances ranged from classical (Bach and Tchaikovsky) to modern (Beatles); they were reorganized with mixed results in the 1970s as the New Swingle Singers.

Merry Christmas and All That Jazz

Most of the classic Christmas songs were written at a time when jazz was a dominant force in American culture. It only stands to reason that almost every Christmas song has been given a good turn by the jazz masters. And a few have even been composed by them.

1. "CHRISTMAS TIME IS HERE"—VINCE GUARALDI

Good grief. For those who do not know Vince Guaraldi by name, his music will certainly ring a bell. He is the pianist whose compositions are forever linked with the Charlie Brown specials of the 1960s. Vince composed the famous "Linus and Lucy" theme for *A Boy Named Charlie Brown*. That is the song to which Snoopy loved to dance, and it was repeated in almost every special. The Christmas special, recorded in 1965, also contained a beautifully peaceful Guaraldi composition, "Christmas Time Is Here." Vince's trio was completed with Fred Marshall on bass and Jerry Granelli playing wonderfully mellow brushes on drums. Since *A Charlie Brown Christmas*, "Christmas

Time Is Here" has been recorded by many artists including Shawn Colvin, Toni Braxton, and Patti Austin.

2. "HAVE YOURSELF A MERRY LITTLE CHRISTMAS"— DEXTER GORDON

At an imposing six-foot-five, Dexter Gordon was given the nickname "The Sophisticated Giant," but the melodies he produced from his tenor saxophone were anything but imposing. Before becoming the front man for his own group, Dexter played for Lionel Hampton, Louis Armstrong, Billy Eckstine, and Miles Davis. Considered one of the all-time great sax men, Dexter had the lead role in the 1986 film *Round Midnight* for which he received an Oscar nomination. Long Tall Dex was also the godfather to Metallica's drummer Lars Ulrich. Dexter recorded "Have Yourself A Merry Little Christmas" in 1980 with Kirk Lightsey on piano, David Eubanks on bass, and Eddie Gladden on drums. Clocking in at just under ten minutes, the quartet flows through this so well, listeners will hardly notice where the time went as faithful friends gather near to us.

3. "JINGLE BELLS"—COUNT BASIE

One of the leading figures of the Big Band era of jazz was pianist William "Count" Basie. The Count's orchestra had hits in the 1930s and 1940s, including "One O'Clock Jump" and "Stop Beatin' Round the Mulberry Bush," and remained an integral part of the jazz scene until Basie passed away in 1984. Always associated with the Kansas City jazz scene, the Count was born in Red Bank, New Jersey, where the local theater is now named in his honor. Basie and his orchestra recorded "Jingle Bells" in 1961 and, like everything they did, it flat out swings. Starting off as a small but swinging party, the full orchestra joins in a minute into the piece and brings the swinging simmer to a full boil. It's a sure-fire hit to replace all the worn-out versions of "Jingle Bells" heard too many times. One of the reasons "Jingle Bells" is such an over-played song is that it's been around; it was composed in 1859 by John Pierpont. Pierpont was living in Savannah, Georgia, at the time of his composition about riding through snow in a one-horse open sleigh, perhaps reminiscing about snowy Christmases of his New England upbringing. So if this song can be composed in Georgia, it most certainly can be sung loudly by people celebrating Christmas in San Diego, Phoenix, Miami Beach, or anywhere else. And if you must, it's okay with us if you sing the "Batman smells" version you learned in elementary school.

4.   "WINTER WONDERLAND"—RED GARLAND

Red Garland may not be the most well-known jazz pianist, but he tickled the ivories for such icons as Charlie Parker, Miles Davis, and Coleman Hawkins throughout the 1950s and 1960s. While not touring with these jazz giants, he recorded several albums with his own trio that included Paul Chambers on bass and Art Taylor on drums. His 1958 recording with his trio, *All Kinds of Weather,* featured such songs as "Stormy Weather" and "Summertime" and a beautiful rendition of "Winter Wonderland." Bassist Chambers took a par-ticularly delightful solo turn, using his bow to establish a unique and subdued approach for this Christmas classic.

5.   "GOD REST YE MERRY GENTLEMEN"—JIMMY SMITH

Jimmy Smith is the king of the Hammond organ and added quite a bit of funk to the jazz scene when he arrived in the 1950s. His 1964 album, *Christmas Cookin'*, featured Jimmy on the cover wearing a Santa suit and driving a red sports car. Not only that, it featured not one but two versions of the formerly staid "God Rest Ye Merry Gentlemen."

The version that opened the album features a full band, while the album ender (though tracks have been added to the CD version) was only Jimmy with his trio, Quentin Warren on guitar and Billy Hart on drums. Pick either version or both, Jimmy's *Christmas Cookin'* is a meal for the ears. "God Rest Ye Merry Gentlemen" has seen almost as many Christmases as St. Nick himself. The origin of this carol dates back to England in the 1500s, although the version with which we are familiar was formed by the 1800s. Smith's version is nothing those olde English carolers in the 1500s could have ever imagined.

6. "SANTA CLAUS IS COMIN' TO TOWN"—BILL EVANS

The often melancholy and introspective sound that Bill Evans created with his piano playing was only slightly evident in his playful recording of "Santa Claus Is Comin' to Town." He built up the tempo as he went along, but the solo piano work took on a more peaceful tone with Evans's soft treatment. Evidently Evans recorded this particular tune several times throughout his career, possibly returning to it with the hope that returns to all of us each December. Haven Gillespie wrote the lyrics to "Santa Claus Is Comin' to Town," and J. Fred Coots set it to music in 1934. Gillespie wrote the lyrics on a subway train in about fifteen minutes. The song was an immediate hit, but Gillespie never cared for it, because it reminded him of the death of his brother, which occurred around the same time as the song was written. "Santa Claus Is Comin' to Town" reminds kids that Santa "sees you when you're sleeping" and "knows if you've been bad or good." All in all, it sounds as if Santa is a little creepy, but no one seems to mind if the man in red is spying on them.

7. "NUTCRACKER SUITE"—LES BROWN AND HIS BAND OF RENOWN

Tchaikovsky completed his orchestral version of the "Nutcracker Suite" in 1892, based on the E. T. A. Hoffman story "The Nutcracker and the Mouse King." It remains one of the most beloved ballets of all time. Because the story takes place at Christmas, the Nutcracker music is now heard most often during the Christmas season. The legendary Les Brown and his Band of Renown recorded one of the most ambitious pieces of Christmas jazz when they tackled Tchaikovsky's "Nutcracker Suite." For six and a half minutes, the big band flew through the entire suite, capturing the highlights of it. Energetic and almost manic, this is truly one of the coolest pieces ever created from classical music. Les Brown conducted his Band of Renown for more than sixty years and is best remembered for introducing Doris Day to the world. She sang "Sentimental Journey" with the Band of Renown—one of the biggest hits of the World War II era. Les and his band accompanied Bob Hope on many of his overseas tours of military bases and appeared on eighteen Bob Hope television Christmas specials.

8. "I'LL BE HOME FOR CHRISTMAS"—OSCAR PETERSON

An absolute wartime tearjerker, "I'll Be Home for Christmas" was written at the height of World War II, 1943 to be exact, by Walter Kent and Kim Gannon. Kent had already struck gold two years earlier with the wartime classic "White Cliffs of Dover." This time he teamed up with Gannon and handed Bing Crosby his second wartime Christmas hit. Crosby had recorded "White Christmas" a year earlier. In the hands of Oscar Peterson, "I'll Be Home for Christmas" received that refined and styled treatment for which this all-time great jazz pianist is known. Peterson has recorded hundreds of albums, teaming up as a trio with guitarist Herb Ellis and bassist Ray Brown in the 1950s and recording with greats Count Basie, Joe Pass, Dizzy Gillespie, and Clark Terry, to name a few. His 1995 recording of Christmas songs, including "I'll Be Home for Christmas," found him with a sextet that included Jack Shantz on flugelhorn.

9.   "OUR LITTLE TOWN"—THE HEATH BROTHERS

There are three Heath brothers with long résumés in jazz history. Between them, they played on nearly 900 albums with just about everyone in jazz. The eldest brother, Percy, was the bassist for the Modern Jazz Quartet for more than forty years. As a teenager, brother Jimmy was already playing sax with Dizzy Gillespie. Younger brother Tootie played drums for John Coltrane and Dexter Gordon. The Philadelphia-bred brothers combined their talents in the late 1970s and early 1980s to record a few albums of their own. Based on "O Little Town of Bethlehem," "Our Little Town" was arranged and performed by Jimmy and Percy with Stanley Cowell on piano, Tony Purrone on electric guitar, and Akira Tana on drums. "O Little Town of Bethlehem" was written by Phillips Brooks in 1867 and was set to music the following year by Lewis Redner. Brooks was a well-known Boston preacher and was inspired to write "O Little Town" after taking a horseback ride from Jerusalem to Bethlehem to perform a midnight Christmas service in 1865.

10.   "WE THREE KINGS"—DAVE BRUBECK

"We Three Kings," based on the visit to the Christ child by the Magi, was written by John H. Hopkins (no, not the *Johns* Hopkins who founded the famous Baltimore hospital) in 1857. The original lyrics have nothing to do with the exploding cigar verse sung in grade school, but do include verses based on the three gifts offered by the Wise Men: gold, frankincense, and myrrh. The Wise Men followed the star that appeared over Bethlehem to find the Christ child. That a Christmas song with an Eastern sound is performed brilliantly by Dave Brubeck in his 1992 recording is no surprise. Brubeck experimented with sounds and time signatures throughout his storied career with songs that include "Blue Rondo a la Turk" and his most famous composition, "Take Five."

That Old-Time Christmas Rock and Roll

Rock and roll was born in the fifties, and with it came a whole new way to celebrate Christmas. Some of these songs come from rock and roll legends, some from people whose only claim to fame is their contribution to December radio fare, and others had nothing to do with rock and roll but were prominent at the time when the genre was defining a hip new way to sing about Christmas

1. "JINGLE BELL ROCK"—BOBBY HELMS

Bobby Helms was a Nashville country singer with a few songs that had charted on both the country and pop charts in the late 1950s. "Jingle Bell Rock" was released by Decca records two days before Christmas in 1957 and was an immediate hit and is now the only song for which the late Mr. Helms is known. Helms wrote "Jingle Bell Rock" with a definite nod toward the standard "Jingle Bells" classic. There is no authentic rock and roll style in the "Jingle Bell Rock," but there are some jingle bells. And it does give us some classic

1950s phrasing, such as "Jingle bell time is a swell time/to go gliding in a one-horse sleigh," although one might suspect the kids were more likely to be gliding in Chevys by the 1950s. The vocalists behind Bobby Helms are the Anita Kerr Singers, who, along with the Jordanaires, were one of the most sought-after backing vocal groups of their time. They made regular appearances on the *Arthur Godfrey Talent Scouts* television program throughout the 1950s.

2. "ROCKIN' AROUND THE CHRISTMAS TREE"—BRENDA LEE

Do you "get a sentimental feeling" when you hear Brenda Lee's "new old fashioned" Christmas classic? Written by Johnny Marks, who also wrote the music to "Rudolph the Red-Nosed Reindeer," Lee was only fourteen at the time she recorded it in 1958. Amazingly, it failed to chart in 1958 or in 1959. It wasn't until 1960 that "Rockin' Around the Christmas Tree" became a bona fide hit. The now-classic song was not young Brenda's first recording of a Christmas song. At her very first recording session, Brenda sang "I'm Gonna Lasso Santa Claus," an amazingly perceptive tune where Brenda observes that Santa doesn't visit the poor kids the same way he visits the rich ones.

Brenda reached her peak as a Nashville country singer in the early 1960s under the direction of producer Owen Bradley. Bradley was also instrumental in the career of Patsy Cline at this time. Brenda had more crossover appeal than Patsy, partially because of her young age in the rock and roll set, and partially because her songs had more of a pop than country sound. Brenda had a string of number-one hits in the 1960s, most notably her gold record "I'm Sorry."

3. "RUN RUDOLPH RUN"—CHUCK BERRY

Rock and Roll Hall of Famer Chuck Berry put the rock and roll in Christmas with his 1958 hit "Run Rudolph Run," a rocking little piece that finds Rudolph rushing Santa through town in order to make all deliveries on time, including a "rock and roll electric guitar" to some deserving young boy. The "Randolph" in the lyric "Randolph ain't too far behind" is a vague reference to Rudolph's cousin, who evidently possessed the more typical brown nose. Chuck Berry is truly one of the most important and influential figures in rock and roll, penning such hits as "Johnny B. Goode," "Roll Over Beethoven," and "Maybellene." Additionally, he brought a swagger and showmanship, such as his famed duck-walk during guitar solos, that influenced John Lennon, Bob Dylan, and Brian Wilson. "Run Rudolph Run" was prominently featured during a rush-through-the-airport scene in the movie *Home Alone*. Although the title is "Run Rudolph Run," the lyric is "run run Rudolph." Confusing, huh?

4. "SANTA BABY"—EARTHA KITT

Every few years, someone convinces a young, pretty singer to cover "Santa Baby." Madonna gave it a good try in the 1980s. But no one has come close to the incomparable Eartha Kitt, who performed this steamy Christmas song to perfection in 1953. Eartha is convincing in her assertion that she has been an awfully good girl in the past year and thus worthy of a sled-full of Christmas cheer, including a yacht, a '54 convertible, and a deed to a platinum mine. If she's not entirely truthful about how good she's been, Santa probably doesn't mind by the third line. Eartha Kitt was discovered by movie director Orson Welles, and her career in film and music began in earnest in the 1950s. She is best known for her turn as Catwoman in television's *Batman* series in the 1960s. In recent years, Eartha has lent her voice to animated shows and movies such as *The Wild Thornberries*, *The Emperor's New Groove*, and a television special titled *Santa Baby*.

5.   "CHRISTMAS (BABY PLEASE COME HOME)"— DARLENE LOVE

Legendary producer Phil Spector created one of the first full-length rock and roll Christmas albums in 1963. It was called *A Christmas Gift For You From Phil Spector* and featured such performers as The Ronettes and The Crystals. Using his legendary "wall of sound," Spector created one of the greatest Christmas albums ever. The highlight of the album was a Spector-penned song called "Christmas (Baby Please Come Home)," performed by Darlene Love. In 1962, Love had hit the top of the charts with "He's a Rebel," which was credited as a Crystals number, but she performed solo for this big Christmas production, which lamented the wonderful holiday season without the presence of her baby. Forty years later, Love continues to usher in each holiday season with another big production of "Christmas (Baby Please Come Home)" on David Letterman's television show. Once Santa hears Darlene perform on *Letterman*, he starts to load his sleigh for his big run. "Christmas (Baby Please Come Home)" has received fair treatment in recent years by artists such as U2 and Mariah Carey.

6.   "LITTLE SAINT NICK"—THE BEACH BOYS

The Beach Boys put out their own holiday good vibrations when Brian Wilson created a new Christmas classic with "Little Saint Nick." Saint Nick has a bobsled that he "spends the whole year workin' out" like a magical surfboard. The reindeer (although only six, including Rudolph) haul him through the snow at such speed that Saint Nick needs some cool shades to keep the snow out of his eyes. "Little Saint Nick" was one of five holiday songs written by Brian Wilson for the Beach Boys' 1964 record simply titled *Christmas Album*. The Beach Boys also lent their harmonies to standards such as "White Christmas" and "I'll Be Home For Christmas" on their holiday treat.

7. "HEY SANTA CLAUS"—THE MOONGLOWS

One of the most successful early R&B groups was the Midwest-based Moonglows. Consisting of Harvey Fuqua, Bobby Lester, Pete Graves, and Prentiss Barnes, the Moonglows had a smooth and soulful sound and were closely associated with famed 1950s disc jockey Alan Freed. Their biggest charting hit was "Sincerely," which reached national prominence in 1955. It was Fuqua who wrote the 1953 recording of "Hey Santa Claus," which showcases their elegant harmonies as the Moonglows implore Santa to "bring my baby back to me," promising to never let her go if Santa makes good on his delivery. Fuqua also appeared as himself in the 1956 rock and roll movie *Rock, Rock, Rock.*

8. "FROSTY THE SNOWMAN"—JAN AND DEAN

"Frosty the Snowman" was written by the songwriting team of Jack Nelson and Steve Rollins in 1949. Nelson and Rollins, who also created the character of Peter Cottontail for Easter, looked at the phenomenon that "Rudolph the Red-Nosed Reindeer" had become that year and worked to create a song based on another wintertime Christmas character. The song was first recorded by Gene Autry (who had first sung "Rudolph") and probably became most recognizable through the voice of Jimmy Durante from the 1969 animated television Christmas show *Frosty, the Snowman*. Many performers recorded "Frosty" between Autry's initial offering and Durante's classic (and continue to do so), but the duo of Jan and Dean gave Frosty a unique doo-wop sound in 1962. Jan Berry and Dean Torrence teamed up to record California beach music in the 1960s. While not quite rivaling The Beach Boys, they did hit gold with "Surf City" which Beach Boy Brian Wilson helped write and also performed on the recording.

9. "HERE COMES SANTA CLAUS"—ELVIS PRESLEY

Another hit Christmas song for Gene Autry, this one was actually written by Autry and Oakley Haldeman in 1947. However, the definitive rock and roll version is performed by The King himself. Elvis recorded this in 1957 and gave it the complete Elvis hip gyrating sound that defined him as Elvis the Pelvis. In addition to giving "Here Comes Santa Claus" some soul, Elvis added spirit to the verses at the end that show a rarely mentioned connection between the Man in Red and the Man Upstairs. There appears to be an acknowledgment on Santa's part that peace will come to Earth "if we just follow the light" while requesting us to thank "the Lord above, 'cause Santa Claus comes tonight." Never one to shy away from his love of Gospel music, Elvis also enjoyed both the sacred and secular music of Christmas.

Burl Ives poses with his character Sam the Snowman and Rudolph. ©1964 Rankin/Bass Productions. *Courtesy of the RankinBass.com/Rick Goldschmidt Archives*

10. "HOLLY JOLLY CHRISTMAS"—BURL IVES

Burl Ives is certainly not a rock and roll pioneer, but his recording of "Holly Jolly Christmas" for the *Rudolph the Red-Nosed Reindeer* television special in 1964 gave him plenty of airplay on the oldies format at Christmastime. He also performed the title number for that show and another popular song, "Silver and Gold." That classic became so well loved, there is an instant recognition for many people of several generations when they hear Burl Ives sing "Holly Jolly Christmas" as they think of Rudolph and the Island of Misfit Toys. Almost all of the songs from the special, including "Why Am I Such A Misfit" and "There's Always Tomorrow" were written by Johnny Marks, the songwriter for "Rudolph the Red-Nosed Reindeer" and many other Christmas classics. For his part, Burl gave voice to the snowman narrator and sang some of the songs. Burl made many folk and children's recordings throughout his long career and is also well know for his hit "On Top of Old Smokey."

Both Types of Christmas Music— Country AND Western

Country music fans have always had a wealth of their favorite artists covering their favorite Christmas songs and creating some new ones. "Silver Bells" reminds us of Christmastime in the city, yet it's out in the country where we can really enjoy that ride in a one-horse open sleigh. Additionally, country music has never been afraid of a little church influence.

1. "CHRISTMAS TIME'S A-COMING"—EMMYLOU HARRIS

No one else in the world sings like Emmylou Harris, an incredible singer in the country music industry since she collaborated with Gram Parsons in the 1970s. After the untimely passing of the hard-living Parsons at age twenty-six in 1973, Harris began her solo career and has given the country music world four decades of both traditional and eclectic music. Her 1979 *Christmas Album (Light In The Stable)* opens with her version of Tex Logan's "Christmas Time's A-Coming," a song that is pure country. The song revels in the approaching cold weather that signals the beginning of the holidays, anticipating the reunion of friends and family with "When it's snowin', I'll be goin' back to my country home." Songwriter Tex Logan is an influential bluegrass fiddler, who has rubbed shoulders with Bill Monroe and Doc Watson. In addition to Harris, Logan's songs have been covered by everyone from Bob Dylan to Diamond Rio.

2. "AWAY IN A MANGER"—JOHNNY CASH

The perennial theme song of every Sunday School's Christmas play, "Away in A Manger" usually conjures up images of five-year-old wise men wearing their bathrobes as they fearfully walk down the church aisle on Christmas Eve to present their gifts to the baby Jesus. "Away in A Manger" first appeared in an 1885 Lutheran publication. No one knows who wrote the words; they have often been attributed to Martin Luther, although there is no evidence to back that up. The words were set to music ten years later by William Kirkpatrick. In the hands of Johnny Cash, "Away in A Manger" is given the sweet and solemn treatment that it is due. Cash's baritone is reverent in order to keep the "little Lord Jesus" sleeping in his manger. The Man in Black is a member of the Country Music Hall of Fame and the Rock and Roll Hall of Fame and had more than one hundred hit songs. He is best known for his hits "I Walk The Line," "Folsom Prison Blues," and "Ring of Fire." Cash and his wife June Carter, of country music's legendary Carter Family, hosted *The Johnny Cash Show* on television from 1969 to 1971. Johnny recorded several Christmas albums; "Away in a Manger" can be found on 1991's *Country Christmas*.

3. "CHRISTMAS LULLABY"—DOC WATSON

In the early 1700s, young Isaac Watts complained to his father that the hymns they sang in church were too boring and needed to become modern—sounds like a common complaint still heard today. His father responded with the challenge to write something more engaging, and Watts produced a hymn called, "Behold the Glories of the Lamb." All in all, Watts wrote hundreds of hymns; many are still being sung today. Whether they are boring or not may be in the ear of the listener, but "We're Marching To Zion" and "When I Survey The Wondrous Cross" remain popular in many church circles. One of the hymns Watts wrote was called "A Cradle Hymn" and is also known as "Hush! My Dear, Lie Still and Slumber." Doc Watson adapted this hymn on his 1990 recording *On Praying Ground* and named the song "Christmas Lullaby." Similar in theme to "Away in A Manger," "Christmas Lullaby" lulls the baby Jesus to sleep, assuring the infant that "Holy angels guard thy bed." Watson has been a world-renowned bluegrass flat picker since he came to prominence during the folk revival of the early 1960s. A childhood illness left Watson blind, but that did not keep him away from music. In fact, he was presented with a new harmonica at Christmas every year when he was a boy.

4. "PRETTY PAPER"—WILLIE NELSON

Before Willie Nelson became an outlaw country superstar in the 1970s, he was successful writing songs for other country artists. The most famous of them, "Crazy," was Patsy Cline's signature song. Roy Orbison recorded Willie's song "Pretty Paper" in 1964, the same year he recorded his biggest hit "Oh, Pretty Woman." Maybe Roy's pretty woman needed her Christmas gifts wrapped in pretty paper that year, but it was another hit for Orbison. Nelson recorded his hit song based on wrapping paper on his 1979 album of the same name. In his typically beautiful yet melancholic style, Nelson contrasts the attention paid to Christmas gifts wrapped with "pretty paper, pretty ribbons of blue" and the neglect often shown toward the downtrodden and needy.

5. "DO YOU HEAR WHAT I HEAR?"—VINCE GILL

A husband-wife songwriting team, Noel Regney and Gloria Shayne, wrote this Christmas standard in 1962. It was written during the Cuban Missile Crisis and is as much a plea for world peace as it is about Christmas. "I am amazed that people can think they know the song—and not know it is a prayer for peace," Regney said in an interview in 1985. Vince Gill, one of the biggest stars of the 1990s country music boom, recorded "Do You Hear What I Hear?" for his 1993 album *Let There Be Peace on Earth*. Gill has won more Country Music Association (CMA) awards than any other performer in history. He is married to former Christian music star Amy Grant, who has several popular Christmas albums of her own, including her version of "Do You Hear What I Hear?"

6. "O COME ALL YE FAITHFUL"—MARTINA MCBRIDE

"O Come All Ye Faithful," also known in its original Latin form as "Adeste Fideles," was written in the eighteenth century by hymn writer John Francis Wade. It was translated into English in 1841 by Frederick Oakeley. "O Come All Ye Faithful" remains a popular expression of joy as it recounts the angels singing and the shepherds leaving their flocks to visit the newborn Christ child in Bethlehem. Martina McBride has had hits on the country music charts since the early 1990s and had a number-one song with "Wild Angels." "O Come All Ye Faithful" is from her 1998 Christmas album, *White Christmas*. Martina strays a bit from her country sound and brings in full orchestration to make the album reminiscent of classic Christmas music.

7. "JOY TO THE WORLD"—PATTY LOVELESS

If you need a little bit of acoustic country sound in your Christmas music, look no further than Patty Loveless's 2002 holiday album *Bluegrass and White Snow: A Mountain Christmas*. Patty is accompanied by mandolins, dobros, and fiddles, though she gives "Joy to the World" a nice traditional sound without overdoing the repetitive "and heav'n and nature sing" lines that can lodge in one's brain during the month of December. Loveless should know a thing or two about a mountain Christmas; she was raised as a coal miner's daughter in Kentucky, just like her distant cousins Loretta Lynn and Crystal Gayle. Patty is joined on "Joy to the World" by Jon Randall and Emmylou Harris. The words to "Joy to the World" were written by Isaac Watts in 1719. Watts also wrote "A Cradle Hymn," but he did not write the music for "Joy to the World." That was a task for none other than George Frederick Handel, who is best know for composing "The Messiah."

8. "A CHRISTMAS TO REMEMBER"—KENNY ROGERS AND DOLLY PARTON

Two of country music's biggest stars from the 1970s teamed up for several recordings during the 1980s. Kenny Rogers may be best known for his roasted chicken these days, but in the 1970s, The Gambler was right up there with Willie Nelson as one of country music's most appreciated male singers. His trademark snow-white beard lends him a strong Santa resemblance, too. Dolly began her career singing with Porter

Wagoner on his television program and became a country music icon by the 1970s. She has one of the most distinct and sincere voices in country music and always brings a smile to the faces of her many fans. Together, Kenny and Dolly recorded several times, including the number-one hit "Islands in the Stream." In 1984 they released a Christmas album called, *Once Upon a Christmas* that included the song "A Christmas to Remember," a song penned by Dolly. The song is about a romantic chance meeting on a Christmas ski trip that resulted in being "curled up by a fireplace in a Tahoe ski chalet with a fast-talking lover and some slow-burning wood."

9.   "UP ON THE HOUSETOP"—REBA MCENTIRE

The red-headed darling of country music, Reba McEntire recorded "Up on the Housetop" on *The Secret of Giving*, her second Christmas album, in 1999. Reba has a good pedigree for a country singer— her father was a professional rodeo rider. She has had eighteen number-one songs on the country charts throughout her career and also has her own television situation comedy. Reba adds some spirit to her version of "Up on the Housetop," a song written in 1866 by Benjamin Hanby. This song finds Santa in the middle of his Christmas run, landing on the rooftops with his reindeer (click, click, click) and then down the chimney to fill the stockings and then back up the chimney again. Who wouldn't go with old Saint Nick?

10.   "MAKING PLANS"—TIM O'BRIEN

It isn't often these days that someone is able to write a Christmas song that measures up to the classics written in the forties, fifties, and sixties. Tim O'Brien's "Making Plans" is one that does so. A simple song about traveling back home to be with family and friends and that "special name" for the holidays is gorgeously constructed and performed by Tim with warm harmonies from his sister, Molly O'Brien. For the last thirty years O'Brien has been a prominent name in the bluegrass industry, first as a co-founder and vocalist for the bluegrass band Hot Rize (and their alter-egos— Red Knuckles and the Trailblazers), and, since 1991, with his own band, The O'Boys. His songs have been performed by Kathy Mattea, Garth Brooks, the Dixie Chicks, and Nickel Creek.

I'll Have a Blues Christmas Without You

Not everyone enjoys Christmas; a lot of people get the blues. Whether it is the high expectations, the lack of daylight, or bad memories of Christmas past, Christmas brings some people down. If you are one of these people, we have just the thing to cheer you up: Christmas Blues. While a few of these songs may lift your spirit, most of them will help you wallow in your bad feelings. If your baby ain't around this Christmas, or nothing is going right, one person to blame may be Santa Claus. At least, he seems to receive a lot of the blame from many singers of the Christmas Blues.

1. **"MERRY CHRISTMAS BABY"—LUTHER "GUITAR JUNIOR" JOHNSON**

Evidently there are a few "Luther Johnsons" in the blues world. Luther "Guitar Junior" Johnson has played for Muddy Waters and Magic Slim and received his "Guitar Junior" nickname for his ability to solo on one string while playing chords on the others. This Mississippi native's version of "Merry Christmas Baby" is more upbeat than some of the others. "Merry

Christmas Baby" was written by Lou Baxter and Johnny Moore. This song is actually cheerful, although definitely blues-y. All is well with his baby and he's got "good music on the radio." The singer is so happy this Christmas, he doesn't even need the aid of a drink to keep his Christmas cheer. Now that's a good Christmas.

2.   "SANDY CLAW STOLE MY WOMAN"—BOBBY PARKER

Darn that Santa! He's supposed to be coming down the chimney and bringing us goodies. When he reached Bobby Parker's house, he stole his woman. Apparently Santa gave her a lift once he spotted her during his Christmas run. Bobby's only hope is that Santa brings her back, but he sees nothing but trouble. Parker has been active in the music industry since playing guitar with Bo Diddley in the 1950s, and "Sandy Claw Stole My Woman" is a Bobby Parker original, recorded in 1995. The blues man with the James Brown hair wrote "Watch Your Step" in 1961, which was subsequently covered by Carlos Santana and The Spencer Davis Group.

3.   "SAM'S CHRISTMAS BLUES"—ANSON FUNDERBURGH AND THE ROCKETS FEATURING SAM MEYERS

Texas blues. Anson Funderburgh serves them up hot, and his singer and harmonica player, Sam Meyers, adds the Delta blues to the mix. It's a great combination that has been pleasing fans since 1982. Funderburgh formed The Rockets in the late 1970s, after spending some time playing for Texas blues legend Lightnin' Hopkins. Meyers, who is legally blind, first recorded in 1957 and once recorded with Elmore James. The veteran blues man made his largest impact in the blues world once he hooked up with Funderburgh's Rockets. In "Sam's Christmas Blues," Sam is dismayed that Christmas has arrived, and while everyone else is happy, he's got the blues. He has not seen Santa or any presents. He states his innocence, proclaiming his goodness throughout the year, yet he's all alone once again for Christmas. Mercy. Meyers wrote the song, which was recorded in 1995 for the Black Top compilation album *Blues, Mistletoe, and Santa's Little Helper,* which features photos of Santa's Little Helper adorned in fishnets, high heels, and an extremely skimpy helper outfit.

4. "DECK THE HALLS WITH BOOGIE WOOGIE"— KATIE WEBSTER

Boogie Woogie piano queen Katie Webster put a fresh spin on this old Welsh Christmas carol with her "Deck the Halls with Boogie Woogie." The original "Deck the Halls" has been recorded by many artists and is one of the most parodied schoolyard carols. Popular kids' versions include "Deck the halls with poison ivy" and "Deck the halls with nitro glycerin." The repeated "Fa-la-la-la-la La-la-la-la" line makes it one of those songs that is tough to forget. Katie's "Deck the Halls" treatment opens with a riff from "White Christmas" then puts a lot of joy back into the song with her rolling boogie-woogie piano licks. She closes with Christmas wishes to all her fans and the old Pearl Bailey beg for a five-pound box of money. Webster began her music career in the 1950s, much against her religious parents' objections. Throughout her life she recorded and played with Lazy Lester and Bonnie Raitt, among others, and was Otis Redding's opening act for three years in the 1960s.

5.   "SANTA'S BLUES"—CHARLES BROWN

Charles Brown is not only the round-headed star of the *Peanuts* comic strip but a blues legend with a strong Christmas connection. He wrote the song best known as an Eagles Christmas hit "Please Come Home For Christmas" and performed the hit "Merry Christmas Baby" (represented on this list by Luther "Guitar Junior" Johnson) while a member of The Blazers in 1947. Brown's piano playing style was low-key and smooth and was highly influential on many up-and-coming jazz and blues pianists including Ray Charles. "Santa's Blues" finds Brown all alone at Christmas, as his baby has left him. He's hoping Santa will "make him glad on Christmas Day." "Santa's Blues" and the rest of Brown's Christmas treats can be found on his 1994 recording *Cool Christmas Blues*.

6.   "I TOLD SANTA CLAUS"—ROOMFUL OF BLUES

The popular large blues band Roomful of Blues released their own Christmas album in 1997 called *Roomful of Christmas*. Their brand of swinging, upbeat blues may please those who do not want to wallow in their Christmas blues. Roomful of Blues has gone through several personnel changes since its inception in 1967, losing guitar hero Duke Robillard and drummer Fran Christina (Fabulous Thunderbirds), but they have always kept their size (roughly nine members) and sound. "I Told Santa Claus" is an old Fats Domino number that is basically a marriage proposal in wrapping paper. The merriest of Christmases will be had if she'll say yes to settling down and starting a family. The woman in question may want to think this over carefully, as the singer's idea of a family is a "boy for you and a ten pound girl for me." Women who have experienced childbirth must wince at that "ten pound" line every time they hear it.

Roomful of Blues. *Alligator Records*

7. "SANTA CLAUS WANTS SOME LOVIN'"—SIR MACK RICE

The playful "Santa Claus Wants Some Lovin'" blurs the lines between Santa Claus and the man of the house, who is informing the woman of the house of the top priority on his Christmas wish list. The stockings have been filled, the children are asleep, the tricycles have been built, and now it's time for Santa to reap his reward. While the mother is in the kitchen putting the finishing touches on the Christmas turkey, Santa has an appetite of a different kind. Songwriter Mack Rice has been producing songs like this and "Mini Skirt Minnie" since the 1950s. His greatest contribution to the world of music was his song "Mustang Sally," covered by many, including Wilson Pickett, Clapton, and made popular again through the 1991 film *The Commitments*. "Santa Claus Wants Some Lovin'" has been covered by several blues greats, including Albert King and Tinsley Ellis.

8. "SANTA CLAUS IS BACK IN TOWN"—ELVIS PRESLEY

Elvis revolutionized rock and roll, but he also made some huge strides with his recorded Christmas music. Best known for "Blue Christmas," The King was not afraid to tackle sacred favorites, then rip up the secular Christmas songs with his often-imitated style. "Santa Claus Is Back in Town" is a blues rocker with more innuendo than might be appropriate for door-to-door caroling (though that may depend on the house and the neighborhood). With his famous background singers, the Jordanaires, providing the "Christmas, Christmas, Christmas" background, Elvis appears as Santa Claus, not in a sled, but in a big black Cadillac. Santa has come to reward a "real good girl," and when he tells her to "hang up her pretty stockings" in preparation for Santa's visit, it is fairly certain that he isn't talking about the stockings that great-aunts knit to hang on the mantle (such as the stockings still kept by both authors). If you are still wondering what Elvis means, Brian Setzer took liberty with the lyric when he recorded his version, changing "pretty stockings" to "fishnet stockings." Hey, hey, the blues is all right.

9. "CHRISTMAS BY THE BAR-B-QUE"—LYNN AUGUST

Zydeco makes a great blues gumbo, and Lynn August mixes up a great one on "Christmas By the Bar-b-que." Whereas many people have a traditional turkey or ham for their holiday feasts, Lynn is looking forward to being at home in the south with his woman and her potato salad, dirty rice, and bar-b-que. Most people would agree that a white Christmas and grilling outdoors with the neighbors don't mix, but Lynn's description of savory Cajun cookin' may change the traditional Christmas dinner menu. Lynn August is a Louisiana native with a long recording career dating back to the 1960s. He performed as a percussionist, piano player, and organist before switching to the accordion in 1988.

10. "SANTA'S MESSIN' WITH THE KID"— EDDIE C. CAMPBELL

Another instance of Santa being a little too flirty with another man's woman. While "Santa's Messin' with the Kid" may be the tune for which Eddie C. Campbell is best known, the Mississippi native has had a long and storied career as a blues guitarist. Campbell has been a sideman for Howlin' Wolf, Muddy Waters, Willie Dixon, and Jimmy Reed. The common blues practice of the singer referring to himself as "The Kid" is prominent in this song, as Eddie C. is becoming a little suspicious of Santa's intentions with his wife as he takes over the house and sits the little lady on his lap. "Santa's Messin' with the Kid" has been covered by several bands. One notable recording is by the legendary southern blues rock band Lynyrd Skynyrd on its 2000 release, *Christmas Time Again*.

Get Down at Christmas

Need a little soul in your Christmas? Ready for some R&B sprinkled with some funk? Over the years, various R&B singers have taken on some standard Christmas songs and given them new life and the soul they've been missing once the tunes have been transported into generic department store background sound. Conversely, some of the originals have been diminished by less notable "musicians" who couldn't help but change something good and drain the soul right out of it. We offer only the good stuff.

1. "SOULFUL CHRISTMAS"—JAMES BROWN

Merry Christmas from the Godfather of Soul! James Brown has several Christmas albums—he is the "hardest working man in show business" after all. James gave us Christmas songs such as "Christmas in the Ghetto" and "Let's Make Christmas Mean Something This Year," allowing him lots of opportunities to scream and grunt through the yuletide season. "Soulful Christmas" is one of the funkiest Christmas songs ever. If you need a tune to get your Christmas dance party going, this one with the funky bass line and rhythm will get even The Grinch on the dance floor. Brown's got his baby, plenty of happiness (good God!), as well as all his fans who graciously go to his shows and buy his records, for which he thanks them in this song. There are several vintage JB squeals in this song—Christmas makes him feel good.

2.   "SOMEDAY AT CHRISTMAS"—STEVIE WONDER

When Stevie Wonder released his Christmas album, *Someday at Christmas,* in 1967, he was only seventeen years old but was already a Motown star from songs like "Fingertips" and "Uptight (Everything's Alright)." He continued to emerge after his Christmas album, making some of the best music recorded in the 1970s with albums such as *Innervisions* and *Songs in the Key of Life.* "Someday at Christmas" was written by Bryan Wells and Ronald Miller and provides social commentary that was beginning to dawn in the 1960s. It is a wish for worldwide peace, and Stevie delivers it perfectly as he sings, "Someday at Christmas there'll be no wars/When we have learned what Christmas is for." One insightful lyric states "maybe not in time for you and me." Almost forty years later Stevie's hope remains unrealized.

3.   "I SAW MOMMY KISSING SANTA CLAUS"—
THE JACKSON FIVE

"I Saw Mommy Kissing Santa Claus" was written by Tommie Connor in 1952 and was first recorded by ten-year-old Jimmy Boyd. The youngster who sang it best was a young Michael Jackson for the *Jackson Five Christmas Album* released in 1970. Older brothers Jackie, Tito, Jermaine, and Marlon were the other members of the Jackson Five, but it was Michael who was the true star performer among the talented family. The group formed in the 1960s, and Michael displayed his vocal and dancing gifts at an early age. They recorded many hit singles for Motown Records, including "ABC" and "I'll Be There." Of course, Michael went on to a monstrous solo career that included his 1982 album *Thriller*, which became the greatest-selling record album of all time. The *Jackson Five Christmas Album* contained many terrific arrangements of popular Christmas songs including "Christmas Won't Be the Same This Year" and a brilliant version of "Santa Claus is Comin' to Town." For "I Saw Mommy Kissing Santa Claus," Michael sings the song to his brothers, reporting the scandalous event that he has witnessed. His brothers have a good laugh as they keep Santa's true identity from young Michael while trying to keep him calm, but Michael isn't buying it.

4. "GIVE LOVE ON CHRISTMAS DAY"—THE TEMPTATIONS

One gift that works for everyone is love. It doesn't come in the wrong size or have an expiration date, and there is never a long line for returns. Properly delivered, love can be re-gifted and returned everywhere all year long. While the Jackson Five first recorded "Give Love on Christmas Day," the Temptations offered a stellar version on their 1980 Christmas album of the same name. The Temptations were at their peak in the 1960s with such hits as "My Girl" and "The Way You Do the Things You Do," blending tight harmonies with smooth choreographed dance moves. Their lineup changed throughout the years, and eventually Otis Williams was the only original member left in the band. In the 1970s, the Temptations were still reaching high on the charts with "Papa Was a Rolling Stone" and

"Superstar." "Give Love on Christmas Day" is a sweet number, offering the reminder that gifts from the store are not the only things we can give to others at Christmas.

5. "THE LITTLE DRUMMER BOY"—THE SUPREMES

There are two kinds of people in the world: those who love "The Little Drummer Boy," and those who find it abhorrent. There is no one in the middle on this one. Whether it is well-loved or deeply despised, those who love it continue to record it and give it airplay. The "pa rum pa pum pums" can drum into one's consciousness and remain there for months. Once excised, the Christmas season begins again. The song was inspired by a Spanish song called "Tabolilleros" and was composed in 1958 by Harry Simeone, Henry Onoroti, and Katherine Davis. "The Little Drummer Boy" became a hit for the Harry Simeone Choral—a version still heard each Christmas season. The song became so popular that it even spawned its own television special in 1968. The Supremes (Florence Ballard, Mary Wilson, and Diana Ross) were hugely popular in the 1960s with hits such as "Where Did Our Love Go" and "Stop! In the Name of Love." Their 1965 Christmas record, *Merry Christmas*, included "The Little Drummer Boy," a song about a boy with no gift to give when he visits baby Jesus at the manger. Without a gift, the boy plays the baby a drum solo, and the baby smiles. For those keeping score at home, there is no Biblical mention of a little drummer boy. And most kids who practice their drums while the baby is napping are sent outside to play football for a long while.

6. "WHAT CHILD IS THIS?"—RAY CHARLES

The words to "What Child Is This?" were written by British hymn writer William Chatterton Dix in the

1860s, but the melody was taken from a sixteenth-century English song called "Greensleeves." Usually when this song is played as an instrumental, it is still referred to as "Greensleeves," possibly because "What Child Is This?" is unmistakably religious. The lyrics recount the story of the baby Jesus, born homeless, sleeping in a manger, with shepherds and wise men coming to guard and visit while the angels sing. Ray Charles was no stranger to gospel music and infused quite a bit of church music into his R&B sound, most noticeably on his hit "What'd I Say." Brother Ray was one of the most influential and well-loved figures in the history of recorded music. The blind piano player lost his vision, probably from glaucoma, when he was six years old, and remained blind to musical boundaries throughout his career. Ray recorded soul, blues, jazz, R&B, country, rock and roll—whatever he felt like playing. It was all music to him. His given name was Ray Charles Robinson, but when he started playing music, he shortened his name to Ray Charles to avoid confusion with the famous boxer "Sugar" Ray Robinson. "What Child Is This?" opened his 1985 album, *The Spirit of Christmas*, a record where all of Ray's genius is heard through Christmas songs.

7. "THE MISTLETOE AND ME"—ISAAC HAYES

Did the same man whose music includes *Hot Buttered Soul* and "The Theme from Shaft" also release a tender Christmas ballad? Ya damn right he did! Can you dig it? Isaac Hayes sang "The Mistletoe and Me" for Enterprise Records in 1969, the same year as his steamy, slow-burning *Hot Buttered Soul.* "The Mistletoe and Me" has full orchestration as Hayes seduces the listener under the mistletoe. A bit of kissing is the only way for him to have a complete Christmas. "The Mistletoe and Me" can be found on some of Hayes's full-length CDs and also the compilation holiday album *It's Christmas Time Again*. Hayes had another rise in popularity the late 1990s with his portrayal as Chef in the *South Park* television series. Right on.

8. "WHAT ARE YOU DOING NEW YEAR'S EVE?" — PATTI LABELLE

There are very few New Year's songs, and these days it seems that all the Christmas decorations are down by December 27 so that stores can put out their Valentine's Day candy. But New Year's falls within the Christmas season, which officially ends with Epiphany on January 6. Philadelphia's Patti LaBelle covered the 1949 Orioles hit "What Are You Doing New Year's Eve?" on her 1990 holiday effort, *This Christmas*. LaBelle's musical career began in the 1960s with an all-girl pop group called the Blue Belles. She changed her name from Patricia Holt to Patti LaBelle then to match the name of the group. Throughout her career, LaBelle has recorded soul, funk, disco, and even rock covers, and hit the top of the charts with "Lady Marmalade" in 1975. She actually toured with The Who at one point in her career. "What Are You Doing New Year's Eve?" is a romantic wish to be holding the one you love tightly when the clock strikes midnight.

9. "NOEL"—SMOKEY ROBINSON AND THE MIRACLES

When the Miracles released their first Christmas album in 1963, it included the traditional English carol, "The First Nowell," with the title simply changed to "Noel," the more common spelling of the word today. "The First Nowell" is the first song of Christmas day, and the opening line tells us that the first nowell was sung by angels to the shepherds, which is true to the Biblical account. This carol dates back to the seventeenth century and probably a bit earlier than that. The version that is sung today probably formed most of its words and melody by the early 1800s. "Noel" requires simple but beautiful harmonies (the kind one author's sisters could never quite figure out, annoying the whole house with incessant singing). For some truly classic harmonies, Smokey Robinson and the Miracles will do the trick. Not only was Smokey Robinson the lead Miracle, but he was also a strong, energetic songwriting force within the 1960s Motown machine. Miracles hits included "I Second That Emotion" and "The Tears of a Clown." The Miracles released two Christmas albums before disbanding in 1972, after which Smokey went on to a solo career.

10. "BORN IN BETHLEHEM"—BLIND BOYS OF ALABAMA

A recent entry into the R&B canon of Christmas music is by a band that had been around since the 1930s. The Blind Boys of Alabama released *Go Tell It on the Mountain* in 2003 and included a wide variety of guest singers to harmonize with them. Featured artists include George Clinton, Solomon Burke, Aaron Neville, Shelby Lynne, and Tom Waits who completely rips up "Go Tell It on the Mountain" with the Blind Boys. For "Born in Bethlehem," Mavis Staples, of the legendary Staples Singers, joins the Blind Boys in a breathtaking version of the Christmas gospel favorite. Probably a more realistic counting song than "The Twelve Days of Christmas," "Born in Bethlehem" (also called "Children Go Where I Send Thee") starts with sending the children one by one and ends with sending the children twelve by twelve. The song does some serious gospel name-checking for Paul and Silas, the ten commandments, the gospel writers, and the little bitty baby borne by the Virgin Mary. The Blind Boys were formed in 1937 at the Talladega Institute for the Deaf and Blind in Alabama. Founding members Clarence Fountain and Jimmy Carter (not the former president) are still testifying with their music today.

Nollaig Shona

Christmas music from different cultures always contains its share of beauty, surprises, and laughs. Celtic music holds a particular warmth for American ears, not only because of the Celtic heritage of so many Americans but because many of the old carols originated in the British Isles. So brush up on your Gaelic, take a cup of courage, join the pipes, sing another chorus, and enjoy your figgy pudding.

1. "WREN IN THE FURZE"—THE CHIEFTAINS

Ireland's musical ambassadors to the world, The Chieftains were formed in 1963, and fans across the globe have been dancing jigs and reels to their music ever since. *The Bells of Dublin* was recorded in 1991 and is simply a fantastic example of the Celtic appeal. Guests include Nanci Griffith, Ricky Lee Jones, Elvis Costello, and the Renaissance Singers. Many carols are represented on *The Bells of Dublin*, including "The Boar's Head" and "Ding Dong Merrily On High," but the highlight of the album is the medley "Wren in the Furze," sung by the Chieftains' own Kevin Conneff.

According to the liner notes, the sport of wren hunting takes place on St. Stephen's Day, December 26, and boys in rural areas play songs and plead for money "to bury the wren." Conneff and his bandmates capture the spirit of this hunt perfectly, with lyrics such as "so it's up with the kettle and down with the pan/Won't you give us a penny to bury the wren." Paddy Moloney plays the tin whistle while Conneff scats Celtic-style.

2. "THE WEXFORD CAROL"—JAMES GALWAY

"The Man with the Golden Flute," famed Irish flutist James Galway, was knighted by Queen Elizabeth II in 2001, so from now on that's *Sir* James Galway to you. Part of Galway's appeal is his ability to bridge the gap between classical, chamber, and popular music. He was the lead flutist for the Berlin Philharmonic Orchestra from 1969 until 1975 when he decided to seek out a solo career. What followed has been a long and popular career that has seen Galway perform the world over. Recently, Galway's flute can be heard on the soundtracks to *The Lord of the Rings* trilogy of movies. "The Wexford Carol" is a traditional Irish Christmas carol that retells the Christmas story, complete with shepherds, wise men, angels, Mary, and "a princely babe, sweet Jesus born."

3. "OICHE CHIUN (SILENT NIGHT)"—ENYA

Born as Eithne Ní Bhraonáin, Irish songstress Enya began her singing career in a band her siblings had formed called Clannad. When she branched out on her own in 1982, she recorded her own style of Irish/New Age music. In 1988, she had a bona fide hit called "Orinoco Flow" (many people call it "Sail Away") that was featured on the music television channel VH1. She has remained popular ever since. Her song "Only

Time" was frequently used as background music for news stories regarding the September 11, 2001, terrorist attacks in the United States. In 1992, Enya recorded her version of "Silent Night," "Oiche Chiun" in the Gaelic tongue. The haunting rendition of this most holy of all Christmas songs is delivered slowly and simply. Despite the fact that she has sold millions of records, Enya will not be on a world tour anytime soon; she seldom performs in public.

4. "GOOD KING WENCESLAS"—LOREENA MCKENNITT

This Christmas favorite often confuses the youngsters. What does a song about a king with a funny name have to do with Christmas? It has no Santa, no reindeer, no wise men, or shepherds. What "Good King Wenceslas" does have is the example of helping out the less fortunate during the Christmas season. "Good King Wenceslas" was written by Englishman John Mason Neale in 1853. The music is from a thirteenth-century carol called "Tempus Adest Floridum." King Wenceslas was not English or Irish but from the area in Europe known as Bohemia. He became king in 922, but his legend of kindness and generosity has been remembered for a thousand years.

Canadian Loreena McKennitt, best known for her 1998 hit, "The Mummer's Dance," recorded "Good King Wenceslas" in 1995 and gave it a Celtic rhythm and charm that it has long needed.

5. "O COME, O COME EMMANUEL/GOD REST YE MERRY GENTLEMEN"—BONNIE RIDEOUT

You don't have to be British to create wonderful Celtic music. Bonnie Rideout was born in Michigan and she studied classical violin at the University of Michigan. Her Scottish heritage won out, however. She is a three-time U.S. National Scottish Fiddle champion and the only American to present eighteenth-century and Highland fiddle styles at the Edinburgh International Festival. In 1996, Bonnie recorded *A Scottish Christmas* with her friends Maggie Sansone (dulcimer), Al Petteway (guitar), and Eric Riglar (pipes). This "celebration of Christmas, Hogmanay, and the New Year" opens with the medley of "O Come, O Come Emmanuel" and "God Rest Ye Merry Gentlemen." Beginning with Bonnie's Scottish fiddle, the group jumps in and transforms the aire into a full-fledged reel.

"O Come, O Come Emmanuel" is one of the oldest Christmas carols around. The medieval monastery favorite was translated from Latin into English by John Mason Neale ("Good King Wenceslas") in 1851. This hymn may date as far back as the twelfth century. Emmanuel is the Hebrew word meaning "God with us." When the angel told Mary that she was to conceive a child, she was to "call his name Emmanuel." The lyrics to "O Come, O Come Emmanuel" contain many references from the Biblical gospels, as well as from the Old Testament prophet Isaiah.

6. "O HOLY NIGHT"—THE IRISH TENORS

"O Holy Night" is one of those songs that requires an extraordinary voice, especially when the song hits "o night divine," the part that goes extra high. This song is made for those people who can hit the high notes. "O Holy Night" is a French carol, written by Placide Clappeau in 1847. Clappeau was the mayor of Roquemaure and also a wine merchant. The music was written by Adolphe-Charles Adam, and the song was translated into English by John Dwight. Extraordinary voices abound with The Irish Tenors— Ireland's answer to world famous Three Tenors. The

Irish Tenors are John McDermott, Ronan Tynan, and Anthony Kearns. Of the three, the Irish tenor many Americans may recognize is Tynan. He's the one who sings "God Bless America" during the seventh inning stretch of all the New York Yankees' playoff and World Series games.

7. "ON A COLD WINTER'S NIGHT/CHRISTMAS EVE"— KEVIN BURKE AND MICHAEL O'DOMHNAILL

Kevin Burke, who was raised in England, is a famous Irish fiddler who has been a part of bands such as the Bothy Band, Patrick Street, and Open House. He has also had a successful solo career and has appeared on a few of folk singer Arlo Guthrie's albums. Irish guitarist Michael O'Domhnaill is best known for his work with the Irish chamber band Nightnoise. Burke and O'Domhnaill were in the Bothy Band together and continue to record together here and there. Their recording of traditional carols "On a Cold Winter's Night" and "Christmas Eve" translate into a peaceful Irish medley. This is an ideal song once the stockings have been stuffed, the kids are finally asleep, and peace comes to the household for a brief time.

8. "NOWELL, NOWELL: TIDINGS TRUE/RIU, RIU, CHIU"— MAGGIE SANSONE AND ENSEMBLE GALILEI

Maggie Sansone is an American hammered dulcimer player who specializes in traditional Celtic music. She formed her own recording label, Maggie's Music, in the 1980s and has produced some of the best Celtic music on this side of the Atlantic. Having already recorded two albums with traditional Celtic Christmas music (*Sounds of the Season I* and *II*) that included harp, fiddle, concertina, and guitar to go with the dulcimer, Maggie turned her attention to "traditional carols, medieval cantigas, and Renaissance dances" on a 1993 recording titled *Ancient Noels*. The result is amazingly beautiful. Although most people may not recognize ninety percent of the melodies on *Ancient Noels*, the tunes sink deep into one's soul and brighten one's spirit on a cold winter night. The medley of "Nowell, Nowell: Tidings True," a medieval carol from Britain, and "Riu, Riu, Chiu," a Renaissance-era Spanish song, are particularly lovely. There is no singing on *Ancient Noels*, but the chorus of "Riu, Riu, Chiu" roughly translates into "God kept the wolf from our lamb."

9. "WE WISH YOU A MERRY CHRISTMAS"— THE HIGHLAND BAGPIPES

You didn't think you'd get through this list without a full assault of the bagpipes, did you? While some may dismiss the playing of the pipes, there is nothing that warms the heart of a Scotsman like bagpipes. (Aye, a wee bit of whiskey and a young dark-haired lass warms the heart, too.) The more pipes, the better! The Highland Bagpipes have an album called *Highland Christmas,* and it's full of bagpipes. "We Wish You a Merry Christmas" dates back to at least sixteenth-century England and is a traditional caroling song— maybe *the* traditional caroling song. It is a real "sing for your supper" themed song, complete with the "now bring us some figgy pudding" ending.

10. "AULD LANG SYNE"—JOHNNY CUNNINGHAM

Canadian band leader Guy Lombardo popularized this song by playing it every New Year's Eve. However, this song may be best performed by a Scotsman. Fiddler Johnny Cunningham performed both traditional and contemporary Scottish music and was a founding member of the Scottish band Silly Wizard. His music was both fun and heart-breaking. "Auld Lang Syne" can be found on his album with Susan McKeown called "A Winter's Talisman." The poem "Auld Lang Syne" was written by Scotland's most famous poet, Robert "My Love is Like a Red, Red Rose" Burns. Some people have made fun of the words to "Auld Lang Syne," as did Billy Crystal in the movie *When Harry Met Sally*, but they actually translate into "old long since," or, better yet, "times gone by." So on New Year's Eve, it is perfectly appropriate to raise a glass to times gone by. For those wondering what to do once Hogmanay or New Year's celebration is over, Scotland offers an annual Burns Supper around Burns's birthday each year, January 25, and features poetry, whisky, and the traditional Scottish dish of haggis.

Holiday Movie Classics

Holiday movies come and go by the hundreds. It seems each year another Christmas flick tries to elicit "tidings of comfort and joy" from the movie-going public. Even with all the new movies coming out, the classics maintain their popularity, those old (and sometimes not-so-old) movies that are shown year after year after year—a welcome part of television viewing between Thanksgiving and Christmas. The following are ten of the all-time classic Christmas movies of the past sixty or so years.

1. *IT'S a WONDERFUL LIFE* (1946)

If there are people alive who have yet to see this Frank Capra masterpiece, we haven't met them. Recent studies show that *It's a Wonderful Life* is on television an average of 4,254 times between Thanksgiving and Christmas . . . and that's per day! Okay, we made that up, but it certainly seems like it. Surprisingly, this movie was a box-office and critical failure when it first debuted in 1946, with repeated television viewings giving the public a second chance at this now-favorite.

The movie centers around actor James Stewart's character, George Bailey, a resident of Bedford Falls, thinking of ending it all on Christmas. He's lost a wad of the bank's cash, and that evil despot of the community, Mr. Potter (played by Lionel Barrymore, Drew Barrymore's great-uncle), is trying to blame him for the townfolks' sudden poverty. All of Bailey's dreams are gone, he's stuck in Bedford Falls when he wants to see the world, and it's just not worth it anymore, despite the fact that he is married to the beautiful Mary (Donna Reed) and lives in a beautiful house with beautiful kids. Despondent, he decides to leap to his death from a bridge.

Then, along comes Clarence, played by Henry Travers (who previously starred in *The Bells of Saint Mary's*, which in a neat nod to Travers was the movie advertised at the Bedford Falls theater during this film). Clarence Oddbody is George's guardian angel with a concern of his own—he has yet to earn his wings. He stops George's suicide attempt and takes him on an often-imitated, never-duplicated romp through an alternate Bedford Falls, showing him what the town would be like—invariably for the worse—if George Bailey and his acts of kindness never existed. Heartened by what he's meant to the town, Bailey comes to realize that he has indeed had—can you guess?—a "wonderful life." And Clarence? As the Bailey daughter exclaims, "Teacher says every time a bell rings, an angel gets his wings!" Ding ding, Clarence!

2. *A CHRISTMAS STORY* (1983)

"You'll shoot your eye out!" One of the more recent movies that can truthfully lay claim to the label of "classic," *A Christmas Story* follows the Parker family—most specifically Ralphie Parker, played by Peter

Billingsley—as the magical day approaches in 1940s Indiana. The comedy's tagline of "A Tribute to the Original, Traditional, One-Hundred-Percent, Red-Blooded, Two-Fisted, All-American Christmas" should give anyone who hasn't seen this film an idea of what to expect.

Ralphie pines for a Red Ryder BB gun for Christmas. That's all he wants, just give him that and he'll be a happy nine-year-old. But his mother comes back with the ultimate mother retort, used to open this entry. Curses! Speaking of curses . . . that's only one of the adventures Ralphie takes the viewer on, ranging from a classmate being triple-dog-dared to see if his tongue will stick to a frozen flagpole (of course), his kid brother so overdressed for warmth that he can't put down his arms (another motherly over-reaction), his father receiving a "prize" of a lamp that looks like a woman's leg (priceless!), and the infamous tire-changing quote of ". . . except I didn't say 'fudge.'"

But while Christmas dinner is ruined by the neighbor's dogs attacking the turkey—leading to waiters at the Chinese restaurant the Parkers go to eat attempting to cheer them up with a hearty "fah-rah-rah-rah-rah, rah-rah-rah-rah"—little Ralphie does indeed receive his Red Ryder Carbon Action 200-shot range model air rifle. As for shooting his eye out . . . of course not. But perhaps only because he wore glasses. In recent years Turner Network Television (TNT) has shown the movie for twenty-four hours straight on Christmas Eve into Christmas Day, so it is easy to catch this one. Check it out on TNT any time during the holiday.

3. *MIRACLE ON 34TH STREET* (1947)

We're talking the original here—not the 1990s remake with the lisping kid from *Mrs. Doubtfire*. As with Coca-

Cola, the original is the only "real thing," baby, with the incomparable Edmund Gwenn playing Kris Kringle, and Natalie Wood starring as the little girl who believes in him, against the negativity of her mother's cynicism. This classic centers around a kind old man who pinch-hits as Santa Claus at the Macy's Thanksgiving Day Parade in New York City after the original man hired turns up drunk. The new Santa is then asked by Macy's Doris Walker (Maureen O'Hara) to play Santa for the rest of the season. Walker soon realizes that the man calls himself Kris Kringle and actually believes that he is the Jolly Old Elf himself! While special things always seem to happen around Kringle, his continued insistence upon his true personage finally sees him taken to a mental hospital. Of course, all is set right in the end, allowing for that special miracle to happen. One bit of interesting minutia about *Miracle on 34th Street*: although it is traditional holiday viewing today, the original movie opened in May. The reasoning? More people go to the movies in the summer.

4. *A CHRISTMAS CAROL* (1951)

Also known simply as *Scrooge*, this classic is based on the Charles Dickens novel involving a crotchety old miser who sees a series of four ghosts during one Christmas Eve—Jacob Marley (Scrooge's former partner), and the Ghosts of Christmas Past, Present, and Future. The specters cure him of his cheapskate ways by showing him how he enjoyed the holiday in the past, how others in his life enjoy it now, and how he might end up in the future if he doesn't shape up. This early version—arguably still the best of the many variations of Dickens's story—starred Alastair Sim as Ebenezer Scrooge; Mervyn Johns as his long-suffering assistant, Bob Cratchit; and Glyn Dearman as

Cratchit's doomed-to-die son, Tiny Tim. The latter's famous line, "God bless us, every one!" resounds throughout the season.

5. *national Lampoon's CHRISTMAS VACATION* (1989)

The third of four "Vacation" movies starring Chevy Chase as the patriarch of the Griswold clan (the others being *American Vacation*, *European Vacation*, and *Vegas Vacation*), *Christmas Vacation* is the holiday no one wants to have but everyone loves to laugh at.

Clark W. Griswold (Chase) and his lovely wife, Ellen (Beverly D'Angelo), decide to invite the whole family over for an "old-fashioned family Christmas." The Griswolds are about to have a swimming pool installed, thanks to an assumed hefty bonus. Clark plans for the best set of Christmas lights in the world as well, and he wants to share it all. As those familiar with the *Vacation* series know, Griswold's plans never seem to turn out as expected. First is the uninvited arrival of the mobile-home-driving redneck Cousin Eddie, played hilariously by Randy Quaid. Then, the lights don't quite work the way Clark intended, the sled lubricant used turns his saucer into an uncontrollable speed demon, and his Christmas "bonus" is really a one-year membership in the jelly-of-the-month club— hardly a way to pay for the pool he's been fantasizing about.

Leave it to Cousin Eddie to save the day, however, getting Clark his bonus and providing tons of laughs in this Christmas comedy classic.

6. *HOLIDAY INN* (1942)

Starring Bing Crosby and Fred Astaire, *Holiday Inn* involves a hotel that opens only on holidays. While the movie covers more than just Christmas, Santa's favorite day is still the holiday most associated with the film. The reason? Irving Berlin's "White Christmas," was heard first in this movie—not, surprisingly, in the film of the same name.

Crosby and Astaire star as two-thirds of a love triangle with Astaire's character, Ted Hanover, stealing a girl from Crosby's Jimmy Hardy—and then Crosby attempting to prevent him from doing the same thing with his new flame when the old one dumps Astaire later on. Along the way there's tons of great singing and dancing with some great Irving Berlin classic songs throughout.

7. *WHITE CHRISTMAS* (1954)

Bing Crosby returns to the "silver-bells screen," this time with Danny Kaye by his side and a "cooperation" theme instead of *Holiday Inn's* competition in this box-office smash from 1954. In fact, the original plan was to reunite Crosby with his *Holiday Inn* co-star Astaire, but the retired Astaire turned down the chance. Danny Kaye was actually the third choice, as hoofer Donald O'Connor was offered the part as well.

Bob Wallace and Phil Davis (Crosby and Kaye, respectively) are a pair of World War II vets who form a top song-and-dance team. Rosemary Clooney and Vera-Ellen are the love interests, Betty and Judy Haynes, who—as luck would have it—are *also* a song-and-dance team! The men follow the women to Vermont, where the women are taking part in a holiday revue at a lodge that, wonder of wonders, happens to be owned by the guys' former military commander, ably played by Dean Jagger. Hilarity and, of course, lots of singing and dancing occur as the four try to save the lodge and find love at the same time.

8. *CHRISTMAS IN CONNECTICUT* (1945)

Barbara Stanwyck starred as Elizabeth Lane in this classic, a journalist who is one of the country's most famous food writers. She waxes poetic in her columns about raising and feeding her family at her Connecticut farm, dazzling America with recipe after delicious recipe. One year, her publisher decides that a sailor named Jefferson Jones (played by Dennis Morgan) who spent weeks adrift after his destroyer was torpedoed—buoyed mainly by memories of the food in Lane's columns—should spend Christmas on her farm sampling her lifestyle. There is only one problem: She has no husband. And no baby. No farm, either. Oh, and she can't cook at all. The recipes come from her chef friend, Felix, played by S. Z. Sakall. Needless to say, Elizabeth Lane spends the movie trying to fake her way through a Christmas in Connecticut and falling in love with a sailor.

9. *THE BISHOP'S WIFE* (1947)

Remade in 1996 as *The Preacher's Wife* starring Denzel Washington and Whitney Houston, the original featured David Niven as the bishop, Henry Broughman, and Loretta Young as his wife, Ellen. As Bishop Henry concentrates on the building of a new cathedral, his wife and his congregation wonder if he's paying too much attention to the plans and too little attention to them.

Enter Dudley, played by Cary Grant. When the bishop prays for assistance with his cathedral, an angel (Dudley) is sent. However, he doesn't help in quite the way that the bishop expected. Dudley spreads good cheer to all, especially the bishop's wife and family, resulting in a bit of the green monster out of the bishop. There is, of course, a happy ending for all involved as the bishop discovers what's truly important. Grant and Niven are outstanding in their roles, although Niven was originally supposed to play the angel with Grant starring as the bishop. Luckily, the switch was made before filming commenced.

10. *THE NUTCRACKER* (1993)

This version of Tchaikovsky's classic, with the New York City Ballet, is perhaps the best version of the famed ballet. Choreographed by George Balanchine, this is the familiar story of a little girl (named Marie in this adaptation and played by Jessica Lynn Cohen) and her dreamland of larger-than-life toys, a Sugarplum Fairy, and Macaulay Culkin as The Nutcracker himself. The narration by Kevin Kline adds to the delight for children both young and old.

Not-so-Classic Holiday Movies

Try, try as they may, some movies don't quite match up to the classics in the previous list. In fact, they are as far away from "classic" as a double bacon cheeseburger is from health food. But sometimes a double bacon cheeseburger is fun to eat, regardless of the consequences. Some of these movies are so bad that they can be entertaining in their own right. Others, approach with caution. Don't say we didn't warn you.

1. *SANTA CLAUS CONQUERS THE MARTIANS* (1964)

Oh my, where to begin with this one? This falls into the "so bad it's good" category. For those who remember *Mystery Science Theater 3000*, this is an example of the kind of movie the show spoofed, and did in one memorable episode. The plot is as follows: Martian children are sad, so very sad. Why? It turns out that they can tune in to Earth TV and see how happy the Earth children are, which somehow makes them sad. Or something like that. The solution, according to a really old Martian guy, is to kidnap Santa Claus so the Martian kids can be happy and carefree like children are supposed to be.

While the Martian leader, Kimar (Leonard Hicks), leads the expedition, the contrary Voldar (Vincent

Beck) tries to sabotage it at every turn, insisting that Santa Claus (John Call) will make the Martian children soft. Nevertheless, the Martians kidnap not only Santa but two Earth children who are forced to direct the Martians to Santa Claus. The three are taken back to Mars where Santa starts in on building a workshop, hoping if he does as asked that he will be allowed to leave in time for Christmas on Earth. He's assisted by the lovable Dropo, a goofy Martian who loves making kids happy. In the end, Voldar's plots to kill Santa fail, Santa and the kids go back to Earth, and Dropo becomes the Martian version of Santa.

Star hunting? Check out a young Pia Zadora as Girmar, one of the Martian children.

2. *JACK FROST* (1998)

Michael Keaton stars in *Jack Frost* as Jack Frost, a musician and family man with a wife (Kelly Preston) and son (Joseph Cross). He pays too much attention to his musician side and not enough to his family-man side and probably would have lived to regret this if he hadn't died in a car accident—quite a start to a holiday feel-good flick. A year later, however, to help his wife and son heal, he comes back to life as a snowman to teach his wife and son that they must go on without him. Frost is able to spend some more time with the two of them, time he didn't spend enough of while he was alive, and when it's time to go, everyone is better for his presence. As a snowman.

3. *CHRISTMAS WITH THE KRANKS* (2004)

Christmas with the Kranks is based on the John Grisham book, *Skipping Christmas*, in which a couple decides that, with their only daughter gone for the holidays, it's the perfect time to skip Christmas celebrations and head to the tropics. The plot is hatched by the husband (played in the movie by Tim Allen as Luther Krank). His wife (Jamie Lee Curtis as Nora Krank) goes along with the plan somewhat reluctantly when Luther crunches the numbers and shows that they can finance their vacation simply with savings by not doing anything Christmas-like. No tree, no cards, no presents, no donations, no decorations, nothing.

With cat-who-ate-the-canary glee the Kranks share their plans with one and all, only to find that others don't think their plan is a good one, especially the neighbors who take pride in the neighborhood camaraderie of house decorating. And, of course, the plot takes the expected twist when their daughter, Blair Krank, reveals at the last minute that she and her fiance will indeed be coming home for Christmas, as she wants to show off the standard family holiday with which she's grown up. Predictable twists and turns and guffaws result, but the movie fell flat with viewers and reviewers. Many of Grisham's books may have made successful movies, but *Skipping Christmas* does not join that list.

4. *THE CHRISTMAS SHOES* (2002)

Based on a song written a few years prior, this made-for-television holiday schlockfest has more sap than a Vermont maple tree. The movie centers around a young boy, Nathan Andrews (Max Morrow) who wants to buy his mother a pair of red shoes for Christmas. The shoes will be his mother's last Christmas present ever, because she's dying from a heart condition. While struggling to acquire this perfect present, Nathan finds a workaholic lawyer, Robert Layton (Rob Lowe) who has problems of his own—a struggling marriage and a daughter he doesn't seem to have time for. Needless to say, young Nathan's quest touches Layton's heart, and he learns (say it with me) the "true meaning of Christmas."

5. *SANTA WITH MUSCLES* (1996)

Whatcha gonna do when the largest Santa Claus in the world comes after *you*? If you're a moviegoer, well, you'll go see something else, it appears. *Santa With Muscles* stars Terry Bollea, known far and wide as Hulk Hogan of professional wrestling fame. During his first stint with the World Wrestling Federation (now known as World Wrestling Entertainment after a tiff over initials with the World Wildlife Fund) someone had the bright idea that Hogan could be a movie star. He wasn't bad in *Rocky III* but he certainly had some bombs. This was one of them.

Hogan stars (so to speak) as Blake Thorne, a strongman with tons of cash but a miserly tinge. One holiday season, however, he's struck on the head, and in the standard plot twist of bad comedies, awakens with amnesia. But—here's the fun part!—when this happens, he's wearing a Santa Claus suit, so he thinks he's the fat man himself. "Santa" must stop the town's evil rich dude—the Million Dollar Man Ted DiBiase of the town, for those rasslin' fans out there—from tearing down an orphanage. This movie also includes appearances from television comic Garret Morris and character actor Ed Begley, Jr., as well as a younger Mila Kunis, better known today for her role as Jackie on television's *That '70s Show*.

6. *PRANCER* (1989)

Rebecca Harrell stars as Jessica Riggs, a girl living with her father (Sam Elliott) and brother Steve (John Duda) on a failing apple farm—failing so much so that her father is considering sending Jessica to live with a relative since her older brother can pull his weight whereas Jessica can't. Oh, and her mother's dead, leading to a fit of tears when a friend tells Jessica there's no God, causing the nine-year-old to fret about where her mother might be, because without God there's no heaven and that's just where she assumed all along her mother was!

Into this comes an injured reindeer, which, through a particularly strained setup, Jessica comes to believe is Prancer—and she must nurse him back to health by Christmas Eve so Prancer can take his (her?) rightful place in Santa's team, all the while keeping the animal away from her father's prying eyes. Even the quality of Abe Vigoda as the local doctor and Cloris Leachman as a neighbor can't save this movie.

7. *SANTA CLAUS, THE MOVIE* (1985)

The movie, brought to us by the same folks who brought us the original *Superman*, seems to follow the same map laid by the Man of Steel. The first half is the "biography" background of Santa Claus, played here by David Huddleston. The second half of the story shapes up (with Dudley Moore as Santa's chief elf, Patch, and John Lithgow in an admittedly excellent turn as the villainous BZ) as a plot to ruin Santa with the help of the outcast Patch. With amateurish special effects, Santa sightings in short supply, and Dudley Moore on board, it's not hard to see why this would fall into a list of the ten worst holiday movies.

8. *JACK FROST* (1997)

Same title but completely different movie than the 1998 one with Michael Keaton listed earlier, both center around a dead man coming back to life as a snowman. This one stars Scott MacDonald as a serial killer who, after meeting his death, returns as a virtually indestructible killer snowman—not quite the tearjerker the Keaton flick was. With a tag line of "he's chillin' . . . and killin'" it is easy to guess that this movie comes with tongue planted firmly in cheek. It's still awful but awful in a slightly funny way.

9. *I SAW MOMMY KISSING SANTA CLAUS* (2001)

A young boy, Justin Carver (played by twins Cole and Dylan Sprouse), catches sight of mommy dearest sharing a smooch with the Man in Red. What Justin doesn't know is that we've secretly replaced Santa Claus with his own father in a Santa Claus outfit! Let's see if he notices. Shocked, Justin still has the where-withal to snap a photo, and not knowing what to do, he shares it with the neighborhood bully.

In a bit of logic that even children had trouble fol-lowing, Justin and the bully come to the conclusion that Santa is putting the moves on Justin's mom—she's hotter than Mrs. Claus, after all—and in order to throw a monkey wrench into that, Justin must be the naughtiest boy in the world. Santa hates naughty chil-dren, after all. What results is pranks, pranks, and more pranks. How low do they go? We even get the old rake-on-the-ground-that-smacks-your-face-when-you-step-on-it bit. The main purpose of this movie is to demonstrate once again the perils of voyeurism.

10. *REINDEER GAMES* (2000)

Nick and Rudy (James Frain and Ben Affleck, respec-tively—get the names? Nick? Rudy? Ho ho ho) are cellmates readying for a Christmastime release. Nick talks incessantly about the female penpal he's going to meet, Ashley (Charlize Theron). When Nick is killed by a shiv in a prison rumble before their release, though, Rudy decides to pretend to be Nick in order to meet the lovely lass. That plan apparently goes awry when Ashley's brother, knowing "Nick's" past, decides Nick would be the perfect guy to help out in a robbery and forces the issue with Rudy/Nick. At the end it turns out Nick really isn't dead, but he set up the whole thing knowing what Rudy would do, so Rudy would make the robbery and Nick could walk away with the cash. The moral is once a bad guy, always a bad guy, and bad guys—in this case—make bad movies.

Ho Ho Ho and
Ha Ha Ha

Christmas is all about happiness, and what's more happy than laughter? So it makes sense that there would be a strong compilation of Christmas comedy movies. We've already discussed *A Christmas Story* and *National Lampoon's Christmas Vacation* in the all-time Christmas classics list. Below are ten more somewhat-recent Christmas comedies worth remembering.

1. *THE GRINCH* (2000)

This 2000 movie is a feature-length retelling of the Dr. Seuss classic starring Jim Carrey as the mean one and directed by Ron Howard, who rose to fame on television as young Opie on *The Andy Griffith Show* and then Richie Cunningham on *Happy Days*. *The Grinch* was the highest-selling movie ticket of 2000, with more than fifty million sold. Anyone in the country for more than a month knows the basic plot behind the story; this version keeps those basics but adds a bit more, including a hilarious look at the Grinch as a child in Whoville, which helps explain his misanthropic attitude later in life. The special effects and costumes in the movie are amazing, and country star Faith Hill snagged a hit with the song "Where Are You, Christmas?" from the movie.

2. *THE SANTA CLAUSE* (1994)

This family comedy stars Tim Allen as Scott Calvin (note those initials, those who enjoy foreshadowing!), a divorced man with a son, Charlie (Eric Lloyd), staying with him for Christmas. The two hear a noise outside on Christmas Eve and see Santa Claus—or at least a man dressed as Santa—up on the roof. He wasn't on the roof for long, though, as a fall left him laying in the yard, dead—quite a Christmas surprise.

The dying Kringle hands Scott Calvin a card, instructing him to put on the Santa suit. Once Scott does that, he's whisked away to the North Pole and finds out that by putting on the suit he's legally obligated to become the next Santa Claus. The next year sees the single dad—who at first is not quite sure the whole night wasn't just a dream—put on weight, grow a beard, and overall become more and more Santa-like. While it improves his relationship with his son, his wife (Wendy Crewson) and her new boyfriend Dr. Neal Miller (Judge Reinhold), a psychiatrist, question his sanity and how fit he is as a father. Tons of laughter, and a good bit of feel-good to it as well.

3. *ELF* (2003)

In the grand tradition of boy-raised-by-wolves movies (best done by *Walk Like a Man* starring Howie Mandel), *Saturday Night Live* alum Will Ferrell stars in *Elf* as a human being, Buddy, raised by elves at the North Pole. If you're not familiar with Ferrell, he's tall—very tall—making the juxtaposition of him and the elves a recurring bit of physical humor. Eventually

Ferrell's six-foot-five frame is too out of place in the North Pole and, since he's a substandard toymaker, he's sent by Papa Elf (Bob Newhart) to find his biological father—in New York City. Close your eyes, then (after you finish reading this sentence of course), and try to picture a six-and-a-half foot man in yellow tights and a green outfit wandering the streets of the Big Apple. You can't help but laugh!

Once Ferrell is reunited with his father (James Caan) the "fish out of water" story continues with Buddy's father slowly but surely accepting him and various holiday hijinks, such as Buddy insisting that a department store Santa is not the real one—he would know, after all! Directed by Jon Favreau—quite a departure from *Swingers*—this movie also includes a cameo by Peter Billingsley, the child star of *A Christmas Story*, as an elf in Santa's workshop.

4. *HOME ALONE* (1990)

It's pretty scary when a lot of people today would see Edvard Munch's wonderful painting "The Scream" and immediately think, "oh, it's a painting about *Home Alone*." But that's how ingrained into pop culture the sight of Kevin (Macaulay Culkin) with hands pressed to his cheeks upon discovery of his holiday abandonment has become.

The film opens with the large McCallister clan readying for a Christmas trip to Paris. Just like any family traveling at the holidays, things are frantic—so frantic, in fact, that without realizing it they leave Kevin behind alone in the Chicago home. Kevin's response, like that of most kids in his situation, is one of pure glee. He can eat ice cream in the morning, he can watch movies Mom won't let him, he can stay up as late as he wants. It's all well and good, of course, until two robbers (Joe Pesci and Daniel Stern, both wonderfully hilarious) pick his house as their next target.

Kevin meets the two head on with booby-traps, pranks, and other assorted responses both verbal and physical that frustrate the pair more and more—keeping them far from their larcenous goal. The movie, which launched Macaulay Culkin's career into the stratosphere, grossed an amazing $500-million-plus internationally.

5. *JINGLE ALL THE WAY* (1996)

Anyone who has ever searched for that one "must have" toy of the season is familiar with the basic plot from this comedy. Arnold Schwarzenegger and comedian Sinbad co-star as two fathers trying to locate the same exact toy for their kids—Turbo Man. Arnold is Howard Langston, stereotypical movie father who's too busy for his kids, and after breaking one too many promises to his son Jake Lloyd (later the young Anakin Skywalker in *Phantom Menace*), he tells him he'll make it up with the hard-to-find toy only to forget about it until Christmas Eve. Sinbad is Myron Larabee who wants the toy simply for the joy it'll bring his son. Unfortunately, what with it being Christmas Eve, the toy is in extremely short supply, and the two fathers wind up battling one another—and part of a Turbo Man float in a parade—for the precious toy. There are also fights with Santa and reindeer as the two try to track down a Turbo Man and make it a merry Christmas. Those with a keen eye, by the way, will notice James Belushi as a department store Santa.

6. *BAD SANTA* (2003)

Some of the entries in this list are family comedies. This one . . . is not. Definitely not! *Bad Santa* stars Billy Bob Thornton as Willie, a department-store

Santa; Tony Cox as Marcus, his elf partner; and then-ten-year-old Brett Kelly as a chubby kid that Willie surprisingly befriends. Willie, however, is no normal Santa, and Marcus (a dwarf) is no normal elf. These two pick a different part of the country each holiday season, work as Santa and his assistant, and then on Christmas Eve clean the place out in a robbery planned through the up-close information gained during their stay in each mall's Christmas Village. Ingenious! Thornton's Santa is also a heavy drinker, doesn't shy away from the curse words, and in general is pretty much the Bizarro Santa in his everyday life in the film.

Brett Kelly enters as a lonely boy, picked on by everyone, who somehow comes to believe that Willie is the real Santa. His constant questions and Willie's responses sadly cannot be reprinted in a family book. Eventually, Willie finds that the boy's father is always gone and he lives with his grandmother who's halfway toward the graveyard herself. Needing a place to stay, he invites himself over and crashes at the kid's pad—and he is "the kid," called solely that by Santa. The kid wins Willie over through such means as giving him a a carved pickle as a present and sharing his Advent-calendar chocolate with Willie (although Willie later eats the entire thing in a drunken stupor and has to replace them with mints and medicine). The ending, while a bit schmaltzy, gives a little bit of heart to a cynical movie. Notable in the film is the presence of John Ritter as a store manager who has to deal with Thornton's behavior; this was his last film role before his untimely death from heart problems.

7. *THE SANTA CLAUSE 2: THE MRS. CLAUSE* (2002)

The follow up to 1994's *The Santa Clause*, this sequel focuses on an apparent contractual need for Tim

Allen's Santa Claus to find himself a woman to wed in order to remain as Santa. How did he miss that in the fine print of the contract? On top of that, his son, Charlie, seems to have made it onto this year's "naughty list"—that's gotta rank up there with embarrassing presidential relatives—so Santa heads back home to try to fix things with his son.

But what about Santa's duties at the North Pole? Not to worry, they make a robot Santa to take his place. However, as often happens when robots are involved (see any episode of *The Jetsons* for proof of that), madness sets in and the robot goes out of control. So now Tim Allen's Scott Calvin must find a wife, help out his kid, *and* then return to the North Pole to save Christmas from the mad robot. Whew! The original cast of main characters returns for this one, with Elizabeth Mitchell added on as Principal Carol Newman, the soon-to-be Mrs. Claus.

8. *IT'S A VERY MERRY MUPPET CHRISTMAS MOVIE* (2002)

This made-for-television Muppet masterpiece takes the basic plot of *It's a Wonderful Life* on a zany spin that only the Muppets could pull off. Kermit the frog, Fozzie the bear, Miss Piggy, and the rest of the gang are thisclose to finally being able to purchase the grand old Muppet Theater and have plans for a magnificent Christmas extravaganza. Unfortunately, along comes Miss Bitterman (Joan Cusack) who wants to build a nightclub on the spot where the theater stands and promises to do just that by hook or by crook. When things look their dimmest for the Muppets, Kermit mopes (a moping Muppet?) and, true to the spirit of George Bailey, wishes he'd never been born. As happened to George Bailey, through some divine intervention (including a turn by actress Whoopi Goldberg as God) Kermit is shown what would become of all his pals if he'd never been born in that murky swamp. It's not easy being green, but apparently being without the green one isn't all that easy either.

9. *THE NIGHTMARE BEFORE CHRISTMAS* (1993)

What happens when the denizens of Halloween-town discover another holiday town out there—Christmastown—and decide to take it for their own? From the wickedly funny mind of director Tim Burton, you get *The Nightmare Before Christmas*.

Jack Skellington, the pumpkin king, stumbles upon Christmastown and, bored with the same old same old at Halloween, decides a little change-up is in order. Santa Claus is thus kidnapped and tortured, while Jack and his pals run Christmas in a slightly different way; "sleigh" and "slay" sound so alike, after all. The movie—a marvel of animation in which twenty-four frames were necessary for just one second of action—is a darkly funny look at how a clash of the two holidays might play out and a great "different" kind of holiday movie.

10. *EIGHT CRAZY NIGHTS* (2002)

Okay, so it's not really a *Christmas* movie but rather a holiday movie, but we gave this animated flick from the warped mind of Adam Sandler the okay not only because it's funny but because we love "The Hanukkah Song"! Any song that can rhyme Hanukkah with yarmulke and harmonica—not to mention "gin and tonic-a" is money in our book! And hey—this is our book!

For those of you unfamiliar with Sandler's work, he revels in the childish and the immature, so if that's not your cup of tea you can probably skip this animated comedy. Otherwise, this film is loaded with it, as animation allows for a lot more childishness than live-action can ever hope for! The basic story involves Sandler's Davey Stone as someone who lost his parents in a car accident on the first night of Hanukkah when he was twelve and has hated the holiday—and a lot more, it seems—ever since. He's a miscreant, a drunk, and just plain horrible to be around until the town eccentric Whitey (voiced by Sandler as well) makes it his goal to help the young man. As with most holiday movies—even the ones not just about Christmas—a schmaltzy ending is to be expected.

not Just a Christmas Carol

While 1951's *A Christmas Carol* told Charles Dickens's tale of an old Scrooge visited by four ghosts, it's hardly the only version of the classic tale. It may be the best, but it wasn't the first and certainly wasn't the last. Some versions live up to its impressive predecessor; others . . . well, not so much. Some kept to the same story, whereas some changed it here and there or in some cases almost completely with only a basic similarity to Dickens's words. Be it a comedy, a musical, a cartoon, or—ayyyyy—starring "The Fonz," they all give the same basic message: Bah humbug is no way to go through life.

1. *A CHRISTMAS CAROL* (1938)

Thirteen years before the most famous iteration of the story came 1938's version with Reginald Owen as Ebenezer Scrooge. The part was originally slated to go to Lionel Barrymore, who played the part of Scrooge on many a radio interpretation of the story, but illness prevented him from appearing in the film and he graciously suggested Owen as his substitute. The film also starred Gene and Kathleen Lockhart as Bob Cratchit and the Mrs. and also employed their daughter, June, in her film debut—the only time all three appeared in the same movie. Anticipating its popularity, MGM produced 375 prints, a record at the time, to ensure as many people as possible could see it at the holidays.

2. *MR. MAGOO'S CHRISTMAS CAROL* (1962)

This one's a hidden treasure. As a matter of fact, before writing this book, one of the authors had never even heard of it. However, friends polled for ideas would always insist "Oh, you have to include *Mr. Magoo's Christmas Carol.* It's awesome!" The other co-author owns a DVD of it and confirmed the need for inclusion.

Mr. Magoo, for those unfamiliar with him, is an animated, perpetually squinting, nearly blind older gent voiced by Jim Backus (Thurston Howell III of *Gilligan's Island* fame) who makes his way around pretty much by luck and bumbling. In this holiday special, Magoo is playing Scrooge in a Broadway production of "A Christmas Carol," with Magoo regular Gerald McBoing-Boing as a hilarious Tiny Tim. With wonderful music numbers such as "A Hand for Each Hand," this is certainly a version of the Dickens classic to check out if you haven't seen it.

3. *SCROOGED* (1988)

Inimitable comic actor Bill Murray stars as Francis Xavier Cross in this loose adaptation of Dickens's story. A rather dark and cynical comedy, it nonetheless provides plenty of laughs and, of course, the happy ending Dickens prescribed. Murray's Cross is a television executive with a heart of . . . well, it is hard to know for sure if he has a heart or not. He broke up with an old girlfriend over work, berates panhandlers, gives towels as Christmas presents, and fires an underling (Bobcat

Goldthwait, who is perfectly manic as the Bob Cratchit character) right before Christmas. Also, he's in charge of putting together a live adaptation of the Dickens classic on Christmas Eve. As Cross asks rhetorically after his eventual transformation, "What kind of schmuck makes people work on Christmas Eve?"

The movie includes co-stars Goldthwait and Carol Kane, as well as cameos during the "show within the show" TV special by Jamie Farr, Buddy Hackett, and champion gymnast Mary Lou Retton, who was cast as Tiny Tim—planning on tossing away the crutches for a few flips before the final "God bless us, every one." That happy ending still includes some good touches of humor with Murray's impassioned speech and Goldthwait holding the production booth hostage to keep it on the air. And anyone who's ever seen the movie surely remembers the closing anthem of "Put a Little Love in Your Heart"—sung with the help of theater audiences everywhere led by Murray.

4. *MICKEY'S CHRISTMAS CAROL* (1983)

The Disney gang puts their spin on the holiday classic in 1983's *Mickey's Christmas Carol*. This half-hour animated short stars Mickey as Bob Cratchit (notice how Mickey's always the main attraction?), Scrooge McDuck (who else?) as his boss Ebenezer Scrooge, Goofy (hee-yuck!) as Jacob Marley the first ghost, and Jiminy Cricket as the Ghost of Christmas Past. Mickey, Minnie, and little Tiny Tim—and imagine how tiny a *mouse* named Tiny must be—live a meager existence under the duck's wing until Marley and the trio of ghosts teach him a thing or two about Christmas.

Of particular note, this was the first animated short starring Mickey Mouse in thirty years, and it was also the last time Clarence Nash provided the famous raspy voice for Donald Duck. Nash died in 1985.

5. *A DIVA'S CHRISTMAS CAROL* (2000)

Many of the adaptations listed in this section are classics unto themselves, taking their place next to the original as standard holiday fare. This one does not.

Produced by music video channel VH1, *A Diva's Christmas Carol* stars Vanessa Williams as pop singer Ebony Scrooge, a diva of the first degree who, after a car accident turned a previous musical trio into a duo, abandoned the surviving bandmate for a solo career. As it stands at the start of the movie, she has no use for anyone or anything that can't make her money. Marli Jacob (played by Chilli of the group TLC, and so named in another oh-so-witty play on the original Dickens name) is the dead bandmate who visits Ebony to warn her of three ghostly visitors, with actress-comedienne Kathy Griffin playing the Ghost of Christmas Past, Duran Duran's John Taylor as the Ghost of Christmas Present, and an episode of VH1's show *Behind the Music* taking the place of the Ghost of Christmas Yet to Come. It's not all a lump of coal, though, as the musical productions in the show, such as "Sleigh Ride" and the new "Heartquake," are impressive and show off Williams's singing.

6. *THE MUPPET CHRISTMAS CAROL* (1992)

Ten years before their spoof of *It's a Wonderful Life* came the fun-loving Muppets' version of the ghostly tale. Michael Caine plays the human lead as Scrooge with Kermit the frog in his standard starring role (he and Mickey Mouse are both such ego hounds!) as Bob Cratchit, with Miss Piggy as his lovely wi . . . as his wife. Stealing the show early on are Statler and Waldorf, the two balcony hecklers from *The Muppet Show* as Caine's past business partners come to warn him, and later The Great Gonzo as Charles Dickens himself and Fozzie Bear as Scrooge's old boss

"Fozziwig," instead of Fezziwig. As with most Muppet movies, the songs are an important part of the show and lend quite a bit to the final presentation, especially Kermit's "One More Sleep 'Til Christmas." If he sounds a bit different on the song, it's because this movie was the first feature-length Muppet outing after the death of their creator, Jim Henson. Steve Whitmire took on the high-pressure role of replacing the legend.

7.   *an american CHRISTMaS CaROL* (1979)

Ayyyyyy, "The Fonz" himself, Henry Winkler, stars in this made-for-television adaptation from 1979, smack dab in the middle of his *Happy Days* popularity. Winkler ranges far from his Arthur Fonzarelli roots as Benedict Slade, a Scrooge-like businessman in New Hampshire during America's Great Depression who encounters three ghosts. These ghosts represent three of the people whose possessions he seized in lieu of unpaid bills, which needless to say put quite a damper on the New England town's Christmas spirit. But, as expected, the ghosts convince the miser to change his tune just in time for holiday joy. Perhaps most impressive is the lack of ego and the range of acting ability shown by Winkler, who at the height of his Fonz-era cool was made up as and played convincingly a miserly old coot.

8.   *a CHRISTMaS CaROL* (1984)

George C. Scott stars in this made-for-television version with what many consider the best rendition of "Mr. Bah Humbug," Ebenezer Scrooge, out of all the many variations on Dickens's original story. Directed by Clive Donner, who was the editor for the classic 1951 version, this adaptation was filmed on location in England, presenting the proper murky grittiness to match the early mood of the film. The supporting cast is especially strong as well with actors David Warner as Bob Cratchit, Roger Rees as Scrooge's neglected nephew, Fred, and Frank Finlay as Jacob Marley's ghost.

9. *TNT'S A CHRISTMAS CAROL* (1999)

Call it *Star Trek: A Christmas Carol*. Before the X-Men, there was X-Mas, as this edition stars Patrick Stewart, Captain Jean-Luc Picard of *Star Trek: The Next Generation*, as the miserly Mr. Scrooge, earning himself a Screen Actors Guild Award nomination in the process. He actually played Scrooge on stage in one-man shows for a number of years prior, surely helping him with this production. Bedecked in a stovepipe hat that would make Abraham Lincoln green with jealousy, Stewart shows off the depth of his acting ability (that he doesn't always demonstrate in other roles) in a strong performance for TNT's (Turner Network Television) entry into the Dickens sweepstakes. Where this version surpasses many others is the special effects with a number of cool ghostly actions and accoutrements to accompany the overall strong acting from the cast.

10. *A CHRISTMAS CAROL* (2004)

One of the latest versions of Dickens's classic, this musical is a made-for-television version of an annual stage production at New York City's Madison Square Garden. Debuting on Thanksgiving weekend in 2004, the star-studded cast includes Kelsey Grammar as Ebenezer Scrooge, Jason Alexander as Jacob Marley's ghost, and Jennifer Love Hewitt as Emily, Scrooge's early love interest. Perhaps more important-ly, however, it includes music from Lynn Ahrens (who thirty years prior was a part of ABC's *Schoolhouse Rock*) and Alan Menken (of *Little Shop of Horrors* fame) who made the Madison Square Garden per-formances literally sing.

No Small Parts, Only Small Actors

There's a saying in the theater: There are no small parts, only small actors. It means that a part is what you make of it. Even bit players can have a huge impact on a production if they give it their all, so don't ever give less than 100 percent just because you're not the star. The following people took that saying to heart, and as a result made a big splash in their respective holiday movies. They weren't the stars, they weren't the main attraction, but they still contributed and stood out, becoming a big part of the movie—certainly not small actors, any of these folks.

1. CAROL KANE

Carol Kane appeared in the Bill Murray vehicle *Scrooged* as the Ghost of Christmas Present, giving the ghost a manic, slightly abusive persona. Indeed, Kane so immersed herself in her role that, in a scene that called for her to pull Murray along by his lip, she actually tore it, forcing a short delay in filming. Each "switch" to a different location necessitated another form of violence inflicted upon Murray's Frank Cross.

Luckily there was no electrocution when she smacked him in the face with a toaster.

2. ZACK WARD

Among his credits, Zack Ward played Mark's brother in 2003's epic masterpiece, *Freddy versus Jason* and co-starred in the Fox network sitcom *Titus*. Those aren't roles to really draw attention. But mention the name "Scut Farkus," and chances are the lightbulb goes off. Ward played the evil villain of *A Christmas Story* fame, the yellow-eyed bully who so tormented Ralphie Parker and the rest of the schoolkids that Ralphie blew up and then beat up Farkus. Interestingly, the Farkus character was not in the book on which the movie was based and instead was added just for the movie. Now it's hard to imagine the story without Farkus.

3. RANDY QUAID

Reprising his role as Cousin Eddie from the original *Vacation* movie, Randy Quaid saves Christmas as the redneck relative no one wants in *National Lampoon's Christmas Vacation*. Showing up at the Griswold abode in his trusty RV, Quaid frustrates Chevy Chase's Clark Griswold and annoys the snooty neighbors with his antics. But when the chips are down and it looks like an overly frugal boss is going to ruin Christmas, it's Quaid who comes to the rescue. Unfortunately he does this by kidnapping Chase's boss and bringing him to the Griswold house, followed by local police. Luckily, the boss—with the help of his incredulous wife—realizes his mistake and reinstitutes the Christmas bonus he'd previous rescinded. Thanks Cousin Eddie!

Quaid was so successful and so loved in this role that a made-for-television sequel with the subtitle *Cousin Eddie's Island Adventure* was made for him and revolved around holidays in the tropics for Eddie and his family.

4. DEAN JAGGER

A popular character actor of his time who won a Best Supporting Actor Oscar in 1949's *Twelve O'Clock High*, Jagger (no relation to Mick) played the inn-owning General Thomas Waverly in the Bing Crosby and Danny Kaye vehicle *White Christmas*. General Waverly is the former commander of the two stars, who play a song-and-dance team that follows a pair of sisters (as "the love interests") to a Vermont inn that the guys are surprised to find being run by Waverly. It's close to failing—but the four put on a show to end all shows. The scene at the end when General Waverly realizes that his former charges have saved his bacon is truly a touching moment in a very entertaining film.

5. KAROLYN GRIMES

Who can forget the famous ending to *It's a Wonderful Life*? "Every time a bell rings, an angel gets its wings." It's the six-year-old child star Grimes as ZuZu Bailey who says those lines, the adorable child uttering the feel-good ending that helped make the movie. More importantly, earlier in the movie, it's the petals from ZuZu's rose that George Bailey finds in his pocket, helping him break out of his funk and finally realize how special life can be. Those petals continue to play a role in pop culture today, inspiring a nineties all-female pop group to name themselves "ZuZu's Petals" in honor of Grimes's character.

6. BOBCAT GOLDTHWAIT

Another actor in 1988's *Scrooged*, Goldthwait plays the Cratchit-like Eliot Loudermilk, fired by Frank

Cross right before the holidays. Goldthwait—who, truth be told, is simply playing a version of his normal persona—takes to alcohol after his firing, then comes back with a shotgun to take revenge against his evil boss. The only problem is that Cross has "seen the light" by that point, thanks to his three ghostly visitors. Goldthwait displays visible confusion at the new attitude (not to mention the belly-kiss Cross gives him), but he joins Cross after being promised a new job with a raise, helping Cross spread his special version of Christmas cheer. He does that by holding the production booth hostage during Cross's final speech, giving the boss the opportunity to "put a little love" in everyone's heart.

7. TONY COX

The vertically challenged Tony Cox plays Marcus in the 2003 dark comedy *Bad Santa*, joining Billy Bob Thornton as a Santa-and-elf criminal team that hits department stores each holiday after spending a month working in the Christmas Village and scouting the safe. Cox gives Thornton a run for the title of foulest mouth in a holiday movie, and his one-liners and insults (especially directed at Bernie Mac or John Ritter), are often as funny as they are foul. Again, this is most certainly not a family movie, and Cox certainly does his part to make sure it stays far away from that designation.

8. JOHN PAYNE

There would have been no miracle taking place on or even near 34th Street were it not for Fred Gailey, played by John Payne in 1947's *Miracle on 34th Street*. With Kris Kringle sent to the looney bin for his delusion of ultimate grandeur, it's left to the lawyer

Gailey to spring Kringle from the hoosegow (one must wonder, however, how much of that is because he truly believes the magical old man and how much is because he's smitten with Maureen O'Hara's Doris Walker). In an unprecedented tactical maneuver, he persuades the U.S. Postal Service to deliver bagfuls of mail addressed to "Santa Claus" to Kringle in court and concludes that if the USPS agrees the man is Santa then the courts should as well. Brilliant!

9.   JOE PESCI AND DANIEL STERN

Pesci and Stern play Harry Lime and Marv Merchants, respectively, the foils for Macaulay Culkin in 1990's *Home Alone*. The name Harry Lime was also used in 1947's *The Third Watch* with the character played by Orson Welles. Here, the main story is about Caulkin's character, Kevin McCallister, saving his house from the two robbers; the responses and expressions of the two bungling burglars are what make the gags and pranks work (especially Pesci; based on other films he's done he seems to be dying to swear loudly, and in fact had to be warned about it during filming). Whether they're grabbing on to hot doorknobs, stomping and falling among ornaments, sticking in tar, or feeling the results of a hot iron, Pesci and Stern's reactions show their great acting ability and help make an unbelievable tale of a little kid repeatedly outwitting two thieves a little more believable.

10.   ZOOEY DESCHANEL

It's not often that the person "saving the day" in a movie isn't the lead character, but that's what happens in 2003's *Elf*, starring Will Ferrell as Buddy the Elf and including Zooey Deschanel as his love interest, Jovie. Jovie works in Gimble's department store, where

Buddy finds himself early in the movie, and Buddy proclaims that she decorates a tree very well. The big oaf is obviously smitten, and throughout the movie the two engage in childlike flirting back and forth, as well as an unknowing duet when Buddy sits outside the showers in the store's locker rooms as Jovie sings "Baby It's Cold Outside." When Jovie tells Buddy she doesn't like singing in public, Buddy discloses to her one of the big elf sayings: "The best way to spread Christmas cheer is singing loud for all to hear."

That advice comes in handy later on, as Santa's sleigh sputters and crashes in New York's Central Park. Unfortunately, his sleigh runs on Christmas spirit, and there's just not enough of it. Buddy attempts to fix the sleigh as New Yorkers surround Central Park, but his efforts fail. Leave it to Jovie, then, to repeat Buddy's words to herself, stand up above the crowd, and start a rousing sing-along of "Santa Claus is Comin' to Town." At first singing all by herself, one by one the main characters and then finally the crowd join in, and Santa's sleigh gets the power it needs from the Christmas spirit and zooms overhead. All thanks to Jovie.

It's Only Christmas Rock and Roll, and I Like It

Rock music was slow to move away from the fifties-influenced Christmas sound to create its own new rich traditions for the holidays. For awhile there wasn't much to be heard except the Beatles' annual Christmas greetings to their fans on the radio now and again. By the 1970s and into the new wave 1980s, Christmas became fun and cool again, delivering some classic chestnuts, as well as a few odd nuts.

1. "HAPPY XMAS (WAR IS OVER)"—JOHN LENNON AND YOKO ONO

There are two kinds of Beatles fans: those who tolerate Yoko Ono because she married John, and those who see her as the one who broke up the Fab Four. (For the second group, go back to listening to McCartney's pop-schlock "Wonderful Christmas Time." Oy.) John and Yoko's year-end wish for world peace was produced by legendary rock and roll session man Phil Spector. It was released in 1971 and continues to be played often each Christmas season. "Happy Xmas (War Is Over)" took on a special poignancy in 1980 when Lennon was shot and killed just before Christmas. The song came into favor once again in 2001 after the terrorist attacks on the World Trade Center in New York City and the Pentagon outside Washington, D.C. The children singing on the recording are from the Harlem Community Choir and are given credit along with The Plastic Ono Band. "Happy Xmas (War Is Over)" was originally released as a single on green vinyl. The B-side was Yoko Ono's "Listen, the Snow Is Falling."

2.   "PLEASE COME HOME FOR CHRISTMAS"—THE EAGLES

The Eagles were the most successful band of the 1970s, charting five number-one singles and selling more albums than any other group during that decade. They were fronted by guitarists Glenn Fry and Joe Walsh and backed by drummer Don Henley who also sang. They were originally formed as a back-up band for Linda Ronstadt. Best known for bringing a peaceful, easy country sound to rock and roll, some of the Eagles' biggest hits were "Hotel California" and "Desperado." "Please Come Home for Christmas" is a Charles Brown composition. Don Henley provides the vocals for the Eagles' Christmas contribution. A typical blues lyric finds Henley home alone on Christmas Eve, his baby having left him, hoping for her return by Christmas, or, if not, by New Year's night. "Please Come Home for Christmas" was released as a 45-rpm single in 1978.

3.   "PEACE ON EARTH/LITTLE DRUMMER BOY"— DAVID BOWIE AND BING CROSBY

Of all the odd duets in the history of recorded music, David Bowie and Bing Crosby must be one of the strangest pairings. The most famous crooner and the most famous glam rocker recorded this duet for Bing's television Christmas special only a month before Crosby's death in 1977. It was not released as a single until the early 1980s (complete with MTV video), where it reached the chart high of number three in Great Britain. Proving that a great singer can sing with anyone, Crosby sounds terrific with The Thin White Duke, quickly transitioning from "The Little Drummer Boy" to a plea for world peace by Bowie, while Bing does his pa-rum-pa-pum-pums behind him. Toward the end, the two harmonize in their plea, hoping for peace and love for every child. Remember, it's all about the kids.

4.   "COMFORT AND JOY"—SIMON AND GARFUNKEL

Unbeknownst to many, Simon and Garfunkel were people who could and would perform a blatantly religious Christmas number. The popular folk-rock duo recorded "7 O'Clock News/Silent Night" on their *Parsley, Sage, Rosemary and Thyme* album, a song that contrasted the beatific "Silent Night" with an evening news broadcast detailing gruesome murders, the Vietnam quagmire, and the death of standup comic Lenny Bruce. But it was not until the release of the boxed set, *Old Friends,* that the 1967 recording of "Comfort and Joy" was available. A short version of "God Rest Ye Merry Gentlemen," "Comfort and Joy" displays the trademark harmonies that make Simon and Garfunkel instantly identifiable. It sounds like something right out of Dickens's *Christmas Carol.* Paul Simon opens with the basic melody, and Art Garfunkel's tenor comes in with the harmonies. Eventually the voices overlap one over another in a round, producing a beautifully haunting version of this ancient English carol.

5. "SANTA CLAUS IS COMIN' TO TOWN" — BRUCE SPRINGSTEEN

The Boss and his E Street Band's live version of "Santa Claus Is Comin' to Town" was first released on a 1975 compilation album called *Christmas of Hope.* Ten years later, at the height of Bruce's *Born in the USA* popularity, it was released as the B-side to "My Hometown." Many bootlegs of this song exist as Bruce and the E Street Band often played it during December shows in the early part of his career. Springsteen's voice is raw as he plays with the audience about how many of them had been good throughout the year. The New Jersey native also teases the band, as he suggests Santa might bring a new saxophone to E Street member Clarence Clemons. Springsteen later contributed his version of "Merry Christmas Baby" to the first *A Very Special Christmas* album, which was created to raise funds for the Special Olympics

6. "FATHER CHRISTMAS" — THE KINKS

The often-overlooked Kinks released "Father Christmas" in 1976. Definitely not The Beatles, but not quite The Rolling Stones or The Who, The Kinks are as much a part of the British Invasion as their more famous contemporaries. Led by brothers Ray and Dave Davies, Kinks hits include "You Really Got Me," "Lola," and "All Day and All Night." Their success in the 1960s had not diminished by the 1980s, and they were still producing popular hits, having influenced many of the British punk bands formed throughout the 1970s. Never afraid to speak their minds, "Father Christmas" is a good example of Ray Davies's songwriting. Catchy and upbeat, "Father Christmas" scolds listeners that Christmas is only beneficial to the wealthy in society. The department store Santa is beat up by a band of thugs who are tired of all the toys going to "the little rich boys." Lyrically this sounds dreadful, but the tune rocks, and the message is clear.

7. "CHRISTMAS DAY"—SQUEEZE

The pop–new wave band Squeeze was a collaboration between songwriters Chris Difford and Glenn Tilbrook. They charted well in their native Britain but only a bit in the United States. Hits such as "Tempted," "Black Coffee in Bed," and "Pulling Mussels (From the Shell)" did receive some U.S. airplay by the late 1980s. "Christmas Day" was recorded in 1979 and displays much of the clever word-play and catchy melodies that gave Squeeze their success. A modern re-telling of the Christmas story, this time Mary and Joseph "tried the hotels, the motels, the bed-and-breakfast locals, but no one seemed to have any room." The chorus name-checks many favorite Christmas items, some of which are very British and go right past the American audience, such as "cracker surprise." Christmas crackers are a British tradition—a small ribbon-wrapped tube that "cracks" when the ribbons are pulled, revealing trinkets, jokes, and a paper crown. After mentioning the inevitable aftershave gift for all dads, Squeeze reminds us not to forget Jesus "who was born on Christmas Day."

8. "RIVER"—JONI MITCHELL

One of the most beautiful and heart-wrenching voices in rock music, Joni Mitchell recorded "River" on her aptly named classic 1971 album, *Blue*. The entire album is full of heartache, and "River" takes place during Christmas. A native Canadian, Joni knows a thing or two about cold weather and wishes to "skate away" on a river. While everyone is singing "songs of joy and peace," Joni made her baby say goodbye and now regrets it. Certainly not a traditional Christmas song in the sense of Santa and reindeer and merry-making. Joni has contributed to Christmas music in her own eclectic way. The piano bridge in the middle mimics a melancholy "Jingle Bells." In addition to her painting, Mitchell continues to write and perform new songs, although she may be best known for her classic songs "Both Sides Now," "Big Yellow Taxi," and the Crosby, Stills, Nash, and Young hit "Woodstock."

9. "2000 MILES"—THE PRETENDERS

One of the leading ladies of rock and roll in the 1980s, Chrissie Hynde fronted The Pretenders beginning in the late 1970s. Originally from Ohio, Hynde moved to England in the early 1970s, perpetuating an "Is she British or is she American?" vibe, to which the answer was "Who cares? She rocks." The Pretenders' successes in the 1980s include "Middle of the Road," "Brass in Pocket," and "Don't Get Me Wrong." Chrissie wrote "2000 Miles," which can be found at the end of the 1984 album *Learning to Crawl*. The song states that "He's gone 2000 miles in the snow/It's very far," but that "he'll be back at Christmastime." Both vague and specific, "2000 Miles" has a catchy, slow, methodical guitar line that is played throughout the length of the song, suggesting the length of the 2,000 miles.

10. "DO THEY KNOW IT'S CHRISTMAS?"—BAND-AID

Bob Geldof's band, The Boomtown Rats, may not be very well remembered, but his relief work for the victims of famine in Ethiopia and throughout Africa in the 1980s will not be forgotten for a long time. As rock and roll became more socially conscious regarding injustices in the world in the 1960s, Geldof put actions to his ideas by organizing a charity single in 1984 called "Do They Know It's Christmas?" The song featured many popular British singers and the memorable "Feed the world/let them know it's Christmastime" chorus. Among the British performers were Sting, U2, David Bowie, Boy George and Culture Club, Phil Collins, Paul McCartney, and Duran Duran. The song immediately charted number one in Britain and hit number one on the U.S. charts two weeks later. A four-minute single was released, but a six-minute extended single was also available. True to his word, Geldof delivered the profits to famine victims. "Do They Know It's Christmas?" co-writer and producer Midge Ure of Ultravox personally delivered the first proceeds to Africa himself. The song and its successful attempt to raise money inspired the Michael Jackson/Lionel Richie "We Are the World" project the following year, which also featured numerous singers.

Geldof organized two simultaneous "Live Aid" concerts in 1985, one in London, the other in Philadelphia. Among the many performers were INXS, Elvis Costello, Dire Straits, Neil Young, Tom Petty, Mick Jagger, Bob Dylan, and, performing at both shows in the same day, Phil Collins. Through his charitable efforts, Geldof raised millions of dollars for famine relief, and more continues to be raised because the Live Aid concerts have been released on DVD. Rock stars: Is there anything they can't do?

Send in the Clowns

Say what you want—and we've said it ourselves—about the annoying attention grabbers that never go away, but the novelty song reaches its pinnacle when it comes to Christmas music. Singing dogs and chipmunks, not to mention tons and tons of sound effects and just plain corny melodies and lyrics are just the thing needed when trimming the tree. The kids love them.

1. "JINGLE BELLS"—THE SINGING DOGS

The "be all and end all" of all Christmas novelty numbers is The Singing Dogs barking "Jingle Bells." The Singing Dogs first appeared in 1955 and have been a harbinger of everything tacky, senseless, and completely fun that Christmas is all about. The official title is "Don Charles presents The Singing Dogs, directed by Carl Weismann" and some debate exists as to whether the dogs barking are real or, shall we say, sampled. Although sampling was not around in the 1950s, taping and mixing dog barks to replicate the song would have taken hours. But this is America, and people will spend hours on the darndest ideas. Regardless of the source, The Singing Dogs have had many imitators throughout the years, including the Jingle Cats, singing frogs, potbellied pigs, and even a whole album of Christmas songs performed by bodily noises. A man named Woody Phillips once created an album called *A Toolbox Christmas* where every sound was produced by a workshop tool. Your wife will claim to hate all of this, except maybe the cats. But your nephews and uncles will love it.

2. "THE CHIPMUNK SONG"—THE CHIPMUNKS

No Christmas is complete without Simon, Theodore, and Alvin urging Christmas to "hurry Christmas— hurry fast," especially since the Chipmunks had been good all year but don't think they can keep it up for much longer. Put together by David Seville and Ross Bagdasarian and first released in 1958, the success of "The Chipmunk Song" created a whole Chipmunk industry for the trio of rodents and their creators. Bagdasarian had modest success writing songs that reached the charts in the 1950s, but when he started playing around with a tape recorder's speed on some vocals, he struck gold. First was a number-one hit called "Witch Doctor," but the real success came later the same year with "The Chipmunk Song," which spent four weeks at the top of the charts. The Chipmunks went on to star in their own television series in the 1960s and recorded a total of five full-length LPs, including one of Beatles cover songs. Wonder if Alvin ever got that hula hoop?

3. **"ALL I WANT FOR CHRISTMAS IS MY TWO FRONT TEETH"—SPIKE JONES AND HIS CITY SLICKERS**

Spike Jones and His City Slickers created some of the most zany and memorable music of the forties and fifties. Not only a novelty act, these musicians could play straight-ahead big band music but preferred song parodies played on instruments such as toilet seats with strings on them while bells, whistles, and gunshots were going off. This was top-drawer comedy in its day, and still elicits chuckles from kids of all ages. Spike Jones started off as a drummer, and it is alleged that he played the brushes on Bing Crosby's classic "White Christmas."

"All I Want for Christmas Is My Two Front Teeth" is the sad-sack story of a kid (voiced by Spike's twenty-eight-year-old son, George) who is having difficulty speaking because he's missing those two teeth right up front. The kid whines about his difficulties for a whole song, complete with the Spike Jones sound effects. "All I Want for Christmas" hit number one on the charts in 1948.

4. **"SNOOPY'S CHRISTMAS"—THE ROYAL GUARDSMEN**

The Royal Guardsmen made a brief career out of singing songs about Charlie Brown's dog, Snoopy, and his imaginary fights against German World War I flying ace, Baron Von Richthofen. The *Peanuts* comic strip was huge during the 1960s, the same time most of the Charlie Brown television specials were being created. The Royal Guardsmen had a million seller in 1966 with "Snoopy versus the Red Baron" and several subsequent follow-up singles with the same theme. "Snoopy's

Christmas" is not much different, except that the battle against the Red Baron takes place at Christmas, and the chorus emphasizes Christmas bells and peace throughout the land. Sound strange? Kids love it.

5. "I WANT A HIPPOPOTAMUS FOR CHRISTMAS"— GAYLA PEEVEY

Now here's a song that lives up to its glorious title. Written by John Fox and recorded in 1953 by young Gayla Peevey, the songs tells the tale of a young girl who wants a hippopotamus as her holiday gift from Santa. She has the whole thing planned out. Santa can bring the beast through the front door rather than trying to push him down the chimney. The girl will keep the hippo in the two-car garage, where she can wash him, feed him his vegetarian food, and give him his massage. A hippo probably doesn't need a massage, but it does rhyme with garage, and after all the song is pure fantasy anyway. There is some evidence that the song was used as a gimmick to raise enough money to bring a hippo to the Oklahoma City zoo in the 1950s. This would make a little more sense, but fifty years later, it's just a fun song.

6. "GRANDMA GOT RUN OVER BY A REINDEER"— ELMO AND PATSY

A novelty song released in 1979 that enjoyed heavy airplay during the 1980s, "Grandma Got Run Over by a Reindeer" has lost a lot of its punch because of repetition but was once a funny record. Old grandma had too much egg nog on Christmas Eve and had a hit-and-run encounter with St. Nick on her walk home. No one seems too upset about the whole ordeal. The only angst is what to do with Grandma's gifts? (Send them back!) Elmo and Patsy are actually only Elmo (Shropshire), and this song was his only recording of note. It appears on an album with the same name as the song. For the 45 rpm single, the B-side was "Percy, the Puny Poinsettia."

"Grandma Got Run Over by a Reindeer" was eventually made into an animated television special for those kids who want the backstory on how Grandma ended up under the sleigh.

7. "NUTTIN' FOR CHRISTMAS"—STAN FREBERG

The old parental ploy that Santa only gives gifts to kids who are well-behaved is given a workout in this famous novelty song. It was such a huge hit during the Christmas season of 1955 that five different versions of "Nuttin' For Christmas" reached the charts that year. In addition to Freberg's version, Art Mooney and Barry Gordon had a popular version, as well as the Fountaine Sisters, Ricky Zahnd and the Bluejeaners, and Joe Ward. Freberg's version is the best. It includes a conversation with a burglar at the end, removing all doubt that this kid "ain't been nothin' but bad." Juvenile pranks such as putting a tack on the teacher's chair or filling the sugar bowl with ants are among the boy's offenses, although the kid sees the real problem as "somebody snitched on me." Freberg was a well-known radio comic in the fifties and sixties, best known for his novelty records that satirized the popular *Dragnet* radio show. He had several other Christmas novelty hits in the 1950s, including "Christmas Dragnet" and "Green Chritma," a scathing piece that vilifies all the Christmas advertising moneymakers who rob the season of the simple joy and peace it is meant to represent.

8. "SANTA CLAUS AND HIS OLD LADY"—CHEECH AND CHONG

Richard "Cheech" Marin and Tommy Chong—Cheech and Chong—were a popular comedy team in the late sixties and early seventies. Almost all of their material was targeted toward hippies and marijuana, so it might be possible that they sold a lot of comedy records to the same kids over and over, partially because their parents would break them and partially because they couldn't remember if they had already bought one yet. Along with "Sister Mary Elephant," "Santa Claus and His Old Lady" was one of their most popular routines. The "story" of Santa and His Old Lady is re-told with references to the couple living in public housing and Santa's old lady making "the best brownies in town." Marijuana-loaded brownies are an interesting piece of seventies culture that may explain some things to the post-hippie generation, if nothing else. By the late 1970s, Cheech and Chong hit the silver screen with movies such as *Up In Smoke* and *Cheech and Chong's Next Movie*, but the act was over by the mid-1980s. Since then, Cheech Marin has had the more successful career, appearing in many movies, including *Tin Cup*, and co-starring with Don Johnson in television's *Nash Bridges*.

9. "I YUST GO NUTS AT CHRISTMAS"—YOGI YORGESSON

This hard-to-find single was a favorite in many households years ago. Yogi Yorgesson is the recording alias for Harry Stewart, who recorded songs with funny accents. With his Scandanavian accent, he was Yogi Yorgesson and recorded "I Yust Go Nuts at Christmas" with every "J" being slurred into a "Y." (The B-side was "Yingle Bells.") This 1949 hit features a poor guy with kids who "flip their lids, while their papa goes in hock." Shopping is a dilemma as he tries to find that perfect gift for his wife. The day before Christmas he looks at nightgowns, the black ones trimmed with red, but, not sure of her size, he buys her a "carpet sweeper." Christmas Day with the extended family proves that dysfunction was not invented in the 1990s. He hugs and kisses his mother-in-law, despite the fact that they don't speak throughout the year. The entire family deteriorates into a pretty good brawl. Yet, he still enjoys the holiday and is happy to sing about it. In later years, the entire song was truncated because radio executives found it to be outdated.

10. "CHRISTMAS WITH THE DEVIL"—SPINAL TAP

The complete opposite meaning of the spirit of Christmas comes from the fictitious heavy metal band, Spinal Tap. The 1984 "mockumentary," *This Is Spinal Tap,* introduced the world to a band that made fun of the excesses and absurdities of modern metal bands. The original movie soundtrack was so popular (actors Michael McKean, Christopher Guest, and Harry Shearer actually performed the music themselves) that subsequent albums, *Break Like the Wind* and *Back from the Dead*, were recorded. "Christmas with the Devil" was released in 1984 and puts evil and violence into the holiday of goodwill and cheer. It opens with "The elves are dressed in leather, and the angels are in chains," and goes downhill from there—exactly as a heavy metal band should do it. Turn it up to eleven.

The B-Side

Everyone knows the standard cartoon Christmas classics—the title songs, the ones that you associate immediately with the specials. "Rudolph the Red-Nosed Reindeer." "Frosty the Snowman." "Santa Claus is Comin' to Town." Those are great, but there's so much more. Below are some of the better "B-sides," the songs that don't get top billing but still amuse, entertain, and make us smile, in addition to the songs from some lesser-known shows.

1. "WHY AM I SUCH A MISFIT?"

By far the best holiday tune out there that's not a title song, this song was written by Johnny Marks for *Rudolph the Red-Nosed Reindeer*. Marks wrote the title song for *Rudolph* as well. "Why Am I Such a Misfit?" is sung by Billie Mae Richards (Rudolph) and Paul Soles (Hermey) and signifies the low point of the two characters in the show. Rudolph demands to know "Why am I such a misfit? I am not just a nit wit! Just because my nose glows. Why can't I fit in?" Hermey feels the same way and sings "Why am I such a mis-

Not a couple of misfits, Rudolph and Hermey the Misfit Elf.
©1964 Rankin/Bass Productions. Courtesy of the
RankinBass.com/Rick Goldschmidt Archives

fit? I am not just a nit wit! They can't fire me, I quit! Seems I don't fit in." The two go off to be "independent . . . together" and sing their back-and-forth lamentations of why they're not accepted in North Pole society.

2.   "WELCOME CHRISTMAS"

The other song from *How the Grinch Stole Christmas*, this classic doesn't have quite the exposure of the main song, "You're a Mean One, Mr. Grinch" (which, by the way, was sung not by narrator Boris Karloff but by Thurl Ravenscroft, later the voice of Frosted Flakes' spokes-animal, Tony the Tiger). Known to some simply as "The Who Song" because it uses the word

"Who" over and over, "Welcome Christmas" is the annual celebratory song that "all the Whos down in Whoville" sing. At the beginning of the story, it's the song that makes the Grinch snarl about having "to stop Christmas from coming, somehow." However, by the end, as he listens to the Whos in their holiday revelry, some say, the Grinch's heart "grew three sizes that day." If a simple song can do that, it must be a good one. It's co-written by Albert Hague and Theodor S. Geisel, the latter better known as Dr. Seuss. Note: for those adults looking for a fun new way to watch this special, try taking a drink every time the word "Who" is uttered. You'll be tipsy by the time this song ends.

3. "EVEN A MIRACLE NEEDS A HAND"

This song is from the 1974 animated television special, *'Twas the Night Before Christmas*, which involves a brainy young mouse who almost ruins Christmas by writing to Santa and indicating his lack of belief in the great man. When all seems dimmest for a happy ending, clockmaker Mr. Trundle breaks into this song, proclaiming "You hope; and I'll hurry. You pray; and I'll plan. We'll do what's necessary 'cause even a miracle needs a hand!" And if you can keep a lump out of your throat when the little mouse Albert chokes back a sob and sings the title line to himself, well then you're just not human.

If you haven't seen this special, yet the tune sounds familiar, you might be a *South Park* fan; the creators spoofed this song in one of their Mister Hankey episodes.

4. MISTER HANKEY, THE CHRISTMAS POO

Speaking of Mister Hankey . . . it may not be a classic cartoon song, but it's different and catchy all the same. It has its genesis in the first *South Park* Christmas episode, as Kyle tells his friends of his fiber-loving pal, Mr. Hankey, only to be committed to a mental hospital because at first Kyle is the only one who sees him. This is perhaps the only Christmas song to use the word "vicariously" in it, promising that "he loves me and I love you, therefore vicariously he loves you." Impressive indeed.

5.   "PUT ONE FOOT IN FRONT OF THE OTHER"

From yet another classic Rankin-Bass cartoon from 1970, *Santa Claus Is Comin' to Town*, "Put One Foot in Front of the Other" highlights the about-face of the Winter Warlock, changing from bad to good which, as Mickey Rooney's Kris Kringle says, is "as easy as taking your first step!" Sung by Rooney and Keenan Wynn as the Winter Warlock, the tune is an ode to teaching old dogs new tricks, and Warlock certainly complies. Soon enough, as Kringle points out, Warlock was taking that first step and "walking out the door."

6.   "HEAT MISER"

We put "Heat Miser" first of the two related songs mostly because it's our favorite of the duo, but it's certainly interchangeable with number seven in the list. "Heat Miser" is written by Jules Bass (yes, of Rankin-Bass) and Maury Laws, and sung by George S. Irving as part of his job doing the voice of the Heat Miser in *The Year Without a Santa Claus*. He's "Mister Green Christmas," "Mister Sun," "Mister heat blister," and "Mister hundred-and-one," and he sings of his love for all things hot and steamy (temperature wise only). It's Broadway in style, complete with backup mini-me singers and a dance routine that'll leave you smiling.

7. **"SNOW MISER"**

In comparison to his brother, the Snow Miser sings that he's "Mister White Christmas," "Mister snow," "Mister icicle," and of course "Mister ten below." Also co-written by Jules Bass and Maury Laws, in the song as well as the show Dick Shawn gives voice to the guy for whom, everything he touches "turns to snow in my clutch!" They both are, as they and their respective mini-selves singing with them proclaim, "too much."

8. **"WE'RE NOT SO BAD"**

From the 1999 classic *Olive, the Other Reindeer* comes the manic and fast-paced "We're Not So Bad." The song is performed at a point in the story where Olive needs a little help in getting to Santa at the North Pole. After suffering a vicious taunting over her goal, Olive makes an impassioned speech and Schnitzel the Reindeer (Blitzen's flightless cousin) has a change of heart and offers the assistance of himself and his friend. He then launches into the rousing "We're Not So Bad," another reminder that somewhere deep down, everyone has a little good in them—and Christmas is the time to bring it out. Schnitzel is voiced by Michael Stipe of the music group REM, and the song is definitely worth REMembering.

9. **"FIRST TOYMAKER TO THE KING"/"NO MORE TOY-MAKERS TO THE KING"**

Also from *Santa Claus Is Comin' to Town*, this pair of songs is in the classic fifties style of song-and-response, with the second song being a rebuttal or response to the first. "First Toymaker to the King" is sung by Tanta Kringle (Joan Gardner, giving voice to Kris's adopted mother) about the responsibilities involved in being the toymaker for the king. The response is from the lovably evil Burgermeister Meisterburger (and really, is there a better villain name then that?) after an "incident" with a toy. He proclaims all toys "illegal, immoral, unlawful" and orders "every jack-in-the-box be sealed" as well as "stuffed animals—unstuff them," and he instructs that, sadly, there will be no more toymakers to the king. Or, at least until Santa Claus has a say!

10. "SILVER AND GOLD"

Another classic from *Rudolph the Red-Nosed Reindeer*, "Silver and Gold" was written by Johnny Marks and sung by Burl Ives in his role as the narrator, Sam the Snowman. The song ostensibly is in connection with Yukon Cornelius and his searches for treasure but has no real connection to the storyline of the show at all. It's still a very pretty song, however, with an important message: that silver and gold only have as much meaning as the happiness they can bring us, and that it "means so much more when I see, silver and gold decorations" on the Christmas tree.

Twelve Ways of Christmas

One of the most bizarre and mysterious of all Christmas carols is the well-loved "Twelve Days of Christmas." The old partridge in a pear tree has seen a lot of action and been the punch line to many Christmas jokes. It remains unclear whether this is just a nonsense song or put together to teach catechism (five gold rings as the biblical Pentateuch, four calling birds as the four gospels, the partridge in a pear tree representing Christ, etc.). On the high church calendar, the season leading up to Christmas is Advent. The twelve days of Christmas begin on Christmas Day and run through January 5. January 6 is called The Epiphany, the alleged day that the wise men showed up. One thing that is very clear is that people have had a lot of fun coming up with new ways to sing this Christmas carol.

1. MITCH MILLER AND THE GANG

Mitch Miller was a huge deal in the pop music world in the 1950s and 1960s. Not only was he in charge of

A&R (artists and repertory) at Columbia Records, he also conducted his "gang," a popular choral group that featured sing-alongs to familiar songs that you may have sung around the campfire. In 1961, *Holiday Sing-Along with Mitch* was released, and it included a traditional take on "The Twelve Days of Christmas" which is still played often during the holiday season. If you grew up in the 1960s, there is no doubt that your groovy parents played this record incessantly on their hi-fi.

2. THE MUPPETS AND JOHN DENVER

Since our lives are not complete without the Muppets, Christmas cannot be complete without Jim Henson's fuzzy puppets, including Kermit and Miss Piggy. For Christmas, the Muppets created *A Muppet Christmas Carol* with Michael Caine and several television specials for the season. In 1979, they teamed up with country-folk star John Denver for a Christmas sing-along. The television special resulted in the album *A Christmas Together*. The Muppets do not add any new items to the list of things "my true love sent to me," but they add to the legacy of this Christmas classic. Miss Piggy, of course, gets the five gold rings verse. Denver teamed up with the Muppets on several occasions, and his trademark moppish yellow hair almost made him seem like a Muppet himself. He rose to fame in the late sixties after penning the hit "Leaving On A Jet Plane," made popular by Peter, Paul, and Mary. Denver then went on to become one the biggest stars in music during the seventies for such hits as "Take Me Home, Country Roads," "Sunshine On My Shoulders," and "Annie's Song." He also starred in the 1977 film *Oh, God!* with George Burns.

3. ALLAN SHERMAN

Allan Sherman was a writer and comedian who wrote for television's *Steve Allen Show* and also produced the popular television quiz show *I've Got A Secret* which was on the air from 1952 to 1967. Sherman turned his attention to song parodies in the 1960s, and is best known for his novelty hit about Camp Grenada, "Hello Muddah, Hello Fadduh." Sherman's parody of "The Twelve Days" is called "The Twelve Gifts of Christmas" and pokes fun at all the pointless gifts exchanged during the holidays. Included in Sherman's list of gifts are a statue of a lady with a clock where her stomach ought to be and a Japanese transistor radio. At the end of the song, Sherman exchanges the gifts, another grand Christmas tradition. So far, however, there are no known songs about re-gifting.

4. FRANK SINATRA AND FAMILY

The Chairman of the Board, no doubt one of the shining lights of twentieth century music, decided to make the twelve days personal by having his kids, Nancy, Tina, and Frank, Jr., record this with him in 1968. The Sinatra "kids" were in their twenties when they recorded this with "Old Blue Eyes." Nancy was already well-known in her own right at this time, having hit the top of the pop charts with "These Boots Are Made for Walking" in 1966. She would later record "Something Stupid" as a duet with her father. Frank, Jr. is a crooner in the style of his father and also conducted his father's orchestra. During the Sinatra family's twelve days, the children bestow gifts upon Frank. Included in the pile are: ten silken hankies, nine games of Scrabble, five ivory combs, and a most lovely lavender tie.

5. JEFF FOXWORTHY

You just might be a redneck if your true love sends you the items on Jeff Foxworthy's "Redneck Twelve Days of Christmas" list. Foxworthy became one of the most popular stand-up comics during the 1990s with his brand of southern redneck humor (or what he called the "gloriously unsophisticated"). An employee for IBM, Foxworthy first tried stand-up comedy on a dare and has since become a Southern icon. In 2003, Foxworthy recorded his "Redneck Twelve Days of Christmas," with the gifts including wrasslin' tickets, shotgun shells, Redman chewing tobacco, big mud tires, and some parts to a Mustang GT. All of the redneck stereotypes are used by Foxworthy, usually to the delight of his redneck audience.

6. MCKENZIE BROTHERS

Merry Christmas and good day, eh? Bob and Doug McKenzie (comedians Dave Thomas and Rick Moranis), hosts of SCTV's skit *The Great White North*, let us know how Canadian hosers sing "The Twelve Days of Christmas" in 1982. Brilliantly imitating all the false stereotypes Americans have of their friendly neighbors to the north, the McKenzie Brothers have a difficult time figuring out just what the twelve days are while they come up with a list of suggestions that would make great Christmas gifts. Their ideas include the ever popular back bacon, turtle necks, French Toast, comic books, cigarettes, and, of course, beer. Beauty, eh?

7. GARRISON KEILLOR

Tune in to public radio just about any Saturday evening and you can hear Garrison Keillor tell stories about his radio hometown of Lake Wobegon,

Minnesota. The two-hour radio program *A Prairie Home Companion* features skits, music, and lots of jokes. The regular sound-effects man on the show has been Tom Keith, and Keillor has had a lot of fun writing scripts that allow Keith to showcase his talent. One tradition that continues almost every year is the singing of "The Twelve Days of Christmas" with Keith providing the sound effects for the lords a-leaping, swans a-swimming, and pipers piping in place of the words. This yearly radio fun can be found on an album called *Now It Is Christmas Again*, recorded by Keillor and his radio friends in 1994.

8. VEGGIE TALES

Veggie Tales has been a hit with the kids since 1993. Brilliantly produced computer-animated videos featuring Bob the Tomato and Larry the Cucumber tell Bible stories with such creativity and humor that their popularity reaches beyond the Sunday school room. The album *A Very Veggie Christmas* was released in 1996 to coincide with the release of the video *The Toy That Saved Christmas*. The theme of the album is a Christmas sing-along party at the house of Bob the Tomato. It's a good party with only one problem: the caterer does not show up on time. The caterer finally arrives with plates of Polish food for the veggies to consume. (Try not to think too hard about that.) The result is the song "The Eight Polish Foods of Christmas" which follows the "Twelve Days" melody while the veggies devour all the pierogies, gwumpkies, hooscheekies, and smoked kielbasas they can handle.

9. HAWAIIAN VERSION

You don't have to have a white Christmas in order to celebrate the season properly. Christmas is enjoyed in

Hawaii, too, which happens to be in a time zone that maximizes the amount of time Father Christmas can spend stuffing your stocking with macadamia nuts. One Hawaiian tradition is the song "Numbah One Day of Christmas" written by Eaton Magoon Jr., Edward Kenny, and Gordon Phelps in 1959. It became an instant classic in Hawaii as the traditional twelve items are replaced by distinctively Hawaiian products, including poi, ukulele, hula lessons, and one mynah bird in one papaya tree. This song is also distinct in that it is written in pidgin English, giving a native island flavor to lines such as "five beeg fat peeg."

10. DESTINY'S CHILD

The variations on "The Twelve Days of Christmas" continue into the twenty-first century. Destiny's Child, one of the most popular groups in R&B today, released an album in 2001 titled *8 Days of Christmas*. While they reduced the number of days by four and added a heavy hip-hop flavor to the whole thing, the title track contains the same feel as the traditional carol, with an altered list of gifts "my baby gave to me." Beyoncé Knowles and company are looking for such items as "a pair of Chloe shades and a diamond belly ring."

Destiny's Child original members Beyoncé Knowles and LaTavia Roberson met when they were nine years old. They received their first major recording contract in 1997 and have been at the top of the R&B charts ever since. They have also contributed to several movie soundtracks, including *Men in Black* and *Charlie's Angels*. The leader of the group, Beyoncé, appeared in the Austin Powers film *Goldmember* as Foxxy Cleopatra.

As Seen on TV and Heard on Your Hi-Fi

An all-too-easy cash-in on the popularity of a television series or star is to try to branch out into the music industry. Christmas music is no exception. Sometimes the results flow naturally and create music that is enjoyed through the years. Other times, well, except for the hard-core fans, the product can be pretty brutal. Here are the some of the stars of the small screen who have increased our holiday cheer, one way or another, through their own albums.

1. **PARTRIDGE FAMILY—a PARTRIDGE FAMILY CHRISTMAS CARD**

This popular television series ran for a few years in the early 1970s and starred Teen Idol David Cassidy as Keith Partridge, his real-life stepmother Shirley Jones as Shirley Partridge, and Susan Dey (an *L.A. Law* lawyer in the 1980s) as well as red-headed troublemaker Danny Bonaduce. The Partridge Family drove around in their multi-colored school bus and performed a song on every episode, although the only actual musicians were Cassidy and Jones. Albums came out under the Partridge Family name and even yielded a number-one hit by Cassidy, "I Think I Love You." In all, ten Partridge Family albums were made, including *A Partridge Family Christmas Card*. Going through the usual standards, Cassidy takes the lead vocals on almost all of them, although Shirley takes the lead on "The Christmas Song." If you were a teenaged girl in the 1970s, this album probably holds a lot of memories for you. If you were the brother of a teenaged girl in the 1970s, it will bring back scarring memories of your sisters performing the whole album, dancing around while singing into their hairbrush microphones. Somehow they got to be Keith and Laurie Partridge while you were only allowed to be the youngest Partridge, Tracy.

2. KATHIE LEE GIFFORD—*IT'S CHRISTMAS TIME*

Kathie Lee's popularity stems from her fifteen years of television sitting next to Regis Philbin, cohosting *Live With Regis and Kathy Lee*. Her perky personality and nonstop chatter about her football legend husband, Frank Gifford, and two children, Cody and Cassidy, endeared her to many fans and made her the object of ridicule for everyone else. She starred in an eponymous Christmas special for a few years during the 1990s and made several albums, including more than one Christmas album. There's just something about Kathie Lee that screams Christmas. Her first Christmas album, *It's Christmas Time*, was released in 1993. It's everything one might expect from Kathie Lee—a great gift for your mother, and a great gag-gift for your brother-in-law. It's bound to show up in your office white elephant gift exchange sooner or later.

3. ALLY MCBEAL—*A VERY ALLY CHRISTMAS*

The popular *Ally McBeal* show ran from 1997 to 2002. With a background of a busy law firm, the show mostly centered around the neurotic McBeal (think Mary

Richards of *The Mary Tyler Moore Show* for the 1990s). *Ally McBeal* always had a lot of music. In fact, the main musical contributor to the show was a singer named Vonda Shepard, who became a mainstream musical star merely from her almost weekly performances on the show. *A Very Ally Christmas* was released in 2000 and mostly featured Shepard, although Ally (Calista Flockhart) took a stab at "Santa Baby," and Robert Downey, Jr. sang Joni Mitchell's "River." There was also a contribution of "Winter Wonderland" by Macy Gray.

4. CLAY AIKEN—*MERRY CHRISTMAS WITH LOVE*

The *American Idol* television phenomenon has created the careers of several singers who have now become household names. Winners and losers alike have been thrust upon the American television viewing audience, and viewers are loyal to their favorites, win or lose. While losers William Hung and George Huff have released their own Christmas albums and the show released a holiday CD that included entries from Ruben, Kelly, and Justin, the choice for this list is Clay Aiken's *Merry Christmas with Love*. Clay looks like he should be singing in a church choir and offers several holiday standards. *Merry Christmas with Love* was released in 2004 and sold more than 270,000 copies in its first week.

5. ROSIE O'DONNELL—*A ROSIE CHRISTMAS*

Before she became a television talk show host in 1995, Rosie O'Donnell was in the cast of television comedy *Gimme a Break* and had many appearances on the music channel VH1. She also had featured film roles in *A League of Their Own* and *Sleepless in Seattle*. The talk show was a natural fit for a comedienne and actress who loved to talk and loved celebrities. It was an immediate hit. Rosie was able to use her fame and celebrity to release her own Christmas album in 1999—*A Rosie Christmas*—where Rosie sang her favorite holiday songs

with some of her favorite singers. Better than those
celebrities who think they can carry the project all by
themselves, Rosie enlisted career singers such as Celine
Dion, Elton John, Cher, Donny Osmond, and even *White
Christmas* star Rosemary Clooney to sing with her.
"Gonna Eat for Christmas" with Gloria Estefan is a highlight. The best news of the whole endeavor is that it
helped raise money for Rosie's For All Kids Foundation.
Another Rosie Christmas followed in 2000.

6. BONANZA—*CHRISTMAS ON PONDEROSA*

Bonanza ran from 1959 through 1973, most of that
time as an American Sunday night institution. Along
with *Gunsmoke*, it was the premiere television Western
and was also the first colorized series on television. It
starred Lorne Greene as ranch owner Ben Cartwright,
and Michael Landon, Dan Blocker, and Pernell Roberts
as the Cartwright sons. Victor Sen Yung played their
Chinese cook, Hop Sing. The family ranch was The
Ponderosa, located outside Virginia City, Nevada.
Greene recorded several albums under the moniker
Ben Cartwright while the show was at the height of its
popularity. As you might guess, *Christmas on
Ponderosa* has a heavily spaghetti western sound, with
a sixties sing-along. It featured all of the main actors
and lots of extra singers. Several Christmas standards,
such as "Deck the Halls" and "Jingle Bells" are includ-
ed, as well as a few Bonanza extras, such as "Santa
Got Lost in Texas" and "Stuck in the Chimney."

7. THE BRADY BUNCH—*CHRISTMAS WITH THE BRADY BUNCH*

One of the most loved and idealized families in television history, the Brady Bunch was "the story of a lovely lady who was bringing up three very lovely girls,"
and, well, unless you've lived in a cave all your life, you

know the whole song of how they all became the Brady Bunch. The show ran from 1969 through 1974, and it remains a favorite of television fans everywhere thanks to reruns and several feature-length films. The Brady kids (Greg, Marsha, Peter, Jan, Bobby, and Cindy) became very popular through the series and had some success recording a few albums on the heels of touring the country as a singing group. The most popular Brady Bunch song was *It's a Sunshine Day*. While that attempt was groovy, *Christmas with the Brady Bunch* offers nothing spectacular except the kids singing standard arrangements to all those Christmas songs we have all heard before. Not even Alice the housekeeper or Sam the butcher could help this out.

8. THE REN AND STIMPY SHOW—*CROCK O' CHRISTMAS*

Not all television stars are humans. Cartoon characters have become beloved for their sincerity—or lack thereof—and humor. And if you are looking for something gross for your Christmas ears, Nickelodeon's *Ren and Stimpy* have just the album for you: *Crock o' Christmas*. Actually, the humor on *Ren and Stimpy* became so lowbrow that Nickelodeon decided to keep some episodes off the air. Too subversive. Not enough "Happy Happy Joy Joy." A regular television odd-couple, Ren is a maniacal Chihuahua, and Stimpy the cat is the kind, but slow, sidekick. The show was satirical and had a lot of sick humor. *Crock o' Christmas* has the same spirit as the show. Several original songs are found here, as well as a few familiar Christmas songs with rewritten words about hairballs and yak shaving.

9. NICK AT NITE—*A CLASSIC CARTOON CHRISTMAS*

If *Ren and Stimpy* is not your idea of cartoon fun, Nickelodeon released *A Classic Cartoon Christmas* in 1996, obtaining the rights to many favorite holiday cartoon Christmas songs. Several selections from the *Charlie Brown Christmas Album*, the *Grinch Who Stole Christmas*'s "You're a Mean One, Mr. Grinch," and several selections from the *Rudolph the Red-Nosed Reindeer* television special appear here. This is just the ticket if you are the type of person who sings "We're a Couple of Misfits" and "Put One Foot in Front of the Other" instead of "Joy to the World" and "Good King Wenceslas" each December. A few of the Muppets songs are also represented here, and a sequel from 1997, *Classic Cartoon Christmas, Too*, provides even more cartoon carols.

10. MARTHA STEWART—*HOME FOR THE HOLIDAYS*

Thank goodness Martha does not sing on this! As with all things associated with the domestic goddess, Martha (or someone who works for her) shows exquisite taste in her music selections. *Martha Stewart Living: Home for the Holidays* is a collection of some very good Christmas music that can be played at any holiday gathering, whether you have hand-decorated your entire house or just picked up some chicken wings from a drive-through. Stewart came to prominence in the early 1990s with frequent appearance on the *Today Show*. By the mid-1990s, she had established a home decorating empire that included her own magazine and several television shows on decorating, cooking, and gardening. An easy object of ridicule because of her intense nature, Stewart ran into a few legal troubles but returned to polite society after jail time more powerful than ever. *Home for the Holidays* includes classic Christmas numbers by Emmylou Harris, Eartha Kitt, and Ray Charles, as well as Judy Garland's "Have Yourself a Merry Little Christmas."

'Tis the Season to Be Jolly

Face it, most Christmas music is about love (obtained or lost), gifts, God, or the weather, with a little bit of world peace thrown in. Christmas is supposed to be fun. There are plenty of novelty songs, which are discussed in a different section. In addition to the novelty delights are some just plain-old fun Christmas songs. Here are a few of them.

1. "MELE KALIKIMAKA"—BING CROSBY AND THE ANDREWS SISTERS

"Here we know that Christmas will be green and bright." When Bing Crosby was not dreaming of a "White Christmas," he must have been dreaming about Christmas in the Hawaiian Islands. "Mele Kalikimaka" is the traditional Hawaiian Christmas greeting and was put into song by Hawaiian native R. Alex Anderson in 1949. Crosby recorded "Mele Kalikimaka" in 1950 with the help of his frequent recording partners, The Andrews Sisters (LaVerne, Maxene, and Patty). The Andrews Sisters charted more than 100 hits between the late 1930s and early

1950s, and are best known for their World War II hit "Boogie Woogie Bugle Boy." "Mele Kalikimaka" is a fun twist to the usual assortment of Christmas music and has been recorded by others, including Jimmy Buffett and Poi Dog Pondering. For the kids, it sounds like spending Christmas in Bikini Bottom with SpongeBob SquarePants.

2. "ST. STEPHEN'S DAY MURDERS"—ELVIS COSTELLO AND THE CHIEFTAINS

We're sure Elvis Costello and the Chieftains do not approve of the practice of poisoning your family during the Christmas season. There are times with some families where the temptation must be great though, and "St. Stephen's Day Murders" tells the story of one such family. St. Stephen's Day is celebrated the day after Christmas in Ireland. Costello wrote "St. Stephen's Day Murders" with the Chieftains' Paddy Moloney and recorded it on the Chieftains' *Bells of Dublin* holiday collection. This is a fun Irish lilt about two sisters named Dawn and Eve Christmas who tire of their extended family's excessive alcohol consumption. While feasting, the drunks are poisoned and the sisters "finally get rid of them." Although this all sounds horrid, the song is a lot of fun. Our own family members are nothing but joy when we gather with them each year, of course, so they have nothing to fear about that special sweet potato pie that's been prepared just for them.

3. "CAROLINA CHRISTMAS"—SQUIRREL NUT ZIPPERS

For a brief period in the 1990s, big band music and swing dancing was all the rage with the kids, and there to provide them with all their musical needs were

North Carolina's Squirrel Nut Zippers. Yes, they named themselves after a candy bar. Formed by Jim Mathus and Katharine Whalen in 1993, the seven-member Squirrel Nut Zippers scored a big hit in 1997 with "Hell." Their 1998 Christmas album *Christmas Caravan* includes the infectious "Carolina Christmas," a swinging tune that will get you up and jitterbugging around the Christmas tree. The song boasts that Christmas in Carolina is "the best around," and it's hard to disagree. It must be great when "Grandma's got the fiddle, and Grandpa's got the bass," but the fact that you can "chill in your underwear" turns it into our kind of party.

4. "JINGLE BELLS"—BARBRA STREISAND

In the most manic version of "Jingle Bells" that you'll ever hear, Barbra opened her 1967 Christmas album with her take on the standard classic. The Funny Girl changes tempo radically several times throughout the song and goes crazy with the jingles. It's a whole lot of fun. Another fun thing about Barbra is that she has given us not one, but two, Christmas recordings. Several other famous Jewish singers are represented with wonderful recordings on these lists, but Streisand was not afraid to go double-dipping for her many fans. And she doesn't stay with the secular Christmas tunes, either. She wasn't afraid to sing "O Little Town of Bethlehem" or "Ave Maria." Additionally, Barbra may have been the first to place *The Sound of Music's* "My Favorite Things" on a holiday album. Since doing this, others have followed. When you have the talent and respect that Barbra commands, you can probably turn any song into a holiday standard.

5. **"MERRY CHRISTMAS FROM THE FAMILY"—**
    ROBERT EARL KEEN

Talk about your dysfunctional family Christmas. Texas singer-songwriter Robert Earl Keen's "Merry Christmas from the Family" is not your standard holiday sing-along for the kids. There is a lot of drinking in this song, references to multiple divorces, cigarettes, and, in some versions, feminine hygiene products. Depending on your point of view, this song is either very sad or very realistic. Keen attended Texas A&M with Lyle Lovett, and they wrote a few songs together, but Keen has never seen the same success that the quirky and gifted Lovett has. Nonetheless, he is a well-respected songwriter with a strong following. "Merry Christmas from the Family" has been covered by country music acts Montgomery Gentry and the Dixie Chicks.

6. **"CHRISTMAS AT K-MART"—ROOT BOY SLIM**

Washington, D.C., cult rock figure of the 1970s and 1980s, Root Boy Slim (Foster MacKenzie III) created one of the all-time great Christmas songs with "Christmas at K-Mart" in 1978. With the backing vocals of the Rootettes, Root Boy sings about the joys of shopping at the crowded discount store during the holiday season. Root Boy suggests purchasing 1970s-novelty-item mood rings but highly recommends "this album by Root Boy Slim." Root Boy is thrilled at the opportunity to shop at K-Mart, as he regards it as a big step up from Christmas shopping at the 7-Eleven. The entire song is a delightful look at the 1970s counterculture, one in which Root Boy freely indulged while producing college radio hits "Boogie 'Til You Puke" and "Mood Ring."

7. "MERRY CHRISTMAS (I DON'T WANT TO FIGHT TONIGHT)"—RAMONES

There's no better way to spend your Christmas than with Joey, Dee Dee, Tommy, and Johnny Ramone. The highly influential, unrelated punkers formed the group in 1974 and soon became a regularly featured band at New York's famed nightclub CBGBs. They went on to record such memorable songs as "Blitzkrieg Bop," "Sheena is a Punk Rocker," and "I Want to be Sedated." By the time they recorded "Merry Christmas (I Don't Want to Fight Tonight)," from 1989's *Brain Drain*, the lineup had changed a bit, but amazingly, everyone in the band still had the last name Ramone! "Merry Christmas" reminds us that Christmas "ain't the time for breaking each other's hearts." Hey! Ho! Let's Go!

8. "RUDOLPH THE RED-NOSED REINDEER"—JEWEL

Singer-songwriter Jewel burst onto the musical scene in 1995 with her best selling *Pieces of You* album, which contained the hit "Who Will Save Your Soul?" *Pieces of You* remained on the charts for two years, and Jewel became so popular that she sang the national anthem at Super Bowl XXXII in her hometown of San Diego. Her other hometown was Homer, Alaska. Not content with mere music stardom, Jewel Kilcher wrote a few books of poetry that sold quite well, too. In 1999, Jewel released *Joy: A Holiday Collection*, which included a playful version of "Rudolph the Red-Nosed Reindeer."

9. "HO HO HO AND A BOTTLE OF RHUM"—JIMMY BUFFETT

There's no better person to spend Christmas in the islands with than the birthday boy himself. Jimmy

Buffett was born on Christmas Day, and his 1996 album *Christmas Island* features his trademark sound. "Ho Ho Ho and a Bottle of Rhum" tells a story about Santa that will delight everyone who wants to spend Christmas in the islands. It seems Santa is tired of his work, tired of the snow, tired of the bad decorations, and tired that "chimney scars cover his buns." He runs off to the Caribbean and enjoys the local lifestyle. Not to worry, after a week in the tropics, Santa is refreshed and ready to resume his yearly run.

10. "O HOLY NIGHT"—BARENAKED LADIES

Ironic goofball popsters Barenaked Ladies (relax! The group is all male and they keep their clothes on) were popular in their native Canada throughout the 1990s, but they didn't become stars in the United States until their 1998 number-one hit "One Week." Success has not spoiled the adolescent fun these guys have had since their inception. In 2004, they released the CD *Barenaked for the Holidays* that includes several original holiday songs and a swinging version of "God Rest Ye Merry Gentlemen" with Lilith Fair organizer and fellow Canadian Sarah McLachlan. Also included are a few Hanukkah songs such as "I Have a Little Dreidel." The sacred hymn, "O Holy Night," is given an instrumental roller-skating-rink-organ treatment that is unique and memorable. This song is usually performed by pop "divas" who try to out-squeal each other when they hit the high notes. Instead of turning it into a piece to show off their singing talents, the Barenaked Ladies let the melody take center stage.

Mass Appeal?

As Christmas is the season of joy and love, we hate to take issue with anyone's music. We all have different tastes. One elf's fruitcake is another elf's yule log. However, there are some songs that are truly bad. For some reason, maybe because they were recorded by well-loved artists, they are played over and over, annoying many Christmas music lovers looking for a bit of originality and variety in their holiday music. We realize we are stepping on some sacred ground here, but hear us out. You can do a whole lot better than these songs. Just because you love the singer and the radio plays it doesn't mean it's good.

1. "LAST CHRISTMAS"—WHAM!

Like a bad fruitcake, this song pops up every Christmas. It is, hands down, the most annoying and ridiculous piece of Christmas pop-schlock ever produced. This song is terrible on so many levels. It's hard to say which is worse—the sappy lyrics or the fact that once you hear it over the department store speakers you absolutely cannot get the melody out of your head. The song has nothing to do with Christmas, except for the fact that the extremely needy and inse-cure singer had his heart broken at the prior year's Christmas. Somehow, his lover was able to "give away" his heart the day after Christmas. How is this even possible? He seems to be taking great delight in giving his heart to an unnamed "someone special" this year in what seems to be more of an act of lover's revenge than a true affection for someone new. Ugh.

In the same way that oldies stations play the Rolling Stones' "Ruby Tuesday" on Tuesdays, pop DJs see the word "Christmas" in the song title and some-how feel compelled to pull "Last Christmas" out each year and play it while the good Christmas music is sit-ting in dust on the shelf. Wham! (Yes! The exclamation point is part of the band's name! Exciting!) is the 1980s British pop duo of George Michael and Andrew Ridgeley. Before Michael went on to a huge solo career, Wham! had a number one hit with "Wake Me Up Before You Go Go." The silver lining to "Last Christmas" is that it is reported that George Michael gave all profits to Bob Geldof's Band-Aid project for famine relief in Africa.

2.   "WONDERFUL CHRISTMAS TIME"—PAUL MCCARTNEY

Picking on a Beatle is a terribly cruel thing to do. We love Paul McCartney, not only for his Beatles contribu-tion, but even for Wings, his post-Beatle band. However, his 1979 Christmas song "Wonderful Christmas Time" is more than we can handle. And it is played nonstop each Christmas season. When you really get down to listening to the lyrics, McCartney's only real full sentence may be "The choir of children sing their song." The rest is just a bunch of sentence fragments to be sung before reaching the ever-repeti-tive "simply having a wonderful Christmas time."

3. "FELIZ NAVIDAD"—JOSE FELICIANO

This may have been a good song at one point, but now it is really hard to tell, because like many other Christmas songs, "Feliz Navidad" has been so over-played that it earned a spot on this list. And, it has very few lyrics except the over-repeated "Feliz Navidad" with "I want to wish you a merry Christmas from the bottom of my heart." "Próspero Año y Felicidad" is not translated in the song, but means best wishes for a prosperous new year. Feliciano is a talented guitarist with a prosperous forty-year music career that has seen him singing the National Anthem at a World Series game in 1968 and singing the theme song to 1970s sit-com *Chico and the Man*. The Puerto Rico native, who has been blind since birth, was raised in New York City. In 1995, New York City Public School 155 was renamed Jose Feliciano Performing Arts School. Recently, the popular West Texas band, Los Lonely Boys, recorded "Feliz Navidad." Apparently, it's not going away for a long while.

4. "AYAYAY IT'S CHRISTMAS"—RICKY MARTIN

With the wealth of wonderful Latino music around, it seems a shame that a song like "AyAyAy It's Christmas" is one of the few Latino entries heard on the local radio station that goes to the twenty-four-hour-a-day Christmas music format each December. Former Menudo singer Ricky Martin, who was born on Christmas Eve, had the country dancing all over the place in 1999 with his smash hit "Livin' la Vida Loca." The handsome singer (Ricky has appeared in the soap opera *General Hospital* as bartender Miguel Morez) has had hit records sung in English and Spanish. But we have to draw the line with his Christmas attempt of "AyAyAy It's Christmas." Somehow Ricky has forgotten that it was Christmas and did not buy a present for his hard-to-please baby. "AyAyAy it's Christmas and I don't have a gift for you." So what does he give her? "AyAyAy" of course. "AyAyAy it's Christmas, and I don't know what to do. AyAyAy it's Christmas, and I don't have a gift for you. I can give you ayayay, all you need is ayayay, un poquito ayayay on this Christmas night, yeah." Yikes.

Ricky Martin surely uttered "Ay ay ay" when viewing the devestation caused by the December 26, 2004, tsunami in Indonesia. While many celebrities and musicians gave monetarily to relief efforts, the generous Martin personally visited orphans in Thailand, bringing much-needed attention to their needs exacerbated by the disaster.

5. "WHITE CHRISTMAS"—MICHAEL BOLTON

Making fun of Michael Bolton is like shooting fish in a barrel and became one of the more popular hobbies of music lovers everywhere when this overly emotive singer reached his zenith in the late 1980s. The (formerly) long-haired soft rock balladeer, who had such hits as "How am I Supposed to Live Without You?" and "Love is a Wonderful Thing," recorded Christmas albums in 1996 and in 2002. The latter included "Georgia on My Mind," a Christmas classic if ever there was one, yes? What the heck is this guy thinking? "White Christmas" can be found on his 1996 entry *This is The Time: The Christmas Album*. It takes effort to make this Irving Berlin classic into a loser, but Bolton's drawn-out emotional treatment of the tune could make a sane person revolt. Bolton has sold more than 50 million records over his career, which is really amazing because it is hard to find anyone who will admit to owning one. Because it is Christmas, the time for goodwill to all, we will mention that Bolton formed the Michael Bolton Foundation in 1993. His charitable group helps children and women living in poverty or in abusive conditions.

6. "WHERE ARE YOU CHRISTMAS?"—FAITH HILL

We have nothing against Faith Hill. Really. The pop country star has an incredible voice and made-for-music-video good looks to go along with her string of pop and country hits such as "This Kiss" and "The Way You Love Me." Additionally, she is married to country superstar Tim McGraw. There is hardly a misstep in this beauty's career. But in 2000 she had a Christmas hit from the Jim Carrey version of *How The Grinch Stole Christmas* with "Where Are You Christmas?" The true crime of this song is that it is dull, dull, dull. While it fit the movie just fine, the popularity of Faith has forced this song onto our airways repeatedly during the Christmas season. It makes you want to shout "just find Christmas already, Faith!" which, thankfully, she does by the end of the song. "Where Are You Christmas?" was written by Mariah Carey, James Horner, and Will Jennings. Evidently Mariah was slated to sing this for the movie soundtrack, but somehow Faith ended up with the job.

7. "HEY SANTA"—CARNEY AND WENDY WILSON

The continued fascination with the singing group Wilson Phillips continues to befuddle people looking for depth when they cruise the radio dial. Maybe a good hunk of their popularity has to do with their musical heritage. Carney and Wendy Wilson are the daughters of Beach Boy Brian Wilson. Chynna Phillips is daughter of John and Michelle Phillips of The Mamas and the Papas. The three women formed Wilson Phillips in 1990 and scored

a number of pop hits with their sugary-sweet harmonies. Although never matching the spine-tingling
harmonies of their parents' respective bands, Wilson
Phillips' songs also never went very deep lyrically. "Hey
Santa" is actually from an album made by just the two
Wilson sisters but continues in the same vein as the
Wilson Phillips sound. The not-unpopular plea to Santa
to bring my baby back is expressed here with nonoffen-
sive sibling harmonies and light lyrics. "Hey Santa/I
wish with all my might/Hey Santa/Bring my baby home
tonight"—just the type of thing pop radio cannot resist.
Wilson Phillips broke up after just a few years together
but have recently reunited and continue to make music
into the twenty-first century. Hey Santa, here's my wish:
bring us some music with soul.

8. "THE CHRISTMAS SHOES"—NEWSONG

At the risk of stepping on many toes, Newsong's
"Christmas Shoes" is awful. This one was made for all
those who go to Hallmark stores merely to read the
cards and weep. The story of the guy who sees a little
boy trying to buy some shoes for his dying mother is
complete over-the-top sentimentality with a tear-jerking
message. It becomes almost too much to bear as it is
played overly often each Christmas season. Does Jesus
really check our shoes as we enter heaven? "Christmas
Shoes" is delivered by contemporary Christian middle-
of-the-road band Newsong from its 2000 album,
Sheltering Tree. It was so well received, Newsong made
an all-Christmas holiday album the following year called
Christmas Shoes. The song became a book, which
became a television movie starring Rob Lowe.

9. "SILVER BELLS"—KENNY G

Maybe the best picture of the effect of saxophonist
Kenny G's music comes from the movie *Wayne's World*

ll when Garth (Dana Carvey) envisioned being in the dentist chair having his teeth drilled while attending a Kenny G concert. Kenny G has been blowing his own "soothing" sound as a solo artist since 1982. His full name is Kenny Gorelick, and he began his career as a member of soul icon Barry White's orchestra. The popular standard bearer for the genre known as (shudder) Smooth Jazz, Kenny G is playing something, but it is definitely not jazz. If you want to hear jazz, this book has lists of both jazz instrumentals and jazz vocals. Nonetheless, Kenny G has a devoted following, has sold more than 30 million albums throughout his career, and is highly popular at Christmas. He went to the Christmas well three times within ten years, first with the 1994 album *Miracles: The Holiday Album*, followed by *Faith: A Holiday Album* in 1999, then *Wishes: A Holiday Album* in 2002. He probably has a few more creatively named Christmas albums just waiting to be made. "Silver Bells" appears to be the Kenny G holiday song that radio stations have latched onto for airplay. Kenny G is pretty much the "socks and underwear" gift that you know you'll receive each Christmas. You know it's coming, but you'd rather have the big screen television.

10. "STEP INTO CHRISTMAS"—ELTON JOHN

We really hate to break on Sir Elton John, but his 1973 Christmas offering "Step into Christmas" offers none of the creativity or originality that marks a career that has given us "Rocket Man," "Bennie and the Jets," and "Goodbye, Yellow Brick Road." Born as Reginald Kenneth Dwight, Elton John has collaborated with lyricist Bernie Taupin and has become one of the most well-loved acts in popular music since 1968. Sir Elton (knighted by the Queen in 1998) had at least one song chart on Billboard's Top 40 every year from 1970 through 1999, a feat no one else has come close to matching.

For "Step into Christmas," John invites his listeners to "hop aboard the turntable" in order to "step into Christmas with me." Elton has done better. Much better. So can you when choosing music for your holiday party mix tape.

Christmas Present

Who says they don't make good Christmas music anymore? While the usual amount of schlock and pap is
produced every year (usually as a quick cash-in for
whichever boy group or newly proclaimed teenaged
diva has emerged from the pages of *People* magazine),
there is still great Christmas music being performed
and created these days if you know where to look. This
list will vary in style, but much of the music was
recorded in the 1990s or early twenty-first century and
hopefully some of it will continued to be heard along
with Bing, Nat, and Frank for many Christmases to
come.

1. "HEY SANTA!"—CHRIS ISAAK

Chris Isaak has always been some kind of rockabilly
cross between Roy Orbison and Elvis Presley. He has
an incredible voice, all the rock and roll moves, and a
photogenic face, too. His good looks have helped him
land acting rolls in *Married to the Mob*, *The Silence of
the Lambs*, and his own cable TV show *The Chris Isaak
Show*. His biggest commercial hit was 1989's "Wicked

Game," a haunting song where Isaak uses his best Roy Orbison imitation to send goose bumps down your spine. In 2004, Isaak released the simply titled *Christmas,* which contained "Blue Christmas" and "Christmas on TV," but also "Hey Santa," a rockabilly Isaak original (not that Wilson Phillips one!) where Isaak implores his baby to come on home. His imploring doesn't seem to be getting him anywhere, but the song is a good ride to take during the Christmas season.

2. "IN THE BLEAK MID-WINTER"—SHAWN COLVIN

Austin, Texas–based songwriter Shawn Colvin has had her share of hits and Grammy nominations. She may be best known for her 1998 Grammy winner "Sunny Came Home," but she also won a Grammy in 1989 for her debut album *Steady On.* In 1998, around the time she was expecting her daughter, she recorded *Holiday Songs and Lullabies*, a combination lullaby and Christmas collection. Shawn's singing and instrumentation is very mellow and beautiful on this recording and the artwork is by Maurice Sendak, author and illustrator of the classic children's book *Where the Wild Things Are.* Of course, Colvin is known to all Simpsons' fans as the voice of Rachel Jordan, Ned Flanders's romantic interest after Maude dies, from the band Kovenant. "In the Bleak Mid-Winter" receives an especially melancholy treatment as Shawn sings of "snow on snow on snow." "In the Bleak Mid-Winter" was written as a poem by Christina Georgina Rossetti in 1872. Her father came to England as a political exile from Italy, and she spent her whole life in England. Music was written in 1906 by Gustav Holst.

3. "CHRISTMAS DAY"—MXPX

Who says punk is dead? This Washington state–based punk outfit was formed when they were in high school and hit it big by 1996 with their album *Life in General*, which contained songs such as "My Mom Still Cleans My Bedroom," "Move to Bremerton," and "Chick Magnet." Popular in the surf and snowboard community, they actually had a snowboard sponsorship at one point. Lead singer and bass player Mike Herrara wrote "Christmas Day" in 1999. It will have you slam dancing and moshing all over the house while you decorate your tree and put up your mistletoe. Careful with the ornaments! Herrara might be missing his girl on Christmas, but he remembers to enjoy the little things during the holiday season because "a little goes a long way on Christmas Day."

4. "HERE WE COME A-CAROLING"—THE ROCHES

The quirky and fun harmonies of the Roche sisters (Maggie, Terre, and Suzzy) found Christmas voice in their 1990 recording *We Three Kings*. "Here We Come A-Caroling" is among the many fine traditional Christmas tunes the sisters sing on this record. The New York City–based sisters performed Christmas carols on city streets when they were young and participated in their first recording on Paul Simon's *There Goes Rhymin' Simon* record. Although never scoring any big hits, they were well-respected enough to have performed on *Saturday Night Live* and released many fine albums since the 1970s. "Here We Come A-Caroling" is also known as "The Wassail Song," and is a traditional British carol. A wassail is a song to wish good health, and songs such as these were sung by beggars and others less fortunate during the Christmas season in old England, hoping to receive a coin or two from the more wealthy in society. The chorus is familiar each Christmas: "Love and joy come to you/and to you glad Christmas too."

5. "BABY IT'S COLD OUTSIDE"—LEON REDBONE AND ZOOEY DESCHANEL

The Will Ferrell comedy *Elf* was a huge hit in 2003, showcasing Ferrell's comedy chops in a sweet story about a human raised as an elf at the North Pole. Whereas the movie had many homages to Christmas movies past, one of the best was Leon the Snowman, who looked an awful lot like Burl Ives's snowman in *Rudolph the Red-Nosed Reindeer*. Leon was voiced by gruff-voiced singer Leon Redbone, who has his own fantastic Christmas album called *Christmas Island*. When Buddy the Elf needed some advice before his trip to New York City, Leon the Snowman was happy to share all he knew. Later in the movie, Buddy's romantic interest Jovie (Zooey Deschanel) sings "Baby It's Cold Outside" in the shower. No voice-overs needed here; that is Zooey's voice. At the end of the movie, a full version of "Baby It's Cold Outside" is performed by Leon and Zooey, and it matches up quite well with the many versions that have been made over the years. The romantic duet has nothing to do with Christmas. It is another cold weather song that is most often heard during the Christmas season. "Baby It's Cold Outside" earned an Oscar award in 1949 for songwriter Frank Loesser, who wrote it for the movie *Neptune's Daughter*. Loesser composed music for Broadway musicals *Guys and Dolls* and *How To Succeed In Business Without Really Trying*. Another famous Loesser composition is the World War II classic "Praise the Lord and Pass the Ammunition." "Baby It's Cold Outside" has seen some action from Johnny Mercer and Margaret Whiting, Buddy Clark and Dinah Shore, Ray Charles and Betty Carter, and even Homer and Jethro with June Carter. Redbone and Deschanel's 2003 interpretation is the equal of any of them.

6. "LES ANGES DANS NOS CAMPAGNES"— BRUCE COCKBURN

Producing another Christmas album with the plain title *Christmas*, Canadian Bruce Cockburn has a real winner with his 1993 holiday album. The singer-songwriter recorded a kicking version of "I Saw Three Ships" and the ancient "Riu, Riu, Chiu," but the highlight of the album is "Les Anges Dans Nos Campagnes" also known as "Angels We Have Heard On High." Cockburn humbly claims that "the groove is written right into it," but if this were entirely true, why was he the first one to find it? "Les Anges Dans Nos Campagnes" is a traditional French carol that was translated into the English language by James Chadwick in the nineteenth century. Cockburn sings it in the original French, but you'll hardly notice. Especially if you are the kind of person who sings the Gloria chorus with the "in eggs shells" pronunciation of "in excelsis Deo." Cockburn is certainly much more of a star in his native Canada than he is in the United States. He had some chart success in the 1980s with "Wondering Where the Lions Are" and "If I Had a Rocket Launcher."

7. "THREE SHIPS"—CYNDI LAUPER

She may be so unusual, but her music is terrific. Cyndi Lauper's career coincided with the rise of MTV's popularity in the 1980s. She had several memorable music videos, some of which included professional wrestlers and an assortment of oddballs, to her songs such as "Girls Just Wanna Have Fun" and "Time After Time." Since then, Lauper has continued to have fun and released a holiday album *Merry Christmas . . . Have A Nice Life* in 1998. "Three Ships" is an old English carol with no known author, and frankly, no real known interpretation of the lyrics. The three "ships" could be the three wise men on their camels, could have been Joseph, Mary, and the baby Jesus, could be just about anything. Lauper makes the lyrics even more obscure by removing the reference to "our Savior" and replacing it with "a little boy." The more traditional religious lyrics are used by Sting in his Celtic version found on *A Very Special Christmas 3*, part of the Very Special Christmas series compilations that contain choice songs from modern day rock and R&B stars.

8. "THE MAN WITH THE BAG"—THE BRIAN SETZER ORCHESTRA

When former Stray Cat Brian Setzer formed his big band in the 1990s, a swinging Christmas album was not far behind. The 2002 *Boogie Woogie Christmas* is all you really need for your holiday party to swing. "Jingle Bells" finds Santa trading in his sleigh for a "'57 Chevrolet." Setzer brings all the big band fun back into Christmas, mixed new-millennium style with his own rockabilly style. "(Everybody's Waitin' for) The Man with the Bag," written by Dudley A. Brooks, Hal Stanley, and Irving Taylor, swings extra-special good under Setzer's guidance. The song tells the story of Kris Kringle's full bag that becomes more and more empty as Christmas night goes by. Of course, everything he's got in his bag will "tingle all your troubles away."

9. **"ON TO BETHLEHEM"—VIGILANTES OF LOVE**

The critically acclaimed band, Vigilantes of Love, was formed in 1990 by Athens, Georgia, native Bill Mallonee. They scored a few hits with "Welcome to Struggleville" and "Real Down Town" throughout the decade. An obscure, fan-only release called *My Year in Review* came out in 1995 with a wonderfully introspective song called "On to Bethlehem," where singer-songwriter Mallonee compares his journeys and difficulties to the long journey the wise men took to Bethlehem at the first Christmas. "On to Bethlehem" was included on a few compilation albums and *My Year in Review* was finally awarded a commercial release in 2002. Independent and slightly obscure, "On to Bethlehem" is a beautiful piece, well worth your own journey to find. While the Vigilantes are no more, Mallonee keeps their spirit alive with his own solo efforts and constant touring.

10. **"MANGER THRONE"—JULIE MILLER**

Singer-songwriter Julie Miller has been creating music with her guitarist husband, Buddy, since the 1980s. Her songs have been covered by Emmylou Harris, Leann Womack, and Lucy Kaplansky. One of her songs, "Broken Things," came to international prominence in 1998 as it was sung by Juliet Turner at the funeral of several of the victims of a car-bomb attack in Omagh, Ireland, that claimed the lives of twenty-nine people. Her recent albums, *Blue Pony* and *Broken Things*, have been supported by guest artists Steve Earle, Emmylou Harris, and Patty Griffin. "Manger Throne" is from a now out-of-print album *He Walks Through Walls*, but a subsequent recording by a band called Third Day with help from singer Derri

Daugherty and Julie can be found on a religious compilation called *City on a Hill: It's Christmas Time.*
"Manger Throne" is a simple song, not unlike "Away in
a Manger" and hits its message when Miller offers her
heart as a "manger throne" for the baby Jesus.

As Seen on TV

Christmas wouldn't be Christmas without the warm, loving, holiday sing-along or variety show hosted by stars big and small. Shows such as these demonstrate what it must be like to be a relative of one of these famous folk, sitting by the fireplace and crooning along with them . . . or maybe not. Whereas some telvision programs are holiday traditions looked forward to by many for years, others were just one-time (now you see it, now you don't) events.

1. BOB HOPE

Who else but the king of the USO could bring the holidays to our nation's troops worldwide and let us in on the fun? On the heels of *The Bob Hope Christmas Show* in 1965, Hope went overseas for *The Bob Hope Vietnam Christmas Show* the following year. He repeated the trip in 1971 for the cameras and made many other trips to the troops besides. The 1980 special, *Bob Hope's Overseas Christmas Tours: Around the World with the Troops 1941–1972* celebrated his many years of service entertaining the soldiers with footage from more than fifty military bases worldwide. His last Christmas special came in 1994, *The Bob Hope Christmas Show: Hopes for the Holidays.*

2. PERRY COMO

Bob Hope wasn't the only one who saw the world for the holidays. Crooner and entertainer Perry Como took the opportunity to bring holiday wishes from all over the world back to viewers in America. Como sent back Christmas wishes and holiday songs from such varied places as Ireland, New Mexico, the Holy Land, the Bahamas, and Austria. He gave us *French-Canadian Christmas*, *Early American Christmas* (including special guest John Wayne), and *Olde English Christmas* as well. Christmas wasn't Perry's only holiday either; he also spent one Easter in Guadalajara.

3. AMERICAN IDOL

Not once but twice those lovable amateur-contestant-turned-professionals shook off the evil criticisms of *Idol* judge Simon Cowell and showed their joy at being rescued from their own personal dead ends and re-created into quasi-celebrities. First up was 2003's *An American Idol Christmas* with winners Kelly Clarkson and Ruben Studdard in addition to runners-up such as Clay Aiken and Christina Christian (but sadly, no Justin Guarini from the wonderful flop *From Justin to Kelly*). In 2004, the network followed that up with *Kelly, Ruben, and Fantasia: Home for Christmas*, starring only the winners of the first three seasons of the show. And for anti-*Idol* fans, although he did not appear on either special, check out the Christmas compilation "Hung for the Holidays" by that also-ran guy from the reject pile, William Hung.

Perry Como chats with children during his Christmas special.
Peppiatt Family Collection

4. **ANDY WILLIAMS**

In addition to appearing on shows hosted by Bob Hope
and Johnny Cash, the impressive baritone Andy
Williams also hosted his own Christmas special for
many years. In 2001, he hosted *Happy Holidays: The
Best of the Andy Williams Christmas Specials.* Andy
and friends perform a wide variety of holiday songs,
including Andy's signature Christmas song, "It's the

Most Wonderful Time of the Year." More forgettable is the 1985 television special *Andy Williams and the NBC Kids Search for Santa,* a cross-promotional mess that included actress Soleil Moon Frye and pals from *Punky Brewster,* Mindy Cohn of *Facts of Life,* Joey "Whoa!" Lawrence then of *Gimme a Break,* Michael Jackson wannabe Alfonso Ribeiro of *Silver Spoons,* and all four original Cosby kids from *The Cosby Show.*

5. *THE OSBOURNE FAMILY CHRISTMAS SPECIAL*

This is not your father's Christmas special. On the heels of the popular reality show, *The Osbournes,* patriarch and heavy metal rock-and-roller Ozzy Osbourne and the rest of the family milked the cash cow for a holiday show in 2003. Joined by such celebrities (and quasi-celebrities) as Mandy Moore, Nick Lachey, Britney Spears, and Triumph the Insult Comic Dog, the highlight was daughter Kelly Osbourne's rendition of "Have Yourself a Merry Little Christmas" performed before her proud papa.

6. *'N SYNC: 'NTIMATE HOLIDAY SPECIAL*

Hear the squeals! See the fainting! Feel the vibrations from thousands of girls jumping up and down animatedly! It's Boy Band supreme, 'N Sync, and they're wishing you a happy holiday! Filmed in front of about 200 special fans (like, omigod, how lucky are *they*?) in the band's Orlando, Florida, hometown, the 2000 show switches between hits and the boys' holiday favorites, and gives each girl watching the special present of knowledge with little bits of inside information about the off-the-stage interests of each band member: Justin Timberlake, JC Chasez, Lance Bass, Joey Fatone, and Chris Kirkpatrick. Merry Christmas!

7. *THE NICK AT NITE HOLIDAY SPECIAL*

Oh no! The Blizzard of 2003 is stranding singing stars left and right, and the only place for them to seek refuge is—what a coincidence—the Nick at Nite Lodge! With *Three's Company*'s Joyce DeWitt as the housekeeper, Martin Mull (*Roseanne*) as the innkeeper, French Stewart (*Third Rock from the Sun*) as the bellhop, and John Schneider (*Dukes of Hazzard*) as the ski instructor, it's a who's who of Nick at Nite classics manning the lodge. The stranded stars range from Vince Gill and Amy Grant to Chaka Khan to Kenny Loggins, and they sing their troubles away while waiting for the snow to stop.

8. **BING CROSBY**

The star of classic films *Holiday Inn* and *White Christmas* surely had a soft spot for the holidays, right? Of course. Performing for years on the radio in holiday concerts with celebrities of the day, Crosby moved his holiday special to television in 1962, and for the next fifteen years hosted a televised holiday special, ending only with his death in 1977. The 1977 edition even aired after his death, taped, of course.

9. **THE MUPPETS**

They did a version of *A Christmas Carol* and they spoofed *It's a Wonderful Life*, but perhaps the most fun watching the Muppets at Christmastime was in 1979's *John Denver and the Muppets: A Christmas Together*. The people and the puppets performed classics such as "Have Yourself a Merry Little Christmas" and "The Twelve Days of Christmas," as well as contemporary songs such as "Little Saint Nick." The special also introduced original songs such as "When the River

Meets the Sea." All the fun of the Muppets is in this special.

10. **KATHIE LEE GIFFORD**

Oh my. Along with her previously discussed albums, Regis's former sidekick gave the world her own holiday special each year for five years, and each year it seemed to get worse and worse. Saccharine sweet, they were the holiday shows everyone loved to hate—most notably Tom Shales, reviewer for the *Washington Post*. Every year his review of Kathie Lee's show was more enjoyable than the show itself, and his grief when the show ended was palpable. Shales wrote such lines as "Kathie Lee Gifford got another hammerlock on Christmas and once again tried to throttle it to death," and, "It was often said that Christmas wouldn't be Christmas without Bing Crosby. But oh brother, would Christmas ever be Christmas without Kathie Lee Gifford."

Classic Christmas Cartoons

Along with some of the movies in the prior lists, holiday cartoons are another favorite Christmas viewing tradition. Shown every year, they're favorites in many a household, with families often sitting down together to watch *Rudolph* or *Frosty* once more. The following are ten of the classic Christmas cartoons, the ones shown and eagerly awaited year after year after year.

1. *A CHARLIE BROWN CHRISTMAS* (1965)

Probably the best-known and most-watched of all the holiday specials, cartoon or otherwise, *A Charlie Brown Christmas* has aired every year since its debut on December 9, 1965, when it was seen in more than fifteen million homes (coming in second for the week behind *Bonanza*). The special has won both an Emmy Award for children's programming and a Peabody Award for excellence in programming.

For the five or six of you who haven't seen this holiday masterpiece, the *Peanuts* gang is putting on a Christmas pageant, and good old Charlie Brown is picked as the director. He and Linus are sent out by the other kids to purchase a Christmas tree for the pageant, and Charlie Brown picks out the scrawniest, droopiest tree there is, much to the dismay of the rest of the crew. Downcast at the rejection, Charlie Brown wails "Isn't there anyone out there who can tell me what Christmas is all about?" Leave it to Linus to step forward with a Scripture quote for everyone (pay attention here: when Linus is quoting Scripture, he actually lets go of his security blanket!). It turns out that the tree, as Linus says, just "needs a little love." With some decorations and tinsel from Snoopy's award-winning doghouse, the tree is transformed into something to be proud of. Merry Christmas, Charlie Brown!

2. *HOW THE GRINCH STOLE CHRISTMAS* (1966)

Dr. Seuss's famous tale comes to animated life in this holiday classic narrated by the inimitable Boris Karloff. That mean, green, Christmas-hating machine (that would be the Grinch) attempts to steal Christmas from the tiny, lovable town of Whoville, dressing up as a very ugly Santa Claus—with doggie pal, Max, as a one-point reindeer—and stealing all the accoutrements needed for the big holiday shindig. When caught in the act by little Cindy Lou Who, the Santa Grinch makes up a lie on the spot, telling her that there was a broken bulb on the tree and he would take it back to the North Pole to fix before returning.

Perched high upon his mountain with a sled full of purloined goodies, the Grinch turned an ear to the town below for the lovely sound of boo-hooing, only to hear the same singing that goes on every Christmas. At this point the Grinch realized that "Maybe Christmas . . . doesn't come from a store. Maybe Christmas . . . perhaps . . . means a little bit more." Thus enlightened he gained the strength of "ten Grinches plus two"—because there isn't much that rhymes with "twelve." Returning the gifts and food to the town below, the Grinch becomes the man of the hour (ahh, sweet forgiveness!) and joins the Whos for a Christmas celebration to end all celebrations.

3. *RUDOLPH THE RED-NOSED REINDEER* (1964)

Rudolph premiered on December 6, 1964, the classic "animagic" claymation everyone recognizes today, made popular by Arthur Rankin and Jules Bass. Based on Johnny Marks's classic song, the cartoon follows Rudolph from birth, through being left out of reindeer games and running away, to his eventual triumphant return to lead Santa's sleigh in a heavy fog. It combines the themes of the Ugly Duckling, believing in yourself, and the Prodigal Son to strike a chord with millions of viewers, then and now.

Rudolph is ably assisted in the show by such legendary characters as Yukon Cornelius, who wants to find gold, and Hermey the Misfit Elf, who wants nothing more than to be a dentist. Rudolph, Yukon Cornelius, and Hermey travel to the magical Island of Misfit Toys. The songs, from "Why Am I Such a Misfit?" to "Silver and Gold," are instantly recognizable and add much to each viewing. As expected, Rudolph brings a happy ending for everyone—even the Misfit Toys, as an alternate finish to the show with Santa rescuing them for Christmas delivery to good boys and girls was added after the initial airing because of an outcry of support for the sad-faced toys.

4. *FROSTY THE SNOWMAN* (1969)

Legend has it he was "a jolly, happy soul," and this cartoon certainly reiterates that fact repeatedly. With a shout of "Happy Birthday!" the anthropomorphic snowman came to life one day, thanks to a top hat from the head of an evil magician. Narrated in the distinctive voice of Jimmy Durante, the story follows the eponymous man of snow from his creation caused by

The "cast" of *Rudolph the Red-Nosed Reindeer.*
©1964 Rankin/Bass Productions. Courtesy of the
RankinBass.com/Rick Goldschmidt Archives.

the magical silk hat of one Professor Hinkle, through
his romp around town with the kiddies, and then—
deviating from the song to help fill up twenty-two minutes of entertainment—a hobo-like jaunt with youngster Karen on the rails to the North Pole so that Frosty
won't melt, with the magician in hot pursuit.

Frosty shows his goodheartedness when he agrees to bring Karen into a greenhouse so she can warm up and avoid getting sick, only to have it backfire when Hinkle locks the door from the outside, leaving Frosty to melt (thankfully for squeamish viewers the cartoon doesn't show the gory details, instead cutting away and then back to the scene with Frosty now a puddle). Leave it to Santa Claus to save the day, however, restoring Frosty to his old self, again with a hearty "Happy Birthday!" beginning.

5. *THE LITTLE DRUMMER BOY* (1968)

Pa-rum-pum-pum-pum, everybody! A little boy is orphaned by bandits of the desert, left only with a lamb, a donkey, and a camel as his companions. Oh, and a drum. Can't forget the drum.

Another in a long line of entertaining Rankin-Bass productions, *The Little Drummer Boy* centers around Aaron, who (in a scene that may disturb very young ones) watches his father knifed and his mother burned to death and professes afterward to hate everyone. He finds solace in his drum, and when he eventually visits the baby Jesus realizes that the only gift he can give the newborn is the gift of music from his drum. The underlying message, of course, is that we all have something that makes us special. If you recognize a couple of voices from the cartoon, you must be *Bullwinkle* fans. Paul Frees and June Forey, who provide voices for Boris Badenov and Rocky J. Squirrel respectively, give voice to Aaron's parents as well.

6. *SANTA CLAUS IS COMIN' TO TOWN* (1970)

The stars come out for this Rankin-Bass production, with famous actor/singer/dancer Fred Astaire providing the voice for the mailman narrator, and a young Mickey Rooney providing the voice for none other than

Santa Claus (Rooney must have enjoyed this holiday experience, as he came back for a sequel as well as the movie *It Came upon a Midnight Clear*).

Astaire's mailman narrates the story as a means of explaining a number of common Christmas tidbits, such as why Santa comes down chimneys, how the reindeer can fly, where Santa acquires the toys, and many more. It traces Santa's story from being dropped off with the Kringles, a toymaking family, through his initial efforts to deliver toys to Sombertown (lorded over by the Burgermeister Meisterburger), being wanted by the law and not only growing a beard as disguise but changing his name too, getting caught and escaping jail, and finally melting not one but two evil hearts on his way toward becoming a legend. And like all good heroes, Santa gets the girl in the end as well, taking redheaded Sombertown schoolteacher, Jessica, as Mrs. Claus.

7. *'TWAS THE NIGHT BEFORE CHRISTMAS* (1974)

While it's not shown quite as much as some of the other cartoons, this classic—yet another gem from the nimble minds of Rankin and Bass—is loosely based on Clement C. Moore's poem of the same name (although the cartoon deviates greatly, actually using the poem more as a launching pad than a base story). Our tale finds us in Junctionville, a town where children are getting their letters to Santa returned unopened, and Santa informs the town they're off his delivery schedule. The reason? A too-smart-for-his-own-good young mouse who wrote a letter to the editor questioning Santa's existence (why does the mouse only get blamed here and not the editor who printed it? Unanswered questions!). Luckily, however, the town's clockmaker comes up with a plan of creating a masterpiece of a clock that, upon the stroke of midnight on Christmas Eve, will blast music skyward in an effort to lure the goodhearted Claus downward.

Ah, but that rascally mouse gets in the way again, inspecting the clock up close only to break it—"kerplunk, kerplooie," he tells his father, who informs him it's up to them to fix the thing after a test run doesn't quite go, ummm, like clockwork. In a race against time mice and man work together to save Christmas for the town and show the little mouse Albert a thing or two about the power of Santa.

8. *THE YEAR WITHOUT a SANTA CLAUS* (1974)

Mickey Rooney again provides the voice of Santa Claus in this Rankin-Bass (yep, they did this one too) staple that ostensibly provides a follow-up to the duo's *Santa Claus Is Comin' to Town* with Rooney as the vocal lead.

Santa is feeling rather taken for granted, underappreciated and even unappreciated in some respects. So, nursing a cold, he decides to take a year off—much to Mrs. Claus's horror. She sends two elves—Jingle and Jangle—along with Vixen (outfitted with socks over antlers to resemble a dog) into Southtown to try to find some Christmas Spirit in order to convince Santa that the show must go on. Things go awry and must be fixed by both Santa and the Missus, with the Missus paying especially memorable visits to the Snow Miser, Heat Miser, and finally Mother Nature in order to get the desired white Christmas for Southtown. Finally, reading a letter from a little girl, accompanied by a heart-tugging rendition of "Blue Christmas," Santa realizes what skipping Christmas would do to children worldwide and hops into his sleigh once again.

9. *FROSTY RETURNS* (1992)

Twenty-three years after the original, *Frosty Returns* is a sequel that really has nothing in common with the first rendition. Frosty this time is voiced by John Goodman, and the story revolves around an inventor who has come up with an aerosol spray that can remove snow with nary a shovel or plow. Brilliant—unless you're completely made of snow and thus facing extinction because of it. Leave it to the children to save the day and convince the town that sometimes snow can be a good thing. *Frosty Returns* not only has Goodman as the main snow dude but also includes an all-star cast of voices, including Jonathan Winters, Jan Hooks of *Saturday Night Live* fame, and Brian Doyle-Murray. It's not quite as good as the original but it's a nice second course for back-to-back Frosty viewings.

10. *OLIVE, THE OTHER REINDEER* (1999)

Not even a decade old, *Olive, the Other Reindeer* is quickly becoming a modern classic. As discussed in another list, the idea for the title resulted from the frequent mishearing of the *Rudolph* lyrics, with "all of the other reindeer" confused with "Olive, the other reindeer." From there came a book by Vivian Walsh and J. Otto Seibold, which begat this Christmas special. The cast is led by Drew Barrymore voicing the title character but also includes such stars as Dan Castellaneta of *Simpsons* fame, Joe Pantoliano, Ed Asner, Tim Meadows, Jay Mohr, and even Michael Stipe of REM.

Not-so-Classic Cartoons

Almost everyone recognizes the ten cartoons on the previous list, but these ten aren't quite so popular and well-known. But hey, that doesn't mean they're not still enjoyable and entertaining! Catch them on TV when you can, because they're not shown very often.

1. *CHRISTMAS IN SOUTH PARK* (2000)

From the demented minds of Trey Parker and Matt Stone came Mr. Hankey the Christmas Poo, the star of a previous *South Park* episode involving the gang thinking Kyle is going crazy because he claims to see a talking piece of poo—Mr. Hankey, who comes complete with his own theme song and standard "Howdy ho" high-pitched greeting. (Mr. Hankey would become a recurring character, with an episode spoofing *'Twas the Night Before Christmas* as well.)

In this special episode, Mr. Hankey hosts a musical revue from the town of South Park, including an in-rounds song about the dreidel (with an ode to Courtney Cox thrown in to boot), a stirring rendition of "O Holy Night" by Eric Cartman, and a holiday party in hell thrown by Satan and attended by such folks as Hitler, Mao Tse Tung, Jeffrey Dahmer, and Michael Landon. In case you've never seen *South Park* and can't tell from this description, their holiday special is most certainly not for children.

2. *A PINKY AND THE BRAIN CHRISTMAS SPECIAL* (1995)

Pinky and the Brain are two laboratory mice introduced on the long-running cartoon *Animaniacs* (from the fertile mind of Steven Spielberg). Pinky is, to be blunt, a doofus, and the Brain is just that—a mouse with a giant brain who puts that mindpower to work for one purpose. As quoted every episode when Pinky asks, "What are we going to do tomorrow night?" the Brain answers, "The same thing we do every night, Pinky. Try to take over the world."

This time around the Brain has concluded that if he can put a toy Brain doll into the hands of every youngster in the world, he can include a mind-control device that would leave all of mankind at his disposal. To accomplish this he sends thousands of falsified requests for the doll to Santa and then travels with Pinky to the North Pole to sneak blueprints for the doll into Santa's workshop. When discovered—their fake elf ears fall off—they escape with a clever "look, a decoy!" and run as everyone looks the other way. Back home at their laboratory, the Brain works feverishly to start the mind-control device on Christmas morning, only to be thrown for a loop when Pinky presents him with a gift: a globe keychain, to finally give Brain "the world." It's enough to make even a megalomaniacal mouse teary-eyed, as Brain simply instructs the world through their brainwashing dolls to have a merry Christmas and then smashes his device in a fit of holiday spirit. *A Pinky and the Brain*

Christmas Special won an Emmy Award for Outstanding Animated Programs (in prime time), and is well worth the effort to see it.

3. *RUDOLPH'S SHINY NEW YEAR* (1976)

Rankin and Bass tackle a different holiday with *Rudolph's Shiny New Year*. It seems Happy, the New Year baby, has run away after folks laughed at his abnormally big ears. If Happy isn't found by midnight on New Year's Eve, then the current New Year— becoming Old Year—must remain in power, a horrible fate as time is supposed to go on. With a thick fog, Santa sends Rudolph to assist Father Time in finding the tyke, and Rudolph searches through past years (after all, where would New Year go hide but Old Years?), picking up compatriots and assists along the way. Also searching for Happy, however, is a monstrous vulture-like bird, who will die when the new year starts but realizes that without Happy the old year will never end, leaving him immortal. Rudolph, with his glowing nose and past ostracization, is the perfect role model for young Happy and his huge ears. He finally locates Happy and convinces the tyke to take his rightful place.

4. *RUDOLPH AND FROSTY'S CHRISTMAS IN JULY* (1979)

Next up after New Year was the Fourth of July for Rankin and Bass. Rudolph and Frosty join forces to try to save a circus from going under, only to face the possible death of Frosty and extinguishing of Rudolph's nose!

The evil Winterbolt—who we're told created the storm that Rudolph's nose eventually led Santa through—has another plan to destroy Christmas. It seems Rudolph will lose his glowing nose if he ever uses it for evil, so Winterbolt and the no-good jealous reindeer, Scratcher, hatch a plot to not only cause just that, but also lead to the death of Frosty, his wife Krystal, and their two kids at the same time. After a complicated series of events that would make Rube Goldberg proud, all seems lost and Winterbolt stands ready to assume power at the North Pole once again. Ah, but that can't be the end of it, and sure enough the circus is saved, Rudolph gets his red nose back, Frosty and family continue living, and Santa continues Christmas. This show doesn't have the same musical magic of some of the other Rankin-Bass products, but it's fun just to see a number of past characters interact.

5. *THE SIMPSONS CHRISTMAS SPECIAL* (1989)

Matt Groening's famous family was introduced to America on *The Tracey Ullman Show*, but had its first half-hour episode as a Christmas special. In it, Homer and Marge Simpson complete sort of a reverse "gift of the Magi"—Marge spends the Christmas money the family has been saving in a jar on tattoo removal for Bart (he was getting MOTHER, but she caught him in mid-tattoo and wasn't quite enthralled with MOTH), proclaiming thanks for Homer's Christmas bonus, while Homer's boss rescinds the Christmas bonus, leading Homer to give thanks for the jar of money. Everyone say it together: D'oh!

Homer's pal, Barney, ponies up a plan, however—twice. First, Barney suggests Homer become a mall Santa to earn extra money, and then when the paycheck totals only $13, Barney suggests Homer bet it at the dogtrack instead and hope for a Christmas miracle. Santa's Little Helper seems like a good choice for a miracle, but the dog comes in dead last. Again: D'oh!

When the owner lambastes the dog, however, Homer and Bart come to the rescue and take it home, only to find that Santa's Little Helper is the perfect Christmas present for the family.

6. *THE FAT ALBERT CHRISTMAS SPECIAL* (1977)

"Hey Hey Hey" turns to "Ho Ho Ho" as Bill Cosby's gang essentially retells the story of the birth of Jesus, with a bit of Dickens's *A Christmas Carol* thrown in as well. Fat Albert, Mushmouth, Rudy, and the rest of the crew are rehearsing their Christmas pageant in the clubhouse when the junkyard's grinchy owner, Tyrone, informs them of his intent to bulldoze the hangout. Soon thereafter, a little boy with his father and very pregnant mother show up—their car broke down and they're very poor, and no one will help them. Albert invites them into the clubhouse and tries to talk some holiday spirit into Tyrone. Only after Mudfoot confronts Tyrone does he see the light and gain the Christmas spirit, and Tyrone greets the birth of the baby with holiday joy. There's no Brown Hornet, but the rest of the Cosby gang don't disappoint.

7. *A FLINTSTONE CHRISTMAS* (1977)

Ignoring the fact that Christmas wasn't exactly around in the Stone Age—after all, Christmas celebrates the birth of Christ—*A Flintstone Christmas* finds Santa with a sprained ankle and Fred and Barney trying to save the day. One problem: Fred has a prior engagement with his boss, Mr. Slate, as he promised to play Santa for a group of kiddies. But in an amazing display of correct priorities, Fred and Barney deliver the toys worldwide before rushing back to Bedrock, albeit a bit on the late side, to appear as Santa for the children. Wilma and Betty berate the guys for being late but back off when the pair explain to their wives what happened, and the four adults, plus Pebbles and Bamm Bamm, watch the real Santa fly back to the North Pole.

If Fred sounds a bit off in this show, it's because the original Fred Flintstone, Alan Reed, died before it was made; Henry Corden filled in, and did a good enough job that he continues to voice the animated Ralph Kramden wannabe today.

8. *YOGI'S FIRST CHRISTMAS* (1980)

A gaggle of Hanna Barbara characters—including Snagglepuss, Huckleberry Hound, and Auggie Doggie—join Yogi, Boo Boo, and even Cindy in this animated tale.

Yogi, as most bears do, hibernates in the winter, and as such has never experienced Christmas. Sad, we know. This year, however, he's awakened by loud holiday music—and just in time. It seems that Jellystone's hotel is going to be shut down because of lack of business. That's fine with the owner's son and the hilarious Herman the Hermit, who both plot to keep the crowds away for different reasons. Leave it to Yogi to save the day, however, as he fights off sleep while entertaining everyone (except for Ranger Smith, of course) on the way to rescuing the failing hotel.

9. *BARBIE IN THE NUTCRACKER* (2001)

Barbie stars in her first movie in this 2001 computer-animated version of the classic *Nutcracker* story. Barbie (voiced by Kelly Sheridan) plays both Clara and the Sugarplum Princess in the movie, which also includes the voice of Tim Curry as the Mouse King. While it may sound horrible, it's not quite as bad as it sounds, and indeed many reviews on Amazon.com included the phrase "pleasantly surprised."

10. *A FAMILY CIRCUS CHRISTMAS* (1979)

Bil Keane's whitebread family from the comic strip of the same name—Billy, Dolly, Jeffy, P. J., Mommy, and Daddy—come to animated life in this predictable cartoon. Billy asks Santa for a special gift this holiday: He wants his recently deceased grandpa back. Yikes, that's gonna be a tough one. However, when the star for the top of the tree goes missing, Billy finds it, thanks to a connection with said grandpa. If you find yourself enjoying this special, you can find more of the same with *A Family Circus Easter* and *A Special Valentine with the Family Circus.*

No Small Parts, Only Small Cartoons

Just like with holiday movies, the holiday cartoons feature some bit players who add quite a bit to each production. Often they steal the show, becoming just as memorable as Santa or Rudolph or Frosty. Below are ten of them from the best Christmas cartoons.

1. MAX THE DOG

He doesn't utter a single word throughout *How the Grinch Stole Christmas*—and in the cartoon world it's not uncommon for the animals to talk or at least think out loud—but Max, the adorable pet of the green monster, steals the show simply with facial expressions and those puppy-dog eyes. He is the recipient of the Grinch's evil soliloquies, his reticent partner-in-crime, a wonderful one-point reindeer, and a joyous sidekick to the Grinch's eventual transformation. Today, Max's appeal remains strong, as he can be seen on everything from neckties to ornaments to even sock puppets. Take that, Triumph!

2. YUKON CORNELIUS

The bearded explorer from *Rudolph the Red-Nosed Reindeer* is often overlooked. After all, there's already Hermey the Misfit Elf (considered for this list but ultimately rejected; his role was slightly too big) in addition to Rudolph and even Santa Claus as big names. But it's Yukon Cornelius who acts as the guide for Rudolph's travels during his runaway stage, keeping the trio away from the Abominable Snowman—the Bumble—while continuing on his plaintive search for peppermint. Yes, that's right, peppermint, not the silver and gold of the song. A deleted scene from the original animation shows Yukon Cornelius finally discovering the elusive underground peppermint stash. So while Rudolph may have saved Christmas, it's Larry D. Mann's Yukon Cornelius who saved Rudolph—and the Bumble as well, rehabilitating the big fella into a productive member of society and the best star-on-the-tree putter-onner this side of the equator.

3. WINTER WARLOCK

Voiced by Keenan Wynn (Col. "Bat" Guano for you *Dr. Strangelove* fans), the Winter Warlock takes an Ebenezer Scrooge–like turn in *Santa Claus Is Comin' to Town*, at first standing as an obstacle to young Kris Kringle's visits to Sombertown. However, after Kringle bestows upon him a gift of a toy train, the evil man's heart melts and he cries icy tears of joy before learning to "put one foot in front of the other" and change his ways. It's the Warlock who saves the day at the end, using his last little bit of magic corn to allow the reindeer to fly and help Kringle and company escape from jail and deliver the toys to all the good girls and boys.

4. PROFESSOR HINKLE

Evil magicians must have been the hip thing during the sixties and seventies. First the Winter Warlock, now Professor Hinkle (brought to life by Billy De Wolfe). It was Hinkle's discarded hat that animated Frosty the Snowman and Hinkle who vowed to get that hat back, providing the chase that sent Frosty and Karen on their trek to the North Pole. Indeed, for one brief moment it appeared that Hinkle had won, melting Frosty and taking possession of the magical headgear. A cameo by the big guy himself, Santa Claus, turns Hinkle into a quivering mess at the thought of having displeased old Kringle. Santa informs the evil magician that if he writes "I am very sorry for what I did to Frosty" a hundred zillion times he just *might* still find something in his stocking the next morning, so Hinkle rushes off to complete his task.

5. CLARICE

Even a young reindeer needs a love interest, right? Clarice was the cutie-pie that appealed to Rudolph, with her flirting comment of "you're cute" sending Rudolph to the air in the reindeer games. Alas, in his macho need to impress Clarice he butted heads and his nose-covering came off, leading to his humiliation. But Clarice wants nothing more than to stand by her man and still walks home with him . . . until her father pulls her away in horror. Still, she waits with Rudolph's mother for his eventual return and tries her best to help as well, and we can only imagine that they have their own little reindeer today.

6. SNOW MISER

Dick Shawn provided the voice for the chilly Snow Miser, one half of a brotherly duo that controlled the weather in *The Year Without a Santa Claus*. When Mrs. Claus wanted to set up a white Christmas for Southtown, it was the Snow Miser she first went to with her request. The wonderful song-and-dance routine that resulted stole the show, even if he wasn't able to grant Mrs. Claus's request.

7. HEAT MISER

The reason Snow Miser couldn't fill that request is because of his brother, the Heat Miser, voiced by George S. Irving. Southtown was in the Heat Miser's realm, so Mrs. Claus traveled to visit him and was treated to another song-and-dance bit. Heat Miser demanded control of the North Pole in exchange for giving up Southtown for just one day—a nonstarter if there ever was one—so the boys' mom, Mother Nature, put her foot down for Mrs. Claus and told the two to cooperate. Together, the duo have only about five minutes of screen time, but more often than not this show is remembered as either "oh, the Snow Miser one" or "oh, the Heat Miser one," depending on which of the two was your favorite.

8. BURGERMEISTER MEISTERBURGER

The mean old mayor of Sombertown in *Santa Claus is Comin' to Town*, the Burgermeister Meisterburger, holds a special place in the lore of Santa Claus. It is he, so the story goes, who outlawed toys after injuring himself on one—"I hate toys! And toys hate me"—which led to the previously mentioned fugitive-like activities of Kris Kringle. Quite a contribution for one little man. The slightly palandromic one is voiced by Paul Frees, a legend of cartoon voiceovers.

The hot and cold brothers, Snow Miser and Heat Miser. *Artwork ©2000 Paul Coker, Jr. Courtesy of the Rick Goldschmidt Archives*

9. SAM THE SNOWMAN

Sam the Snowman—"What's the matter? Haven't you ever seen a talking snowman before?"—is the narrator for *Rudolph the Red-Nosed Reindeer*, and voiced by the incomparable Burl Ives. Ives greatly adds to the tale, with his version of "Holly Jolly Christmas" being perhaps the most recognizable version of the song still today.

10. SPECIAL DELIVERY KLUGER

Following in Burl Ives's footsteps, Fred Astaire voices the narrator for *Santa Claus Is Comin' to Town*, Special Delivery Kluger. It's Astaire's Kluger who ties the story together for the children, as the show features flashbacks that give the details behind Kluger's basic story to the children. And as with Ives, it's Astaire's version of the title song that is the most recognizable today.

Merry Birthday!

Almost everyone knows someone born on Christmas Day. Both one author's brother, Davide, and a college roommate, Weldon J. Wirick IV—known far and wide as "Mongo"—share their yearly celebrations with Jesus. Such a birthday may make Mom and Dad happy—that tax break for having a kid before the end of the year is a nice Christmas present, and a baby wrapped in swaddling under the tree sure is a dandy photo op—for the birthday child it usually means a lifetime of "double dipping," friends and relatives who buy one gift for both occasions. Those people are certainly the scourge of the earth, if Mongo is to be believed. Nonetheless, there's been no shortage of these Christmas birthday folk who rise above that double dipping and go on to lead not only valuable but even famous lives. Following are ten of them.

1. JIMMY BUFFETT

The captain of the Parrotheads, singer/songwriter Jimmy Buffett was born on December 25, 1946. The original beach bum, Buffett gained his popularity through such songs as *Margaritaville*; *Changes in Latitudes, Changes in Attitudes*; and *Cheeseburger in Paradise*. None of his songs met with much critical acclaim—he was fond of saying he had never won an award for any of his songs, but a duet with Alan Jackson titled *It's Five O'Clock Somewhere* changed that fact—but they struck a chord with his audience, the Parrotheads, who have made him a success story that still tours regularly. In fact, his tours make more money than his albums. Today Jimmy Buffett has evolved from a simple beach bum into a singer, songwriter, pilot, and author (he has three number-one books, and was only the sixth author to hit number one on both the fiction and nonfiction *New York Times* bestseller lists). He is also a businessman with restaurants and even his own brand of tequila on the shelf.

2. LARRY CSONKA

Born on the same day as Buffett in Stow, Ohio, Larry Csonka was one of the best running backs to put on a football uniform. In his career, he played in the American Football League, National Football League, and even the World Football League before finishing his career in the NFL again. With teammate Jim Kiick, the two were known as Butch Cassidy and the Sundance Kid, and the duo led Miami to three straight Super Bowls in the early seventies, two of them resulting in championship rings. He rushed for 1,117 yards for the 1972 Miami Dolphins, the last team to go through an NFL season undefeated. Retiring after the 1979 season, he was inducted into the Pro Football Hall of Fame in 1987, and in 2002 his number 39 was retired by the Dolphins.

3. SIR ISAAC NEWTON

It wasn't a Christmas tree he was sitting under when, as the story goes, an apple fell on his noggin and led to the discovery of gravity (and really—how can you "discover" gravity? It's like Columbus discovering America and those thousands of indigenous people). But Newton was a Christmas baby, albeit under the Gregorian calendar, born December 25, 1642.

An alchemist, scientist, mathematician, and philosopher, he was one of the fathers of the scientific revolution and responsible for a number of theories still taught and proven today. All joking about gravity aside, he was the first to demonstrate that there are natural laws of motion and laws of gravity that govern things, and in a moment of history that millions of high school and college students curse each year, Newton was one of two people to independently develop the theory of calculus.

4. HUMPRHEY BOGART

The legendary actor starred in such well-known and still-popular films as *Casablanca*, *The Maltese Falcon*, *The Caine Mutiny*, and *The African Queen*, the last for which he won an Academy Award for Best Actor. Born December 25, 1899, he started his career as a stage actor in New York and eventually moved to Hollywood and was a B-movie player throughout the twenties and thirties. That status changed with his performances in *High Sierra* and *The Maltese Falcon* in 1941, in which he told his sexy client, a murderess, "If they hang you, I'll always remember you," before turning her in. Suave.

But it was 1943's *Casablanca* that put him square-ly in America's eyes. Although he never uttered the phrase that most people associate with the movie, "Play it again, Sam," Bogart is still remembered for his role as Rick Blaine, and *Casablanca* is still considered a classic today. All told, Humphrey DeForest Bogart appeared in seventy-five feature films.

5. CAB CALLOWAY

Born Cabell Calloway on Christmas 1907 in Rochester, New York, this "Highness of Hi-De-Ho" was a bandleader, singer, and eventually an actor as well. His best-known song is surely "Minnie the Moocher," the story of a "low-down hoochie coocher." Originally recorded in 1931, it and Calloway experienced a resurgence in the 1980s, as Calloway appeared as Curtis in the hit film *The Blues Brothers*, serving as a musical delay for fans waiting on the headlining siblings.

Calloway was also the angel Gabriel in the 1969 Halmark Hall of Fame television special, *The Littlest Angel*, starring *A Family Affair's* Johnny Walker as a shepherd boy newly arrived in Heaven.

6. CONRAD HILTON

A Christmas 1887 baby, born in San Antonio (back when it was still part of the New Mexico Territory), Hilton was one of America's great tycoons. Starting with one hotel in Cisco, Texas, he grew his business and in 1946 formed the Hilton Hotels Corporation, which branched out to credit cards, car rentals, and other services for the traveler. He is also the great-grandfather of Paris Hilton, Hollywood bon vivant and star of *The Simple Life* and its sequels. Paris wasn't the only Hilton with a fondness for Hollywood, however, as Conrad married Zsa Zsa Gabor, and his son Conrad, Jr., married Elizabeth Taylor.

7. CLARA BARTON

Clara Barton is the best-known early advocate for the Red Cross, pushing for its recognition by the United States government and becoming the American branch's first president in 1882 upon formal recognition by President Chester A. Arthur. She held that post until her retirement in 1904.

Barton began her professional career at age fifteen as a teacher and would continue in that profession until a mild nervous breakdown forced her retirement from teaching. From there she worked at the U.S. Patent Office in Washington, D.C., but the start of the Civil War brought a higher calling for Barton. She resigned her post and dedicated herself to the care of soldiers in the field. Eventually she was appointed "lady in charge" of the hospitals for the Army of the James, and the following year President Abraham Lincoln placed her in charge of investigating the fate of tens of thousands of missing Union soldiers. She was born on Christmas Day 1821.

8. ROD SERLING

You enter a world where reds collide with greens and songs float above the air. Garlands are everywhere, and a fat man gains admittance to your house in the dead of night, only to leave things rather than take. You see a signpost up ahead. You are entering . . . The Christmas Zone.

Rod Serling, born December 25, 1924 in Syracuse, New York, was the creator of *The Twilight Zone*, an Emmy-winning sci-fi show of the late fifties and sixties that remains a cult hit today. In addition to writing most of the episodes, Serling was also the host of the show. Perhaps inspired by his date of birth, one memorable *Twilight Zone* episode followed a gentleman playing Santa Claus in a production of *The Night Before Christmas*, as the Christmas spirit and the Twilight Zone collided.

9. RICKEY HENDERSON

Henderson is arguably the greatest base stealer in baseball history. He holds the single-season record of 130 stolen bases, achieved in 1982, and has half-again more stolen bases than Lou Brock, the man he passed for the career record in 1991. Amazingly, at this writing he has yet to retire, biding time with minor league and independent league teams while waiting for one more call from the big leagues to show his stuff. Henderson (the Man of Steal) is also famous for his ego, proclaiming after breaking Brock's record, "Today, I am the greatest of all time." He was born December 25, 1958, in Chicago.

10. ANWAR SADAT

Born Christmas Day 1918 in Cairo, Anwar Sadat led Egypt into the Yom Kippur War with Israel in 1973, three years after becoming president of the African nation. In 1977, however, he became the first Arab leader to officially visit Israel, taking Menachem Begin up on his invitation and starting the ball rolling on a peace accord. This resulted in the Camp David Peace Agreement, earning Sadat and Begin the Nobel Peace Prize, and also earning Sadat a lot of animosity in the Arab world. A crackdown on Muslim organizations in 1981 further inflamed his detractors, and on October 6, 1981, Sadat was assassinated.

Merry . . . Arrrgh!

The Lord giveth, and the Lord taketh away. Just as babies don't stop coming because it's Christmas, Christmas does not stop the Angel of Death from claiming more souls. In fact, more people die of heart attacks on Christmas Day than any other day of the year. Perhaps if Mr. Death were a bit nicer during the year, someone might give him a gaily wrapped present and make his Christmas a happy occasion, one where he ignores his duties bringing death and sadness for awhile. Until then, however, his icy finger will still find its mark on Christmas, taking names and ending lives, such as the following ones.

1. BILLY MARTIN

A one-time teammate and long-time drinking buddy of Yankees legend Mickey Mantle, Alfred Manuel "Billy" Martin is perhaps best known for his on-again, off-again (and on-again, off-again, lather, rinse, repeat) relationship with Yankees owner George Steinbrenner, complete with multiple hirings and firings as manager of George's Yanks.

Prior to managing the Yankees, Martin led the Minnesota Twins, Detroit Tigers, and Texas Rangers ballclubs. In one of the "hate" portions of his love-hate relationship with Steinbrenner, Martin briefly managed the Oakland Athletics before returning to the pinstripes. He is famous for his legendary temper, both on the field and off, as on-field he would engage in shouting matches with umpires, often complete with dirt-kicking fury. His temper showed off the field as well, as one of his stints managing the Yankees ended after a fight with a marshmallow salesman.

Finished with managing—at least for the moment—Martin was working as a special assistant to Steinbrenner when a one-car accident near his home in New York took his life on Christmas Day 1989.

2. ELENA AND NICOLAE CEAUSESCU

Nicolae Ceausescu was the Communist Romanian dictator from 1965 through 1989; Elena was his wife. Both died on Christmas Day 1989, although hardly from natural causes.

Ceausescu formed almost a cult of personality in Romania, formally the president but having a monarch-like scepter made for him. He appointed family members, including Elena, to important government posts. His downfall began when he ordered military forces to fire on anti-Communist protesters on December 22, 1989. That merely fanned the flames of the protests, and Nicolae and Elena were captured, tried, and then executed by firing squad on December 25, 1989. It was the only violent overthrow of a Communist government in the Eastern Bloc.

3. JON-BENET RAMSEY

Still unsolved, the murder of little Jon-Benet Ramsey shocked the city of Boulder, Colorado, as the six-year-old beauty queen was found dead in her family's home on December 26, 1996, likely murdered on Christmas Day. Officially, the cause of death was asphyxia by strangulation.

The case drew nationwide attention, with Ramsey's picture broadcast on television and printed in newspapers, and debates launched as to whether her family had anything to do with the horrific crime. A federal judge ruled that a preponderance of evidence led to the conclusion that an intruder was responsible, and a later DNA test indicated the killer was male and not genetically related, but no one has been arrested, much less tried, for her death.

4. CHARLIE CHAPLIN

Known as "The Little Tramp," Charlie Chaplin was by far the most famous actor of early Hollywood history with his trademark bowler hat and square mustache as he portrayed the refined vagrant that made him a star. One of the most versatile talents of the silent film era, he acted, directed, produced, and later in life even wrote the musical score for many of his movies.

Born in London in 1889, Chaplin made his way to America in 1912 with a comedy troupe, rooming at one point with Arthur Stanley Jefferson—better known as Stan Laurel. With his "Little Tramp" persona, Chaplin flourished in film, ascending up the ladder rapidly. How rapidly? In 1914, Chaplin worked for Keystone for $150 a week. In 1917—just three short years later—he signed a one million dollar deal with First National, the first actor to sign a deal of such magnitude. And in 1919 he was one of the founders of United Artists, with Mary Pickford, Douglas Fairbanks, and D. W. Griffith.

His professional success, however, was often overshadowed by his private life. At various times he married women—girls, really—who were sixteen, sixteen, and seventeen, respectively. Further, Chaplin's politics leaned to the left, and J. Edgar Hoover targeted him during the era of McCarthyism. While Chaplin was on vacation in England in 1952, Hoover persuaded the government to revoke his re-entry permit (Chaplin kept his British citizenship), and Chaplin simply decided to stay in Europe, settling in Switzerland. He briefly returned to the United States in 1972 to pick up an honorary Oscar for "the incalculable effect he has had in making motion pictures the art form of this century."

Chaplin was knighted in 1975, and died on Christmas 1977 in Vevey, Switzerland. Even in death he couldn't escape notoriety as thieves kidnapped his body to extort money from relatives. His body was found in March and the bad guys arrested.

5. DEAN MARTIN

No relation to Billy Martin, singer, comedian, and entertainer Dean was born Dino Paul Crocetti in 1917, and was a prizefighter for a time before changing his name and hitting the club circuit and then the silver screen. Teaming with Jerry Lewis, the duo rocked the stage scene with a top comedy act and transferred to Hollywood for their first film in 1949. The two were regulars on the new medium of television as well, sometimes hosting *The Colgate Comedy Hour* together before breaking up in 1956.

Both went on to more success, with Martin forming the infamous Rat Pack with Frank Sinatra and Sammy Davis, Jr., among others, and helping make Las Vegas a place to be with their performances. The group also made their mark in Hollywood, including the original version of the recently remade *Oceans Eleven*. Between his partnerships with Lewis and the Rat Pack, Martin appeared in more than fifty films in all. He died of acute respiratory failure on Christmas Day 1995.

6. YOSHIHITO

Yoshihito, the 123rd Emperor of Japan, reigned from 1912 until his death on December 25, 1926.

The emperor contracted meningitis shortly after birth, and was in poor health both physically and mentally. Perhaps because of this, he was rarely seen in public. At one of his more memorable public appearances, the 1913 opening of the Diet (Japan's ruling body), he rolled his prepared speech up into a telescope and, closing one eye, peered through the peephole instead of reading his remarks. He undertook no official duties from 1918 until his death, when he was succeeded by his son Hirohito.

7. KAREL CAPEK

Who? How do you pronounce that? And why should you care? Pronounced "CHAP-eck," Karel Capek was born in Czechoslovakia in 1890. An author, he gained his greatest fame as a science fiction writer long before science fiction was a genre of its own. He's perhaps most famous for coining the word "robot," giving millions of nerds and geeks something to dream about building in their basements. Later in life, Capek's work focused on condemning Nazi, Fascist, and even Communist governments. Because of this, the Gestapo ranked him "public enemy number two" in his home country. He died of double pneumonia on December 25, 1938, refusing to leave his country or even eat in the face of Nazi aggression.

8. W. C. FIELDS

Anyone who has ever read a quote book or book of insults surely will recognize many of Fields's bon mots. "A woman drove me to drink, and I never had the courtesy to thank her." "Marriage is better than leprosy because it's easier to get rid of." "Anything worth having is worth cheating for."

One of the early masters of the one-liner, Fields worked in vaudeville, film, and Broadway. His most famous film role was in *My Little Chickadee* alongside Mae West, whom he called "a plumber's idea of Cleopatra." He died on Christmas Day—a holiday he claimed to despise—in 1946. About Christmas, Fields once joked "Christmas at my house is always at least six or seven times more pleasant than anywhere else. We start drinking early. And while everyone else is seeing only one Santa Claus, we'll be seeing six or seven."

9. DENVER PYLE

Before his most well-known stint as Uncle Jesse on *The Dukes of Hazzard,* Denver Pyle made a career out of playing a slow-talking Southern gent, appearing on shows such as *Gunsmoke, Bonanza,* and *The Life and Times of Grizzly Adams.* He was a television regular with more than 220 guest appearances and more than 120 series roles over five decades.

Pyle also developed a close relationship with John Wayne, appearing in many of The Duke's later films. (Hmmm. Friends with The Duke. Played Jesse Duke. If he had lived, British royalty might have been next. Or perhaps college down in North Carolina.) He died of lung cancer on December 25, 1997, just two weeks after receiving a star on Hollywood's Walk of Fame.

10. **JOHNNY ACE**

Let's take a quiz, boys and girls. Say you're an up-and-coming rhythm and blues singer in the 1950s. It's Christmas Day, and you're playing a holiday dance in the city of Houston. You get a five-minute break and go backstage. Do you (a) hit the restroom quickly; (b) find something to eat and drink; (c) scope out the groupies and plant some mistletoe over them; or (d) pick up a gun with one bullet in the chamber and play Russian roulette?

If you're Johnny Ace—real name John Alexander—you choose option d, with predictable results (even more predictable because this is a list of people who died on Christmas . . . although he could have choked to death with option b). As many others have found, he garnered more fame in death as his records were in high demand after his demise, and his label released other discs to meet demand. He was just twenty-five at his Christmas death in 1954.

The World Doesn't Stop on Christmas

Just like the Angel of Death, history doesn't stop simply because it's Christmas. Disasters occur, laws are enacted, rulers are inserted or removed, and surrenders are, umm, surrendered. The point is, as the Beatles sang, "ob-la-di, ob-la-da, life goes on." Whatever ob-la-di, ob-la-da means we don't know, but below are ten events throughout world history that occurred on Christmas Day.

1. GORBACHEV RESIGNS

Mikhail Gorbachev was leader of the Soviet Union from 1985 until his resignation on Christmas Day 1991. In that time he introduced the concepts of "glasnost" (openness) and "perestroika" (reform) to a stagnating Communist Party and abandoned the Brezhnev Doctrine, allowing Eastern European countries to turn to democracy if they wished. They did, effectively ending the Cold War and earning "Gorby," as some affectionately called him, a Nobel Peace Prize.

Elected as the first executive president of the Soviet Union in 1990, Gorbachev quickly lost power, finding himself under house arrest for three days as a result of a coup attempt that ultimately failed. He returned to power but found his support dwindling. He resigned his position on December 25, 1991, and the Soviet Union itself was dissolved the next day.

2. CHARLEMAGNE CORONATED

The son of Pepin the Short (who instituted the first European coinage system), Charlemagne reigned from AD 771 until his death in 814. His reign was marked by constant battle and fighting, including the conquest of Saxony (in present-day Germany). He attempted a conquest of Spain but never fully succeeded. Charlemagne forced Catholicism on his subjects and ordered mass slaughter of those who refused. In 800 at a Christmas Mass celebrated by Pope Leo III, Charlemagne was crowned emperor for those actions, a title out of use since 476.

3. BEGIN MEETS SADAT

Menachem Begin, prime minister of Israel, traveled to Egypt to meet its president, Anwar Sadat, on December 25, 1977. This was thirty-six days after Sadat became the first Arab leader to officially visit the Jewish nation.

The result of these two historic meetings was the 1978 Camp David Accord, arranged by President Jimmy Carter, that brought peace between Israel and Egypt, for which both Sadat and Begin received the Nobel Peace Prize. Although popular worldwide, neither man gained much personally from the move. Begin saw his ruling party split over the process, and Sadat was assassinated a few years later by opponents of Israeli negotiations.

4. CIVIL WAR PARDONS GRANTED

The years immediately following the American Civil War were tough years, no doubt about it. The process of putting a nation back together was an arduous one. President Abraham Lincoln was a firm believer in leniency for the rebel fighters and even granted some pardons during the Civil War itself; the Confiscation Act of 1862 authorized the president to pardon anyone involved in the rebellion. Lincoln reasoned that the nation would not heal quickly if the Southerners were treated poorly.

President Andrew Johnson followed in Lincoln's footsteps, vetoing many attempts by Congress to levy overly strict conditions on readmittance to the Union by the Southern states. Most of those vetoes were overridden, and Johnson would later face an impeachment over his decisions. But there was no overriding his decision on Christmas Day 1865 to grant an unconditional pardon to all Civil War participants, except for civil officials and high-ranking military officers. Merry Christmas, indeed.

5. HONG KONG SURRENDERS

The United States wasn't the only victim of Japanese aggression in December 1941. One day after the attack on Pearl Harbor, the Japanese Army attacked the then-British colony of Hong Kong on the south coast of China. British forces held off the attack for a few weeks, but on Christmas Day 1941—after seventeen days of fighting—they were forced to surrender. It would take the Brits almost four years to regain control of Hong Kong, reclaiming the city on August 30, 1945, after the Japanese surrender effectively ended World War II.

6. GANSU EARTHQUAKE

On December 25, 1932, an earthquake measuring 7.6 on the Richter scale hit in the Gansu province of China, killing an estimated 70,000 people. This was a mere twelve years after a December 16 earthquake—this one measuring 8.6—that killed 200,000 in the same province. Both rank in the top fifteen of earthquake killers worldwide according to the United States Geological Survey.

7. WASHINGTON CROSSES THE DELAWARE

It's the boat trip so famous they put it on a state quarter! Oh, and there's a painting of it too. *Washington Crossing the Delaware* by Emanuel Leutze is an amazingly impressive piece of art.

The event on which both quarter and painting are based occurred on December 25, 1776, late at night. After losing the Battle of Long Island, General Washington and his troops bunkered in Valley Forge, Pennsylvania, outside of British-held Philadelphia. Across the river in Trenton, New Jersey, were the Hessians—German troops fighting with the Redcoats. Banking on the Hessians' reputation for heavy drinking and partying on holidays, Washington planned a daring Christmas night raid, but first he had to get across the river. With freezing temperatures and ice, that was no easy task, but all 2,000 men made it over, regrouped, and proceeded to rout the unsuspecting Hessians. The battle lasted all of forty-five minutes, and afterward the rebels had food, supplies, ammunition, and most importantly, a much-needed victory and momentum. Quite a Christmas present for the American Revolution.

8. WILLIAM THE CONQUEROR CORONATED

William's cousin, King Edward the Confessor, died in January 1066, after allegedly promising William that he would succeed the childless monarch. Not so fast! Harold Godwinson, who William claimed had pledged support to his ascension, reneged and was named king himself later that month, becoming King Harold II. As you can imagine, that didn't sit well with William. And as you can guess from his name—William the Conqueror—he went out and, well, conquered. He assembled an invasion fleet and an army, and landed near Hastings, setting up a base. In October 1066, King Harold's troops and William's troops met on the battlefield in what would later be named the Battle of Hastings. Harold also met his death, however, as shown in a tapestry with an image of an arrow through the eye. The remaining noblemen quickly surrendered to William, and on December 25, 1066, he was crowned King of England at Westminster Abbey.

9. HIROHITO BECOMES EMPEROR

In another list we noted that Emperor Yoshihito died on Christmas Day 1926. With Yoshihito's death, Hirohito became the new emperor on that same day, reigning until 1989 as the 124th Emperor of Japan. Within that timeframe, he was the emperor during Japan's military aggression in World War II.

Depending on the source, he was either a powerless figurehead or Asia's version of Hitler. Although many wanted to see him tried for war crimes after the war, the man who made the radio announcement of Japan's unconditional surrender retained the throne, partially on the advice of General Douglas MacArthur, who saw him as a symbol of continuity that the

Japanese people needed. He remained an active leader until his death—albeit more of a figurehead—and was extremely helpful in restoring Japan's diplomatic image with visits to foreign heads of state.

10. CHRISTMAS TRUCE

Okay, sometimes the world *does* stop for Christmas. At least, it did on Christmas morning in 1914 right in the middle of World War I. German and British troops were faced off in Belgium, but shortly after midnight on Christmas Day the German guns and artillery fell silent, and the sounds of *Stille Nacht—Silent Night—* filled the No Man's Land between the two groups of fighters. The British responded in kind, with English versions of Christmas carols, and shouted greetings led to a crossing of the No Man's Land—the trench-free zone that was usually packed with danger—as the troops exchanged gifts such as whiskey and cigars. Unfortunately, higher ups made sure this kind of thing didn't happen again, ordering artillery strikes on Christmas Eve for the rest of the war and rotating troops more often to prevent the kind of familiarity that breeds—gasp—such human kindness.

The Toy's the Thing

There are two types of people in the world: those who go all-out for that "elusive" Christmas toy (wanting nothing more than to see the look of surprise from their child or niece or nephew when they unwrap the "it" thing to have) and those who realize that these fads, these shortages, are usually created by the companies in an effort to cause havoc (and they decide that if little Johnny really has to have that gift, he can have it for his birthday in March when the stores will be overflowing with it). Sometimes the thrill of the chase can overwhelm just about anyone, though. Below are ten toy fads that thrilled many.

1. ETCH-A-SKETCH

Originally called "L'Ecran Magique" (the magic screen) by its creator, Arthur Granjean, the Etch-a-Sketch caught the eye of the Ohio Art Company at a toy fair in Nuremburg, Germany. Although company execs initially passed on the red-framed toy, they eventually decided to take a chance and manufacture the item in the States. They're surely glad they took that chance. Demand for the toy was so great upon its release in 1960 that the company kept its manufacturing plant open until noon on Christmas Eve so the toy could be shipped immediately to the West Coast and purchased for last-minute placement under the tree.

2. SUPER BALL

The toy that helped name the Super Bowl was a simple piece of rubber, manufactured to bounce and spin like no other ball before it. The trick? The ball was under 3,500 pounds of pressure per square inch. Give it a good throw and it could go three stories high! At the height of its peak in 1965, Wham-O was producing 170,000 balls per day in mid-November. From its introduction in mid-1965 until Christmas, seven million Super Balls were sold, each for under a buck.

3. PET ROCK

For those of you not familiar with the Pet Rock, it's exactly as described in its name: a rock that one would keep as a pet. It was a tongue-in-cheek invention from the mind of Gary Dahl, who was tired of pets that had to be fed, walked, cleaned up after—in other words, taken care of. The Pet Rock was a pet one could simply have and . . . it would sit there, not needing you to do a thing for its survival.

Dahl introduced the Pet Rock at a gift show in San Francisco in August 1975, then brought his creation to New York. Thanks to some savvy marketing and coverage by magazines such as *Newsweek* and most of the nation's newspapers, by October Dahl was shipping an amazing ten thousand Pet Rocks every single day. By Christmas 1975 more than a million Pet Rocks had been sold, and kids everywhere had an easy pet to take care of. So did their parents.

4. CABBAGE PATCH KIDS

The gimmick for this doll was that children didn't "buy" a Cabbage Patch Kid they "adopted" her (or him), receiving a certificate of adoption with every single doll. Originally called Little People by their creator, Xavier Roberts, Cabbage Patch Kids were perhaps the first toy to inspire riots in the stores, as parents would push and shove and sometimes punch to get hold of one of these precious commodities. The toy company Coleco took them to the big time in 1982, and they were the "it" toy for Christmas in 1983. Sales plummeted as the decade progressed and Coleco went bankrupt in 1988, but Hasbro and Mattell picked up the baton and were rewarded with a resurgence in popularity in 2004, as those who were children at the doll's first peak had children of their own and succumbed to the lure of nostalgia.

5. TEENAGE MUTANT NINJA TURTLES

Heroes on a half-shell! Originally a tongue-in-cheek response to action figures such as GI Joe, the Teenage Mutant Ninja Turtles—who lived in sewers and ate pizza—were originally panned at the 1988 Toy Fair. The green good guys had the last laugh, though, as sales of merchandise by Christmas of the same year totalled more than $40 million, and the guys (named after Italian artists) followed that up with roughly $100 million in sales the next Christmas.

6. TICKLE ME ELMO

"Hee hee hee hee hee! Hee hee hee hee hee! That tickles!" That high-pitched screech was heard in many a household on Christmas Day 1996, and for that we have one person to thank: Rosie O'Donnell. Well, maybe not *just* O'Donnell, but were it not for her, the red-furred one might have languished on the shelves. Tyco, the manufacturer, had sent Rosie's producer more than two hundred Elmos as a promotional device, and on an October episode of Rosie O'Donnell's talk show, she tossed one Elmo into the audience each time someone said the magic word (for the record, it was "wall"). Rosie's core audience was moms with kids, and that one boost started a snowball that resulted in more than a million Tickle Me Elmos being sold during the 1996 holiday season. That still wasn't enough, as demand for the toy far outstripped supply, and cagey capitalists auctioned off the giggler, often for as much as $3,000. Yup, thousand. Desperation for Elmo ran so high that one *San Francisco Examiner* columnist tabbed the dolls "Ransom Me Elmo," and the Associated Press had an "all-Elmo" brief that they distributed each day, with news only about the hard-to-find gift.

Today, Tickle Me Elmo has fallen to the third-best-selling Elmo doll, having been surpassed by both Chicken Dance Elmo and YMCA Elmo. Neither, though, produced the same fever as the original.

7. TAMAGOTCHI

The Tamagotchi is perhaps the first toy that was a fad in two countries, as it took Japan by storm at Christmas 1996 before hitting the shores of the United States and being the hard-to-find gift for Christmas 1997 here. The Tamagotchi roughly translates from the Japanese for "lovable egg," and is a virtual pet in an egg-shaped device on a keychain. It gained its popularity in Japanese cities, because many children lived in conditions too cramped for real pets, and the virtual pet—which required the owner to play with, feed, and clean up after it to make it grow up big and strong—was a fun substitute. Bandai sold roughly half a million of the plastic creatures in the first two months, and demand was such that the $16 to $18 toy was selling for as much as $400 on the black market. Like Cabbage Patch Kids, the Tamagotchi made a bit of a comeback in 2004 with Tamagotchi Connection, which added an interactive feature allowing each Tamagotchi to play with the Tamagotchis owned by other kids.

8. FURBY

Half Tamagotchi and half Gizmo (the cute Gremlin), Furby was allegedly an alien pet with its own language. Kids could play with Furby, teach Furby, and learn Furby's language at the same time Furby learned English. The hysteria over the toy was amazing, as the initial lot of 1.3 million were sold even before the toy was actually released in October 1998, resulting in the same black-market shenanigans as seen with Tickle Me Elmo and Tamagotchi. Its popularity was short-lived, however. Its manufacturer, Tiger, sold forty million worldwide in 1998; by 2000, that number had dropped to one-tenth of that total and today Furby sightings are almost nonexistent.

9. PLAYSTATION2

The PlayStation2 wasn't supposed to be a hot Christmas toy, but because of some bad luck, it became one. It was originally scheduled for release October 26, 2000, but because of a scarcity of one of its components, Sony cut the original shipment of one million units in half, promising another 100,000 units per week through the end of the year. That led Sony exec Jack Tretton to admit, "I don't think everybody who wants one will get one." His comments helped fuel the fire, as technology-savvy consumers parked on the Internet in search of a PlayStation2. So many people camped on the Internet, in fact, that Amazon.com suffered a half-hour outage because of traffic overload, and websites for Kmart and Best Buy reported Internet problems as well.

10. YOUNIVERSE ATM MACHINE

We started this list with the Etch-a-Sketch and a simple rubber ball, and we end it with a toy Automated Teller Machine. How times have changed. The YOUniverse ATM Machine, manufactured by Summit Products, Inc., is at its most basic a piggy bank that comes with an ATM card. Kids can punch in their personal identification number (PIN), have their name show up on the toy's screen, and look into the fake security camera and pretend they are smiling for the tellers who they know must be watching. Unlike a real ATM, the entire cash stash is produced upon a correct PIN, and the kids can take as much or as little of it as desired.

The toy started out slow in 2002 but hit the big time in 2004, going from 50,000 sales the year of its debut to roughly two million in 2004. Toys R Us alone sold 10,000 in four days, and the toy's debut on QVC and the Home Shopping Network resulted in a sellout in minutes. The ATM has been a hit on eBay as well, often going for close to three times its retail price of $29.95. Other versions now compete with YOUniverse, such as BankAmerikid and The Barbie ATM Machine.

Tasty Treats

What are the holidays without tasty treats all over the place? Many people make a New Year's resolution to lose weight, and most of that weight to lose comes from over-indulging in sweet holiday goodness. Below are some of the tastiest of the tasty, the standard goodies seen in homes, office parties, and stores all over.

1. FRUITCAKE

It's become so much of a traditional Christmas gift that it's turned into a monumental joke. Indeed, there are some families that pass the same fruitcake from person to person each and every successive Christmas. But why? Why is the fruitcake so associated with Christmas?

Some sources claim that in eighteenth-century England, fruits were so scarce that they were only used in baking at various holidays. Others point out that it's a good way to use excess fruits and nuts dried for the long winter. Whatever the reason, there sure are a lot of them out there. More than five million fruitcakes are purchased every year, and people take them seriously. At the Harry and David retail store, no one person knows the entire recipe: One shift mixes the first half, another mixes the second half, and a third shift mixes the two halves together. And if you want the fruitcake to end all fruitcakes, check out the self-proclaimed "world's largest fruitcake" from Gladys's Bakery in Texas—150 pounds of fruity goodness for the low, low price of $998.95.

2. FUDGE

It's not just a curse-substitute from *A Christmas Story*. As elementary school music teachers everywhere proclaim, "every good boy deserves fudge," and at Christmastime fudge stands out as a holiday treat for all the good boys and girls. Every grandma has her own recipe, it seems, and of course every grandma's recipe is best. The biggest fudge, however, belongs to

Gladys of Gladys' Bakery poses with her Texas-shaped fruitcake.
Gladys' Bakery

Eagle Family Foods. The company unveiled a chunk of fudge in November 2004 that weighed in at 2,100 pounds and measured eighteen inches high by sixty-two inches wide by forty-eight inches deep, according to a company press release. To make the monstrous concoction, bakers used "292 pounds of pure milk chocolate chips, 861 pounds of semi-sweet chocolate chips, 821 pounds of Eagle Brand Sweetened Condensed Milk (equivalent to 938 of the traditional 14 oz. cans) and 126 pounds of butter." No word on how many calories the fudge has.

As for your fudge, want a quick and easy hint for making it special for Christmas? Smash up some candy canes to mix in for a minty holiday touch.

3. CANDY CANES

Speaking of candy canes, that's another holiday standard (and, as mentioned earlier, even a Halloween standard for one of the authors who passes them out to trick-or-treaters. Hey, they're in the stores!).

According to one legend, candy canes were created in Cologne, Germany, in 1670, when the choirmaster handed out sugary sticks to his young singers in order to keep their mouths occupied with something other than talking during down times in a long holiday service. He bent them into the J-shape, allegedly, to resemble a shepherd's crook. The canes were at first all white, with the now-standard red stripes coming in the early twentieth century. Mass production came in 1955 when Gregory Keller invented a machine to automate the creation of the candies. Keller's brother-in-law was Bob McCormack of Bobs Candies, which used and improved upon Keller's machine to become the largest candy cane vendor in the world. Today, nearly two billion candy canes will be sold overall in the month before Christmas.

4. GINGERBREAD

Be they men, houses, cookies, or just plain loaves of bread, gingerbread is a delicious and standard Christmas food for many. According to popular legend it was England's Queen Elizabeth I who "invented" the gingerbread man, as she requested ginger-spiced cakes to be baked in the shape of some friends for the holiday. The world's largest gingerbread man was baked in late 2003 by the Hyatt Regency Hotel in Vancouver, Canada, and measured almost fourteen feet tall by five-and-a-half feet wide, and weighed in at more than 370 pounds.

Moving on to abodes, gingerbread houses are a fun holiday activity for the young and young at heart, with only your imagination limiting the many ways you can decorate your creation. (One of this book's authors, for example, created a maroon-and-orange-themed Hokie Gingerbread House for a holiday charity event.) And for another baking tip, add a teaspoon of cardamom to your gingerbread for an extra little kick.

5. MILK AND COOKIES

How does Santa get so jolly—okay, okay, fat? Milk and cookies left out for him at every house he visits surely can't help any efforts at weight maintenance. In the grand tradition of bribery, folks have been leaving treats for Santa (and in some cases, carrots for the reindeer as well) for ages. It's not always milk and cookies, though. In England, for instance, children sometimes leave sherry and mince pie.

6. LOG CAKE

Nothing says Christmas more than sitting before a roaring fire, so log cakes are a natural Christmas treat, shaped like a fireplace log and sometimes impressively decorated to look just like one. For a simpler log cake, all you really need is a jelly roll pan, a cream filling, and a frosting or ganache. Or if you're the Northland Spectrums in Edmonton, Alberta, Canada, you can set a Guinness world record for the world's largest Christmas log cake, checking in at more than 5,500 pounds and measuring seventy-two feet in length.

7. FIGGY PUDDING

You sing about it—demand it, really: "and bring it right here"—but have you ever actually *had* figgy pudding? Charles Dickens has Mrs. Cratchit serving it in *A Christmas Carol*, so it's been around for quite awhile. If you've had it, you're one step ahead of many! For those that haven't, the question remains: What *is* figgy pudding? And is it any good?

While there are certainly figs in the dish, it's less a pudding and more a soft bread—an English pudding, they say. It's steamed in water in the oven, and sliced rather than spooned into portions. In addition to the figs (chopped, thank you very much) recipes include some or all of nutmeg, cinnamon, orange or apple peels, dates, rum, bourbon, and molasses. And yes, its fans say, figgy pudding is very good.

8. EGG NOG

One of two drinks on this list, egg nog is a thick, creamy, dairy drink that clogs arteries and leaves a coating thicker than Guinness on a glass. It was brought over to America from Europe, a cousin to the milk-and-wine punches. But man, is it good—and it's not just people today who think so! George Washington not only fathered our country, but left behind a tasty egg nog recipe with ingredients of one pint brandy, one-half pint rye whiskey, one-half pint

Jamaica rum, one-quarter pint sherry, eggs, twelve tablespoons sugar, one quart of milk, and one quart of cream. With that much liquor in the recipe it's no wonder his last instructions were "taste frequently."

And what's a nog? Well, there are two different explanations. In George Washington's time, rum was commonly referred to as "grog," which some think was shortened into "egg nog" with the egg mixer. Others claim that the drink was originally served in wooden mugs called "noggins," which sounds more likely.

9. ADVENT CALENDAR

Advent, of course, is the period of time before Christmas for Christians to prepare for the birth of Jesus. A countdown to Christmas can be traced back to the nineteenth century, with Advent clocks or Advent candles marking how much longer until the joyous day. Early in the twentieth century came the Advent calendar we're familiar with today—cardboard doors for each day of Advent, with a little piece of candy behind each door to add to a child's eagerness.

10. HOT CHOCOLATE WITH SCHNAPPS

Not specifically a holiday beverage, this is one that's just good to drink in cold weather, warming you up in more ways than one. Some prefer peppermint schnapps to add a festive touch to their hot cocoa—even stirring with a candy cane for extra mintiness—while another tasty mix is hot chocolate with butterscotch schnapps. Guaranteed to warm you right down to your toes.

All You Need Is
a Reason

Okay, so you don't want to celebrate Christmas? Or perhaps you enjoy the season so much you want to celebrate as many things as you can? What else is there to celebrate in the wintry days surrounding December 25? What other excuses for a party can you come up with—like you really *need* an excuse this time of the year, but if you insist? Below are ten other holidays that you can celebrate instead of or in addition to Christmas. Egg nog optional.

1. HANUKKAH

Also known as "The Festival of Lights," Hanukkah is an eight-day-long Jewish holiday commemorating the rededication—"Hanukkah" translates as "dedication"—of the Temple of Jerusalem in 165 B.C. According to Jewish legend, there was only enough oil to light a candle for one day for the dedication ceremony; miraculously the candle stayed lit for eight days, allowing for more oil to be found to keep it lit. Today the candles in a menorah are lit one per night to symbolize the growth of the miracle.

The feast starts on the twenty-fifth day of Kislev, which corresponds to December in the Roman calendar, but the exact dates vary from year to year.

2. KWANZAA

Kwanzaa is "an African American and Pan-African holiday celebrated by millions throughout the world African community" according to the Official Kwanzaa website. Taking place from December 26 through January 1, the "celebration of family, community, and culture" comes from the phrase "matunda ya kwanza," meaning "first fruits." The second A of Kwanzaa came from the specific makeup of the organization introducing the holiday; seven children each wished to represent a letter of Kwanzaa, so a seventh letter—the second A—was added to accommodate all seven children.

Kwanzaa is modeled on "first fruit" celebrations of ancient Africa, which lasted seven days. Because of this, Kwanzaa is also a seven-day holiday. With those seven days come the "Nguzo Saba," the Seven Principles. The purpose of the Seven Principles is to introduce and reaffirm the importance of these ideas in African culture and community. They are "Umoja" or unity, "Kuji-chagulia" or self-determination, "Ujima" or collective work and responsibility, "Ujamaa" or cooperative economics, "Nia" or purpose, "Kuumba" or creativity, and "Imani" or faith.

3. NEW YEAR'S EVE

Should old acquaintance be forgot and never brought to mind . . . chances are there's a ton of alcohol involved, and New Year's Eve often sees a bunch of the bubbly popped and consumed during its celebration. For this, we have the ancient Babylonians to thank, as they first celebrated the beginning of a new year roughly four thousand years ago.

January 1 wasn't always the start of a new year, and today the Chinese and the Jewish both celebrate new years on different days, to name but a couple of exceptions. New Year's Eve celebrations have been around only since the early 1900s, however. Superstition dictated that the events of the forthcoming year would depend on how one started it, and starting the new year right at midnight with friends, family, and fun was certainly a good omen for the forthcoming year.

4. WINTER SOLSTICE

The winter solstice is that point in the earth's orbit when one of the two hemispheres is most tilted away from the sun. In the Northern Hemisphere that corresponds to either December 21 or December 22, depending on the year. It corresponds to both the shortest amount of daylight and the longest nighttime of the year, and is considered to be the official start of winter.

There have been a number of celebrations worldwide centering on the winter solstice, including the Chinese Dong Zhi, the ancient Roman Saturnalia, the Celtic and neopagan Yule, and the Persian Yalda, celebrating the birth of the Sun god Mehr. Christmas, as mentioned elsewhere in this book, was placed on December 25 partially to supersede some of the pagan celebrations of the winter solstice.

5. BOXING DAY

You know Leonard and Hagler, Ali and Frazier. Foreman and Klitschko, Lennox and Tyson. But do you recall, the most famous boxer of all? What?

Ohhhh . . . it's not *that* kind of "Boxing Day," is it? Oops.

Boxing Day is primarily a European holiday, although it's also celebrated and an official day off in many former British colonies (not including the United States). The origin of the holiday is in dispute, because some claim it comes from the practice of servants receiving presents from their employers on December 26, after the family celebrations; others maintain that December 26 was the day priests cracked open the collection boxes to donate the holiday proceeds to the poor. Whatever the origin, today Boxing Day is still celebrated on December 26 and is traditionally a day of sport. In Australia, for instance, a major cricket match and a major yacht race start on this day. Canada—perhaps based on its proximity to America and her commercialism—sees many stores, particularly electronics stores, using the holiday as an excuse to sell off leftover Christmas merchandise at greatly reduced prices.

6. COLLEGE FOOTBALL BOWL GAMES

Boxing Day may be a traditional "day of sport" in those countries, but in the United States we have college football bowl games! Ahh, what a wonderful time of year, when college teams journey to cities grand (New Orleans, Los Angeles) and not-so-grand (Detroit in wintertime; Shreveport, Louisiana) for an end-of-season reward for colleges called a bowl game, a contest against a team they might not normally face in a city they might not normally visit. The host cities are usually a tourist destination—the better for drawing each team's fans—and many of the bowl games have other activities, including parades.

The grand finale of the bowl season is the Bowl Coalition Series, or BCS. Comprised of the Sugar Bowl, the Orange Bowl, the Fiesta Bowl, and the Rose Bowl (the Rose Bowl being "the granddaddy of them all," the oldest bowl game there is), the BCS is an attempt to find a "true" college football national champion, or as "true" as one can get without a playoff system. The four bowls rotate amongst themselves each year, with each bowl hosting a matchup of the number-one versus number-two team every four years. The only problem has been determining which team is number one and which team is number two, as the BCS has caused about as many problems as it originally fixed, with vigorous debates each year on the relative merits of three and sometimes even four schools that supporters claim should be in the national championship game. While minor and somewhat major changes are made to the BCS seemingly every year, the goals still remain the same: crown a college football champion, bring lots of fans to the host cities, and make lots and lots of money. For the fans, it's their last look at college football until August. Oh, the humanity.

7. FEAST OF THE THREE KINGS

Also called the Feast of the Magi, the Feast of the Three Kings commemorates the day when the three kings—the three wise men—visited Jesus in the manger, bringing their gifts of gold, frankincense, and myrrh. In some cultures, this day marks the exchange of presents, rather than or in addition to Christmas Day. In others, it marks the official end of the Christmas season, as decorations and Christmas trees are taken down, with children pillaging the trees for their edible decorations.

8. ORTHODOX CHRISTMAS

As discussed elsewhere in the book, with the switch from Julian to Gregorian calendars, a number of days were "lost"—skipped over in an effort to realign the calendar with the true movements of the sun. As a result, what was once December 25—Christmas—was actually January 7 in the Gregorian calendar once it was adopted worldwide (and will be until 2099, when further conflicts between the two calendars push the date back to January 8). Some religions, mostly of the Eastern Orthodox, refused to realign the celebration of Jesus's birth, and celebrate Christmas on January 7.

9. HOGMANAY

Hogmanay is a Scottish celebration of the New Year, starting December 31 and often lasting until January 2. One of the national customs of Hogmanay is "first-footing," where the first person to set foot in a household after midnight (the start of the new year) presents symbolic gifts as a wish of good luck to the homeowner.

Perhaps the most spectacular Hogmanay custom takes place in Stonehaven, in northeast Scotland. Here, the locals construct flammable balls up to three feet wide, which they connect to a six-foot long fireproof chain. As one can imagine by the use of the words "flammable" and "fireproof," those balls are then set on fire, with the chain used to swing them around and around as the person walks through the town to the harbor, where the fireball is cast into the water to be put out.

10. FESTIVUS

Another pop culture reference brought to us by the wonderful minds behind *Seinfeld*. Festivus, celebrated every December 23, is the brainchild of Frank Costanza, George's brash and opinionated father. Calling it "A Festivus for the rest of us,"—everyone loves rhymes—Festivus, as the slogan implies, is a celebration for people who don't particularly care to celebrate any of the other holidays of the season.

Included in the celebration of Festivus are the Festivus pole, a long, thin, heavy pole with no decorations whatsoever; the "Airing of Grievances," where you inform family and friends of all the ways they've disappointed you throughout the past year; and the "Feats of Strength," where the head of each family chooses one person to test his strength against. Festivus ends, then, only when this head of family is pinned to the ground in a wrestling match. According to legend (or as much of a "legend" as a television show can make), you're only allowed to turn down participation in the feat of strength if you have something else to do. Thus, Kramer was able to pass along his place of honor to George, setting up a father/son grudge match to end the holiday.

Say That Again?

We've reached the end of our book, and what better way to close than with a hearty "Merry Christmas!" We'll go one better than that—or ten better, actually—with our last list. It's a simple list, but one that will help as the world around us gets smaller. Below are ten translations of "Merry Christmas" into other languages. Enjoy!

1. **FELIZ NAVIDAD (SPANISH)**

2. **JOYEUX NOEL (FRENCH)**

3. **BUON NATALE (ITALIAN)**

4. **FROHE WEIHNACHTEN (GERMAN)**

5. **GUN TSO SUN TAN'GUNG HAW SUN (CHINESE/CANTONESE)**

6. **SROZHDESTVOM (RUSSIAN)**

7. **NOLLAIG SHONA (IRISH)**

8. **MELE KALIKIMAKA (HAWAIIAN)**

9. **GAJAN KRISTNASKON (ESPERANTO)**

10. **ERRY-MAY ISTMAS-CHRAY (PIG LATIN)**

Bibliography

Gulevich, Tanya. *Encyclopedia of Christmas*. Detroit, MI: Omnigraphics, 2000.

Studwell, William E. "The Naming of The Deer." Northern Illinois University Public Affairs Office, November 18, 1998.

Waller, Richard. "The Physics of Santa Claus." *Spy Magazine*, January 1990.

Wernecke, Herbert H. *Christmas Customs Around the World*. Louisville, KY: Westminster Press, 1959.

WEBSITES

encyclopedia.thefreedictionary.com
lyricsplayground.com
www.4noel.com
www.allmusic.com
www.amazon.com
www.catholicherald.com
www.census.gov
www.christmas.com
www.christmasradionetwork.com/songs
www.dot.gov

www.historychannel.com
www.hymnsandcarolsofchristmas.com
www.imdb.com
www.mcadenville-christmastown.com
www.mistletunes.com
www.nationalgeographic.com
www.officialkwanzaawebsite.org
www.realchristmastrees.org
www.rienzihills.com/ChristmasSing
www.rottentomatoes.com
www.snopes.com
www.songfacts.com
www.visitrudolphwi.org

Index

Ace, Johnny, 251
Advent calendar, 270
Aiken, Clay, 185
"All I Want for Christmas Is My Two Front Teeth," 165
American Christmas Carol, An, 147
American Idol, 212
Andrews Sisters, The, 189
Armstrong, Louis, 67
August, Lynn, 102
"Auld Lang Syne," 118
Australia, 29
Autry, Gene, 61
"Away in a Manger," 90
"AyAyAy It's Christmas," 197

Baboushka, 32
"Baby It's Cold Outside," 206
Bad Santa, 138
Bailey, Pearl, 68
Band-Aid, 160
Barbie in the Nutcracker, 230
Barenaked Ladies, 194
Barton, Clara, 243
Basie, Count, 74
Beach Boys, The, 84
Begin, Menachem, 254
Bennett, Tony, 65
Berry, Chuck, 83
Bethlehem, Georgia, 16
Bethlehem, Pennsylvania, 16
Bethlehem, West Virginia, 16
birthdays on Christmas, 239–44
Bishop's Wife, The, 127
Black Friday, 5
Blind Boys of Alabama, 111
Blitzen, 56
"Blue Christmas," 64
Bogart, Humphrey, 241
Bolton, Michael, 198
Bonanza, 186

Bondi Beach, 29
"Born in Bethlehem," 111
Bowie, David, 156
Boxing Day, 273
Brady Bunch, The, 186
Brazil, 34
Brian Setzer Orchestra, The, 208
Brown, Charles, 100
Brown, James, 105
Brown, Les, and his Band of Renown, 77
Brubeck, Dave, 79
Buffett, Jimmy, 193, 239
Burgermeister Meisterburger, 236
Burke, Kevin, 117
by the numbers, 5–10

Cabbage Patch Kids, 261
Calloway, Cab, 242
Campbell, Eddie C., 103
candy canes, 20, 267
Capek, Karel, 249
cards. *See* greeting cards
caribou, 48
"Carolina Christmas," 190
carols, 2
cartoons: characters, 233–38; classics, 217–24; not-so-classic, 225–31; songs, 171–76
Cash, Johnny, 90
Ceausescu, Elena and Nicolae, 246
Chaplin, Charlie, 247
Charlemagne, 254
Charles, Ray, 108
Charlie Brown Christmas, A, 217
Cheech and Chong, 168
Chieftains, The, 113, 190
China, 8
"Chipmunk Song, The," 164
Chipmunks, The, 164
Christkindel, 32

Christmas, Florida, 13
"Christmas (Baby Please Come Home)," 84
"Christmas at K-Mart," 192
"Christmas by the Bar-b-que," 102
Christmas Carol, A: made in 1938, 143; made in 1951, 124; made in 1984, 147; made in 2004, 148; versions of, 143–48
"Christmas Day," 159, 205
"Christmas Eve," 71
Christmas in Connecticut, 127
Christmas in South Park, 225
Christmas Island, 11
"Christmas Lullaby," 90
"Christmas Medley, A," 72
Christmas on Ponderosa, 186
Christmas Shoes, The: song, 200; movie, 131
"Christmas Song, The," 60
Christmas Story, A, 122
"Christmas Time Is Here," 73
"Christmas Time's A-Comin'," 89
"Christmas to Remember, A," 93
Christmas tree, 41–46; care of, 44, 45; conservation and, 43; first, 41; kinds of, 44; number of, 42; nutrition and, 45; official, 42; spiders on, 46; White House, 3
Christmas truce, 258
Christmas with the Brady Bunch, 186
"Christmas with the Devil," 169
Christmas with the Kranks, 130
cities with holiday names, 11–17
Civil War pardons, 255
Clarice, 235
Classic Cartoon Christmas, A, 187
Cockburn, Bruce, 207
Cole, Nat "King," 60
college football bowl games, 274
Colvin, Shawn, 204
Comet, 55
"Comfort and Joy," 157
Communism, 4
Como, Perry, 212
Cornelius, Yukon, 234
Costello, Elvis, 190
Cox, Tony, 152
Crock o' Christmas, 187
Crosby, Bing, 59, 156, 189, 215
Csonka, Larry, 240
Cunningham, Johnny, 118
Cupid, 55

Dancer, 54
Dasher, 53
deaths on Christmas, 245–51
December 25, 19

"Deck the Halls with Boogie Woogie," 99
Denver, John, 178, 215
Deschanel, Zooey, 153, 206
Destiny's Child, 182
"Dig That Crazy Santa Claus," 70
Disney World, 7
Diva's Christmas Carol, A, 146
"Do They Know It's Christmas?" 160
"Do You Hear What I Hear?" 92
Donder, 55
Donner. See Donder
Droppa, Laura, 111

Eagles, The, 156
Eastern Europe, 4
Eckstine, Billy, 71
egg nog, 269
Eight Crazy Nights, 141
Elf, 136
Elmo and Patsy, 166
Enya, 114
Esperanto, 274
Etch-a-Sketch, 259
Evans, Bill, 76
"Even a Miracle Needs a Hand," 173
evergreens, 21

Family Circus Christmas, A, 231
Fat Albert Christmas Special, The, 229
Father Christmas, 32
"Father Christmas," 158
Feast of the Three Kings, 275
Feliciano, Jose, 197
"Feliz Navidad," 197
Festivus, 276
Fiedler, Arthur, and the Boston Pops, 62
Fields, W. C., 250
figgy pudding, 269
"First Toymaker to the King," 175
firsts, 1–4
Fitzgerald, Ella, 69
"Five Pound Box of Money," 68
Flintstone Christmas, A, 229
flowers, 7
food, 265–70
Fortress of Solitude, 40
fortune telling, 27
Foxworthy, Jeff, 180
Freberg, Stan, 167
Frosty Returns, 224
Frosty the Snowman: cartoon, 219; song, 85
fruitcake, 265
fudge, 266
Funderburgh, Anson, and the Rockets, 98
Furby, 263

Galway, James, 114
Gansu earthquake, 256
Garland, Red, 75
Germany, 32
Gifford, Kathie Lee, 184, 216
Gill, Vince, 92
gingerbread, 268
"Give Love on Christmas Day," 107
"God Rest Ye Merry Gentlemen," 75
Goldthwait, Bobcat, 151
"Good King Wenceslas," 115
Gorbachev, Mikhail, 253
Gordon, Dexter, 74
Grandfather Frost, 32
"Grandma Got Run Over by a
    Reindeer," 166
Greece, 26
greeting cards, 2, 8; robins and, 22
Grimes, Karolyn, 151
Grinch, The, 135
Guaraldi, Vince, 73
Guatemala, 25
Gurtshaw, Amy, 111

Hanukkah, 271
"Happy Xmas (War Is Over)," 155
Harris, Emmylou, 89
"Have Yourself a Merry Little
    Christmas," 62, 74
Hayes, Isaac, 109
Heat Miser: character, 236; song, 174
Heath Brothers, The, 78
Helms, Bobby, 81
Henderson, Rickey, 244
"Here Comes Santa Claus," 86
"Here We Come A-Caroling," 205
"Hey Santa," 199, 203
"Hey Santa Claus," 85
Highland Bagpipes, The, 118
Hill, Faith, 199
Hilton, Conrad, 242
Hinkle, Professor, 235
Hirohito, 257
historical events on Christmas, 253–58
"Ho Ho Ho and a Bottle of Rhum,"
    193
Hogmanay, 276
Holiday Inn, 125
holiday season: length of, 20
holidays, other, 271–77
"Holly Jolly Christmas," 88
Home Alone, 137
Home for the Holidays, 188
Hong Kong surrenders, 255
Hope, Bob, 211
Horne, Lena, 70
hot chocolate, 270
Hoteiosho, 34

How the Grinch Stole Christmas,
    218

I Saw Mommy Kissing Santa Claus:
    movie, 133; song, 106
"I Told Santa Claus," 100
"I Want a Hippopotamus for Christmas,"
    166
"I Yust Go Nuts at Christmas," 168
"I'll Be Home for Christmas," 77
"In the Bleak Mid-Winter," 204
Irish Tenors, The, 116
Isaak, Chris, 203
Italy, 29, 31
*It's a Very Merry Muppet Christmas
    Movie*, 140
It's a Wonderful Life, 121
It's Christmas Time, 184
"It's the Most Wonderful Time of the
    Year," 64
Ives, Burl, 88

Jack Frost: made in 1997, 133; made in
    1998, 130
Jackson Five, 106
Jagger, Dean, 151
Jan and Dean, 85
January 7, 20
Japan, 34
Jewel, 193
Jingle All the Way: movie, 138; song,
    70
"Jingle Bell Rock," 81
"Jingle Bells," 74, 163, 191
John, Sir Elton, 201
Johnson, Luther "Guitar Junior," 97
Jolly, Texas, 15
Jones, Spike, and His City Slickers,
    165
"Joy to the World," 93
Jultomten, 33

Kane, Carol, 149
Keen, Robert Earl, 192
Keillor, Garrison, 180
Kenny G, 200
Killantzaroi, 26
King of the Bean, 26
Kinks, The, 158
Kitt, Eartha, 83
Kluger, Special Delivery, 238
Kwanzaa, 272

La Befana, 31
La Quema del Diablo, 25
LaBelle, Patti, 110
"Last Christmas," 195
Lauper, Cyndi, 207

Lee, Brenda, 82
Lennon, John, 155
"Les Anges Dans Nos Campagnes,"
    207
"Let It Snow," 61
lights: in windows, 22; on trees, 3, 22
Little Drummer Boy, The: cartoon, 221;
    song, 108
"Little Saint Nick," 84
log cake, 268
Love, Darlene, 84
Loveless, Patty, 93

magnetic North Pole, 40
"Making Plans," 94
"Man with the Bag, The," 208
"Manger Throne," 209
Mari Lwyd, 27
Marteria, Ralph, and His Orchestra, 70
Martin, Billy, 245
Martin, Dean, 61, 248
Martin, Ricky, 197
Mathis, Johnny, 63
Max the Dog, 233
McAdenville, North Carolina, 16
McBeal, Ally, 184
McBride, Martina, 92
McCartney, Paul, 196
McEntire, Reba, 94
McKennitt, Loreena, 115
McKenzie Brothers, 180
"Mele Kalikimaka," 189
"Merry Christmas (I Don't Want to Fight
    Tonight)," 193
"Merry Christmas Baby," 97
"Merry Christmas from the Family," 192
Merry Christmas with Love, 185
Meyers, Sam, 98
Mickey's Christmas Carol, 145
milk and cookies, 268
Miller, Julie, 209
Miller, Mitch, and the Gang, 177
Miracle on 34th Street, 123
"Mister Hankey, the Christmas Poo," 173
mistletoe, 21
"Mistletoe and Me, The," 109
Mitchell, Joni, 159
Moonglows, The, 85
movies: bit players in, 149–54; classics,
    121–28; comedies, 135–42; not-so-
    classic, 129–34; versions of A
    Christmas Carol, 143–48
Mr. Magoo's Christmas Carol, 144
Muppet Christmas Carol, The, 146
Muppets, The, and John Denver, 178,
    215
music. See songs
MxPx, 205

'N Sync: 'Ntimate Holiday Special, 214
narwhal, 39
National Christmas Tree Association,
    42, 44
National Lampoon's Christmas Vacation,
    125
Nelson, Willie, 91
New Year's Eve, 272
Newsong, 200
Newton, Sir Isaac, 241
Nick at Nite, 187, 215
Nick at Nite Holiday Special, The, 215
Nightmare Before Christmas, The, 141
"No More Toymakers to the King," 175
"Noel," 110
Noel, Missouri, 15
North Pole, 37–40; climate of, 37;
    explorers to, 38; geography of, 37;
    travel through, 38
North Pole, Alaska, 12
North Pole Marathon, 40
Norway, 28
"Nowell, Nowell: Tidings True/Riu, Riu,
    Chiu," 117
"Numbah One Day of Christmas,"
    181
Nutcracker, The, 128
"Nutcracker Suite," 77
"Nuttin' for Christmas," 167

"O Come All Ye Faithful," 92
"O Come, O Come Emmanuel/God
    Rest Ye Merry Gentlemen," 115
"O Holy Night," 116, 194
"O Little Town of Bethlehem," 69
O'Brien, Tim, 94
O'Domhnaill, Michael, 117
O'Donnell, Rosie, 185
official holiday, 2
"Oiche Chiun (Silent Night)," 114
Olive, the other reindeer: cartoon, 224;
    character, 57
"On a Cold Winter's Night/Christmas
    Eve," 117
"On to Bethlehem," 209
Ono, Yoko, 155
Orthodox Christmas, 275
Osbourne Family Christmas Special,
    The, 214
"Our Little Town," 78

Papai Noel, 34
Parker, Bobby, 98
Parton, Dolly, 93
Partridge Family, 183
Partridge Family Christmas Card, A,
    188
Payne, John, 152

"Peace on Earth/Little Drummer Boy,"
    156
Peevey, Gayla, 166
Pesci, Joe, 153
Pet Rock, 260
Peterson, Oscar, 77
physics of Santa Claus, 6
Pig Latin, 274
*Pinky and the Brain Christmas Special,
    A*, 226
PlayStation2, 263
"Please Come Home for Christmas,"
    156
Poland, 27, 34
polar bear, 39
postage stamps, 4
Prancer: movie, 132; reindeer, 54
Presley, Elvis, 64, 86, 102
Pretenders, The, 160
"Pretty Paper," 91
Prima, Louis, 71
"Put One Foot in Front of the Other,"
    174
Pyle, Denver, 250

Quaid, Randy, 150
Queen Elizabeth, 4

Ramones, 193
Ramsey, Jon-Benet, 246
Redbone, Leon, 206
reindeer, 47–51; antlers, 49; appearance
    of, 49; and caribou, 48; classifica-
    tion, 47; diet of, 50; domestication
    of, 48; hooves, 50; location of, 48;
    meat, 50; Olive, 57; Santa's, 53–57;
    sleigh and, 3; trivia, 51
Reindeer Games, 134
Ren and Stimpy Show, The, 187
Rice, Sir Mack, 101
Rideout, Bonnie, 115
"River," 159
robins, 22
Robinson, Smokey, and the Miracles,
    110
Roches, The, 205
"Rockin' Around the Christmas Tree," 82
Rogers, Kenny, 93
Roomful of Blues, 100
Roosevelt, Teddy, 44
Rosie Christmas, A, 185
Royal Guardsmen, The, 165
Rudolph, Wisconsin, 15
*Rudolph and Frosty's Christmas in
    July*, 227
Rudolph the Red-Nosed Reindeer: car-
    toon, 219; character, 56; song, 61,
    193

Rudolph's Shiny New Year, 227
"Run Rudolph Run," 83
Russia, 32

Sadat, Anwar, 244, 254
Salvation Army, 21
Sam the Snowman, 238
"Sam's Christmas Blues," 98
"Sandy Claw Stole My Woman," 98
Sansone, Maggie, and the Ensemble
    Galilei, 17
"Santa Baby," 83
Santa Claus, Georgia, 13
Santa Claus, Indiana, 12
"Santa Claus and His Old Lady," 168
Santa Claus Conquers the Martians, 129
"Santa Claus Is Back in Town," 102
Santa Claus Is Comin' to Town: cartoon,
    221; song, 76, 158
"Santa Claus Wants Some Lovin'," 101
Santa Claus, The Movie, 133
Santa Clause 2, The: The Mrs. Clause,
    139
Santa Clause, The, 136
Santa with Muscles, 132
"Santa's Blues," 100
"Santa's Messin' with the Kid," 103
Scandinavia, 27
Schiek, Susan, 111
Scrooged, 144
Second Christmas Day, 27
Serling, Rod, 243
Sherman, Allen, 179
shipping, 9
shooting in Christmas, 28
shopping, 5, 6
"Silent Night," 23, 68, 114
"Silver and Gold," 176
"Silver Bells," 63, 200
Simon and Garfunkel, 157
Simpsons Christmas Special, The, 228
Sinatra, Frank, 62; and Family, 179
Singing Dogs, The, 163
sleigh and reindeer, 3
"Sleigh Ride," 62
Slim, Root Boy, 192
Smith, Jimmy, 75
"Snoopy's Christmas," 165
snow, 8
Snow Miser: character, 235; song, 175
"Someday at Christmas," 106
songs: albums from TV stars, 183–88;
    bad, 195–202; the blues, 97–103;
    cartoon, 171–76; Celtic, 113–19;
    classic, 59–65; classic rock,
    155–61; country, 89–95; fun,
    189–94; jazz instrumentals, 73–79;
    jazz vocals, 67–72; novelty, 163–69;

oldies, 81–88; recent, 203–210; soul, 105–112; versions of "Twelve Days of Christmas," 177 82
Soulful Christmas," 105
Spain, 33
spiders, 46
Spinal Tap, 169
Springsteen, Bruce, 158
Squeeze, 159
Squirrel Nut Zippers, 190
St. Nicholas: history of, 35
"St. Stephen's Day Murders," 190
Star Man, 34
"Step into Christmas," 201
Stern, Daniel, 153
Stewart, Martha, 188
Streisand, Barbra, 191
Super Ball, 260
Superman, 40
Supremes, The, 108
Sweden, 33
Swingle Singers, The, 72

Tamagotchi, 262
Teenage Mutant Ninja Turtles, 261
television: albums from television stars, 183–88; cartoons, see cartoons; holiday specials, 211–16
Temptations, The, 107
Tharpe, Sister Rosetta, 69
Three Kings, 33
"Three Ships," 207
Tickle Me Elmo, 261
TNT's A Christmas Carol, 148
toys, 259–64
traditions, 19–23; international, 25–29
translations of "Merry Christmas," 274
travel, 9
turkey, 1
Turkey, 35
'Twas the Night Before Christmas, 222
"Twelve Days of Christmas," versions of, 177–82
"2000 Miles," 160

United Kingdom, 28, 32
"Up on the Housetop," 94
urn of fate, 29

Veggie Tales, 181
Very Ally Christmas, A, 184

Vigilantes of Love, 209
Virginia Tech Hokies, 268, 289
Vixen, 51

Wales, 27
Ward, Zack, 150
Washington, Dinah, 68
Washington, George, 256
Watson, Doc, 90
"We Three Kings," 79
"We Wish You a Merry Christmas," 118
"We're Not So Bad," 175
Webster, Katie, 99
"Welcome Christmas," 172
"Wexford Carol, The," 114
Wham! 195
"What Are You Doing New Year's Eve?" 110
"What Child Is This?" 108
"What Will Santa Claus Say (When He Finds Everyone Swingin')?" 71
"Where Are You Christmas?" 199
White Christmas: movie, 126; song, 59, 198
White House tree, 3
"Why Am I Such a Misfit?" 171
William the Conqueror, 257
Williams, Andy, 64, 213
Wilson, Carney and Wendy, 199
Winter Solstice, 273
Winter Warlock, 234
"Winter Wonderland," 65, 69, 75
Wirick, Weldon J., IV, 239
Wonder, Stevie, 106
"Wonderful Christmas Time," 196
wren hunt, 28
"Wren in the Furze," 113

Xmas, 23

Year Without a Santa Claus, The, 223
Yogi's First Christmas, 230
Yorgesson, Yogi, 168
Yoshihito, 249
YOUniverse ATM Machine, 264

"Zat You, Santa Claus?" 67

The Authors

Phillip Metcalfe is a technical writer whose lifelong obsession with music began when he pilfered his mother's Andy Williams and Brothers Four LPs. His vast music collection includes folk, rock, jazz, blues, classical, bluegrass, metal, R&B, country, and world music. He continues to look for something different every day without completely draining the family bank account. He lives in Sterling, Virginia, with his wife Teresa and son Aaron. The family keeps their fingers on the pulse of the music world by hosting a series of house concerts in their living room.

Kevin Cuddihy is an acquisitions editor at a publishing company, and once played Santa Claus while in high school. He appears regularly in the *Washington Post* humor column, "The Style Invitational," and has written numerous freelance articles on his beloved Virginia Tech Hokies for TechSideline.com. He lives in Fairfax, Virginia.